1-2-3 for Windows

CHEAT SHEET

by Jennifer Fulton

alpha books

A Division of Macmillan Computer Publishing
201 W. 103rd Street, Indianapolis, Indiana 46290 USA

To my husband Scott, whose patience and understanding knows no bounds.

©1994 Alpha Books

International Standard Book Number: 1-56761-488-4

Library of Congress Catalog Card Number: 94-70690

96 95 94   8 7 6 5 4 3 2 1

Interpretation of the printing code: the rightmost number of the first series of numbers is the year of the book's printing; the rightmost number of the second series of numbers is the number of the book's printing. For example, a printing code of 94-1 shows that the first printing of the book occurred in 1994.

Printed in the United States of America

Publisher   *Marie Butler-Knight*

Managing Editor   *Elizabeth Keaffaber*

Acquisitions Manager   *Barry Pruett*

Product Development Manager   *Faithe Wempen*

Senior Development Editor   *Seta Frantz*

Production Editor   *Michelle Shaw*

Copy Editor   *Audra Gable*

Cover Designer   *Tim Amrhein*

Designer   *Barbara Webster*

Indexer   *Greg Eldred*

Production Team   *Gary Adair, Dan Caparo, Brad Chinn, Kim Cofer, Lisa Daugherty, David Dean, Jennifer Eberhardt, Beth Rago, Bobbi Satterfield, Carol Stamile, Karen Walsh, Robert Wolf*

Special thanks to Christopher Denny for ensuring the technical accuracy of this book.

Contents

Part 2 Creating Your First Worksheet

Part 3   Working with Worksheets

Part 5   Formulas and Functions

Part 8 Special Features

Introduction

My husband used to tell his consulting clients to purchase computer books from used bookstores whenever they could. His reasoning was simple: the person who first used the book to learn the program step-by-hard-earned-step would inevitably have marked it up and highlighted certain passages. Discovering these old markings is like borrowing the previous owner's expertise. With this Cheat Sheet, the important need-to-know stuff is already highlighted for you. Because in today's "gotta get it done yesterday" kind of world, you can't afford to waste your time learning things you won't use anyway.

Why You Need This Book

This book cuts through the technical stuff that most manuals use to fill their pages. You'll learn what you need to know, not what someone else wants you to know. To minimize the time you spend learning to use your new program, this book comes with lots of features to get you up and going now:

- The chapters in this book are short, which makes finding what you need to know easy.

- In each chapter, the stuff you need to know right now for basic survival is covered first. Later, when you're feeling adventurous (or you've gotten yourself into a situation you'd like to get out of *fast*), you can read the stuff at the end of the chapter, in a section called "Beyond Survival."

- Along the way, the stuff you need to remember is highlighted for you. So feel free to skim when you're in a hurry.

- The most important points are also repeated in the margins, where you can find them fast.

- If that's not enough, this book also comes with three tear-out reference cards, which you can keep in a handy place so you don't even have to open the book if you don't want to.

How This Book Is Organized

There are eight parts in this book, each organized around a particular topic.

Part 1 covers the basics you need to know in order to use a Windows program such as Lotus 1-2-3 for Windows. If you're already familiar with using Windows programs, you can skip over most of this section.

Part 2, "Creating Your Worksheet," gets you up and going, covering such skills as moving around the worksheet, entering data, selecting ranges, and saving your work. These are skills you'll use all the time in 1-2-3.

Part 3, "Working with Worksheets," covers tasks such as starting a new worksheet or adding changes to an old one. You'll also learn how to work with multiple worksheets in this section.

Part 4, "Formatting Your Worksheet," tells you how to make all your hard work really look professional. You'll learn how to change the way your text and numbers look, and how to add color and shading to emphasize important figures.

Part 5, "Formulas and Functions," covers the basics of adding number-crunching formulas to your worksheets. And if you get into trouble, there's a help section to get you out of it fast.

Part 6 covers the ins and outs of printing your worksheet.

In Part 7, "Getting Graphical," you'll learn how to add a chart to your worksheet to summarize important trends. You'll also learn how to add arrows, text boxes, and other graphics to draw attention to important information.

Part 8, "Special Features," helps you get real mileage out of your program. In this part, you'll learn how to create databases for tracking large amounts of data, such as inventory, employee addresses, client contacts, and more. You'll also learn how to automate dreary tasks and to perform complex analyses.

At the end of the book are two appendices to help you install 1-2-3 for Windows and use 1-2-3's built-in formulas.

Acknowledgments

Thanks to Barry Pruett for coming up with such a great idea for a book—and for letting me write one. Thanks to Seta Frantz for all her suggestions. Special thanks to my husband who helped me keep it together under an aggressive deadline.

PART 1

The Basics

When you first learned to drive a car, chances are that you already knew which pedal did what. If you're familiar with other Windows programs, chances are that you've already found the "pedals." But even so, there's a bit more you need to know in order to put 1-2-3 into drive. In this section, you'll learn about the following topics:

- Starting Lotus 1-2-3 for Windows

- Taking a Look Around

- Working with Worksheets

- The Wonderful World of Windows

- Selecting Commands

- Working the Smart Way with SmartIcons

- Getting Help

- Exiting Lotus 1-2-3 for Windows

Cheat Sheet

Starting Windows

1. Start your computer.
2. At the DOS prompt, type WIN and press Enter.

Starting Lotus 1-2-3 for Windows

1. Double-click on the Lotus Applications program group.
2. Double-click on the Lotus 1-2-3 program icon.
3. Select an option in the Welcome box and click OK. To start a new worksheet, select Create a new worksheet.
4. Complete additional steps as necessary. To start a new worksheet, select a SmartMaster from the list or select Create a plain worksheet. Click OK.

Starting Lotus 1-2-3 with a Worksheet Open

1. Double-click on the Main program group window to open it.
2. Double-click on the File Manager icon to start the program.
3. Double-click on a worksheet file name.

Starting Lotus 1-2-3 Whenever You Start Windows

1. Start Windows as usual.
2. Double-click on the Startup program group to open it.
3. Double-click on the Lotus Applications program group to open it. You now have two windows open.
4. Press and hold the Ctrl key. Click on the Lotus 1-2-3 icon and hold the mouse button down. Drag a copy of the icon into the Startup group window. From now on, 1-2-3 will automatically start whenever you start Windows.

Starting Lotus 1-2-3 for Windows

To use any program, such as Lotus 1-2-3 for Windows, you must first start it. Think of a program as a car—once a program is started, you can put it into drive and make it do something for you. After a program is started, it's said to be *running*. When you're done with a program, you turn it off, which is called *exiting* (see Chapter 8). In this chapter, you'll learn how to start and exit Lotus 1-2-3 for Windows.

Basic Survival

Starting Windows

Lotus 1-2-3 for Windows requires Windows in order to work, so before you can start 1-2-3 for Windows, you must have Windows up and running. If you already have Windows running, skip to the next part for instructions on how to start the Lotus 1-2-3 program. If you don't have Windows running, follow these steps:

1. Turn on your computer.

2. At the DOS prompt (C> or C:\>), type WIN and press Enter. After a few seconds, you should see something like the following figure. (Your screen will not look exactly like mine; one of the things that makes Windows so nice is that you can easily customize it to the way you want—which I have.)

Type WIN to start Windows

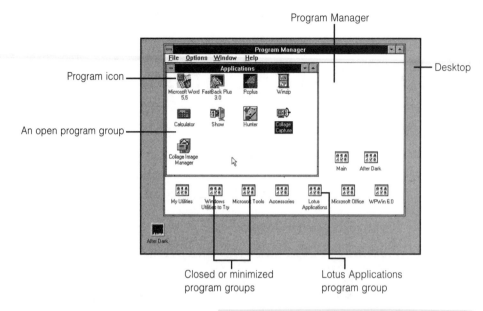

Program Manager

Program icon

An open program group

Desktop

Closed or minimized
program groups

Lotus Applications
program group

When you start Windows, the first thing you see is Program Manager, the main program that manages your applications. Program Manager appears as a large window or box, and it sits on the Desktop, a kind of "carpet" that covers the entire screen. You can arrange your applications anywhere on the Desktop once they are up and running. (You can run many applications at the same time with Windows, which is one of the things that makes Windows so popular and easy to use.)

Program Manager uses *program group* windows to organize your applications. In the figure, the Applications group window is open; inside you see many *icons,* pictures that represent various applications. In my case, I've placed most of my DOS applications within the Applications window. When a group window is closed (minimized), it appears as a tiny icon within the Program Manager window. The Lotus 1-2-3 for Windows application has its own program group window; inside you'll find icons representing the various programs and utilities that come with Lotus 1-2-3.

Starting Lotus 1-2-3 for Windows

After you have successfully started Windows, you can start Lotus 1-2-3 for Windows.

1. Double-click on the Lotus Applications program group. The program group window opens. If you can't locate the Lotus Applications program group, click on the Window menu (at the

Double-click
= Click
twice fast

top of your screen) to open it. Click on Lotus Applications in the list. If you don't see it listed, the program may not yet be installed, or you may have installed it into a different program group. (The Lotus Applications program group is the group window into which the Lotus program icons are normally installed; if you selected a different group during installation, open that group instead.) Turn to Appendix A for instructions on how to install Lotus 1-2-3.

Lotus 1-2-3
program icon

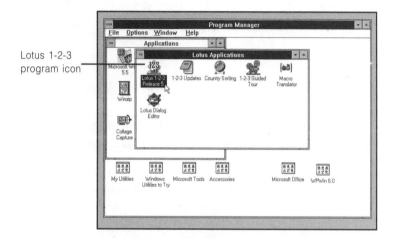

2. Double-click on the Lotus 1-2-3 program icon. Lotus 1-2-3 displays a Welcome box.

3. Select an option from the Welcome to 1-2-3 dialog box. You can create a new worksheet, open an existing worksheet, or start the tutorial.

Click here to create
a new worksheet.

Click here to open an
existing worksheet.

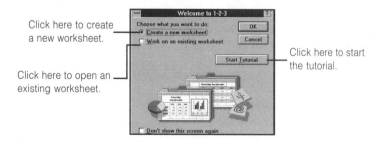

Click here to start
the tutorial.

4. Click OK. If you opted to create a new worksheet, the New File
dialog box appears. Stand by for more instructions. If you opted
to work on an existing worksheet, check out Chapter 17. If you
opted for the tutorial, Chapter 7 is right up your alley.

Select a SmartMaster from this list.

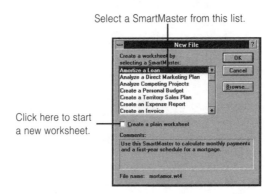

Click here to start
a new worksheet.

5. If you want to start a new worksheet, select a SmartMaster from
the list (for details see Chapter 16) or select Create a plain
worksheet. Click OK.

If you want to open an existing worksheet or start the tutorial,
turn to the appropriate chapter for more help.

6. When you elect to create a plain worksheet, 1-2-3 opens with a
blank worksheet ready for you to use.

Lotus 1-2-3 for Windows
opens a blank worksheet.

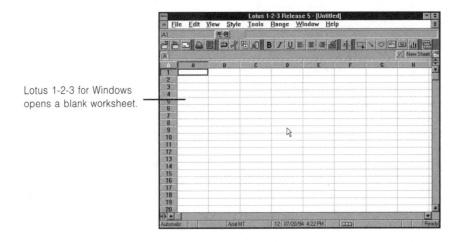

The Welcome box is a new feature to version 5, and personally, I like it. I think it makes it easier to start a new worksheet or open an existing one. But if you've used previous versions of Lotus 1-2-3 and are pretty confident in opening worksheets and starting new files, you may not want to mess with the Welcome box every time. You can turn this option off by opening the Tools menu and selecting the User Setup command. Select the Skip New File and Welcome screens option, and click OK. (If you don't know how to select menu commands or deal with dialog boxes, skip to Chapter 5.)

Beyond Survival

Starting Lotus 1-2-3 for Windows with a Worksheet Open

If you use the same worksheet (such as an expense worksheet) all the time, you can save yourself some time and trouble by creating an icon that starts Lotus 1-2-3 with the Expense worksheet (or whatever) already open and ready to use. Here's how:

1. From Program Manager, double-click on the Lotus Applications program group window. (If the group window is already open, skip this step.)

2. Click on the Lotus 1-2-3 program icon. The icon is selected (highlighted).

Drag = click and hold left button; then drag mouse.

3. Press and hold the Ctrl key as you drag the icon to an open space in the group window. A new copy of the Lotus 1-2-3 icon is created.

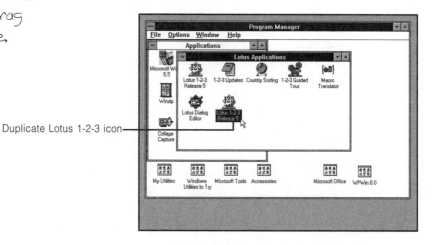

Duplicate Lotus 1-2-3 icon

4. Click on the duplicate icon to select it.

5. In the menu bar at the top of the Program Manager window, click on the File menu to open it. Click on the Properties command. The Program Item Properties dialog box appears.

Type the name of
the worksheet here.

Leave a space after the command,
then type the path.

6. In the Description text box, type a new name for the icon (such as Expense Report).

7. Press Tab to move to the Command Line field.

Path =
drive:\
directory\
filename.WK5

8. Type the path to the worksheet file. The path is the location where the file that you want to open resides on your disk, for example, C:\JEN\EXPENSE.WK5 or H:\123R4W\EXPENSE.WK5. Therefore, a file name takes on the following form: drive:\directory\filename.WK5.

9. Click on OK or press Enter.

Now that you have your icon, just double-click on it to start 1-2-3 with your expense worksheet. If you're familiar with Windows, you can go about this another way. Open File Manager, locate your worksheet file, and drag the file into the Lotus Applications group window. (You may have to resize both windows to make them visible on-screen.)

If you're only going to use a worksheet once or twice, these steps may be too much trouble. But you can still start Lotus 1-2-3 with a worksheet open, without having to go through all these steps. Just open File Manager and double-click on a worksheet file. Because files within File Manager are "associated" with the programs in which they were created, double-clicking on a worksheet file causes Lotus 1-2-3 to start with the file you selected.

Starting Lotus 1-2-3 Whenever You Start Windows

If you use 1-2-3 every day, why not start it at the same time you start Windows? It's easy:

1. Start Windows as usual. (See the steps earlier in this chapter if you need help starting Windows.)

2. Double-click on the Startup program group to open it. If you can't find a group called Startup, click on the Window menu and select Startup from the list.

3. Double-click on the Lotus Applications program group to open it. You now have two windows open: the Startup and the Lotus Application group windows.

4. Press and hold the Ctrl key. Click on the Lotus 1-2-3 icon and hold the mouse button down. Drag a copy of the icon into the Startup group window.

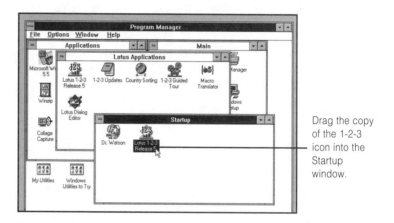

Drag the copy of the 1-2-3 icon into the Startup window.

The next time you start Windows, Lotus 1-2-3 will start automatically. You can delete the 1-2-3 icon from the Startup group at a later time if you decide you no longer want 1-2-3 to start every time you start Windows. Just open the Startup group window as you did in step 2 above, click on the 1-2-3 icon, and press Delete. Click on the Yes button to confirm the deletion.

By the way, removing the icon from the Startup window does not affect the icon within the Lotus Applications window, so you can still start 1-2-3 with the directions found at the beginning of this chapter.

Cheat Sheet

The Basic Parts of a Lotus 1-2-3 for Windows Screen

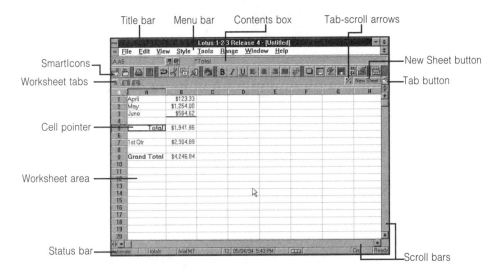

Title bar   Displays the name of the current worksheet.

Menu bar   Displays the names of 1-2-3's menus.

Cell pointer   Marks your current location in the worksheet.

Contents box   Displays the contents of the current cell.

Worksheet area   The area into which you enter data.

Scroll bars   Allow you to move around to other areas of the worksheet.

SmartIcons   These icons (buttons) let you perform common tasks with the mouse.

Worksheet tabs   You can have more than one worksheet in the same file. These tabs display the names of each worksheet and enable you to move between them.

Tab-scroll arrows   Move you to the previous or next worksheet in the file.

New Sheet button   Adds a new worksheet to the file.

Tab button   Controls whether the worksheet tabs are displayed.

Status bar   Displays the status of the worksheet and provides a way to change data's appearance.

2

Taking a Look Around

Whether you've chosen to create a new worksheet or make changes to an existing one, there are many elements on-screen that help you get your work done. In this chapter, you learn what most of those elements are and what they are used for.

Basic Survival

The Parts of a Lotus 1-2-3 for Windows Screen

Once you start Lotus 1-2-3, you see a screen similar to the one shown below:

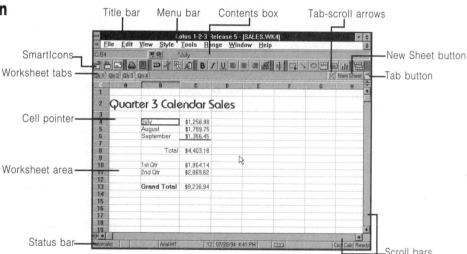

Title bar   Displays the name of the worksheet on which you're working.

Menu bar   Displays the names of 1-2-3's menus. Each menu listed here (such as File, Edit, and so on) can be opened to display a list of commands. You use these commands to work with the data in your worksheet.

Cell pointer marks current location

Cell pointer   Each one of the rectangles you see is a *cell*. The *cell pointer* (dark outline) marks your current location in the worksheet. You learn more about cells in Chapter 3.

Contents box   This displays the contents of the current cell.

Worksheet area   A worksheet is made up of lots of cells. You enter data into cells in the worksheet area. You're seeing only part of the entire worksheet in this window.

Scroll bars   These help you move around to other (unseen) areas of the worksheet. More about scroll bars and how they work in Chapter 9.

Use SmartIcons to get things done fast.

SmartIcons   These icons (buttons) let you perform common tasks with the mouse. What you see here is the default SmartIcon set, which is a collection of the most commonly used SmartIcons. There are other sets to which you can switch; each one makes it easier to complete a certain task. You find out all about SmartIcons in Chapter 6.

Worksheet tabs   You can have more than one worksheet in the same file. For example, you could have a 1st, 2nd, 3rd, and 4th Qtr. worksheet in a file called BUDGET.WK5. These tabs display the names of each worksheet and enable you to move between worksheets easily.

Tab-scroll arrows   These enable you to move to the previous or next worksheet.

New Sheet button   Adds a new worksheet to the file.

Tab button   Controls whether the worksheet tabs are displayed. Worksheet tabs, the tab-scroll arrows, the New Sheet button, and the Tab button are discussed in Chapters 18 and 19.

Status bar   Displays the status of the worksheet and provides you with a quick way to change your data's appearance. To activate any portion of the status bar, just click on it. For example, you could click on the Font Selector to select a different text style.

Beyond Survival

A Closer Look at the Status Bar

The status bar is made up of several parts:

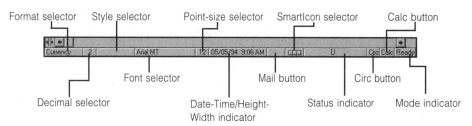

Format selector   Style selector   Point-size selector   SmartIcon selector   Calc button

Font selector   Mail button   Circ button

Decimal selector   Date-Time/Height-   Status indicator   Mode indicator
                                Width indicator

Format selector   Click here to change the format of numbers within selected cells. You learn more about number formatting in Chapter 24.

Decimal selector   Click here to change the number of decimal places.

Style selector   Click here to format selected cells with a named style. You learn how to create and use styles in Chapter 28.

Font selector   Click here to change the typeface of the text.

Point-size selector   Click here to change the size of text. Chapter 23 discusses formatting in more detail.

Can change text & number formats with status bar

Date-time/Height-width indicator   Click here to switch from displaying the date and time to displaying the height and width of the current cell.

Mail button   An envelope icon appears here when you receive electronic mail (a message or a file sent over a network from someone else in your office to your computer using a program such as Lotus Notes, cc:Mail, or Microsoft Mail).

SmartIcon selector   Click here to select a different SmartIcon set. You learn more about SmartIcons in Chapter 6.

Status indicator   This area of the status bar displays information about the current status of the worksheet using the following codes:

U	Current cell/worksheet is unprotected (data can be changed).
Pr	Current cell/worksheet is protected.
Zoom	Full window view is active.
Cmd	1-2-3 is processing a command.
Group	Group mode is active.

Circ = problem with a formula

Circ indicator Indicates that a formula contains a circular reference (a reference to itself). You learn how to fix this problem in Chapter 31.

Calc indicator Results in the worksheets need to be recalculated to be accurate. (Recalculation is discussed further in Chapter 31.)

Mode indicator Indicates which of these modes 1-2-3 is in:

Ready	Ready to receive input (data).
Point	You're currently selecting a range of cells.
Label	You're entering what 1-2-3 believes is text.
Value	You're entering what 1-2-3 believes is a number, a formula, or a function.
Edit	You're editing the contents of a cell.

Cheat Sheet

What's a Cell?

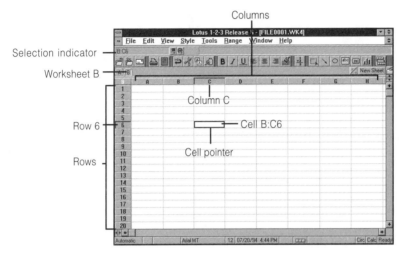

A worksheet is comprised of *rows* and *columns*.

A *cell* is created by the intersection of a row and a column.

The *cell pointer* indicates the current cell (location).

Cell Addressing

A file originally contains only one worksheet.

You can add up to 255 worksheets to a file.

Worksheets are originally labeled A, B, and so on, but you can change their names.

A cell's address is a combination of its worksheet name, its column, and its row. For example, cell B:C6 is the third cell in the sixth row of the second worksheet.

A cell's address is displayed in the *selection indicator*.

3

Working with Worksheets

Lotus 1-2-3 stores its data in worksheets. When you start 1-2-3, you are presented with a single blank worksheet into which you can enter your information. You can add more worksheets to the file as needed. In this chapter, you learn what a worksheet is and how it functions.

Basic Survival

What's a Cell?

A worksheet is just a page with columns and rows. A single worksheet contains 8,192 rows and 256 columns. Each rectangle formed by the intersection of a column and a row is called a *cell*.

Row +
Column =
Cell

The rows are numbered from top to bottom in the worksheet, from 1 to 8,192. The columns are labeled from left to right in the worksheet, from A to Z, then AA, AB, AC, and so on, BA, BB, BC, and so on, up to IV.

The current cell is indicated by the *cell pointer*, a dark outline around the edges of the cell. You learn how to move the cell pointer from place to place in Chapter 9.

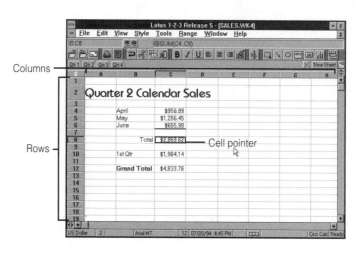

Cell Addressing

Each cell has its own address, or location, within the worksheet. A complete cell address includes the name of its worksheet, followed by its column letter and its row number. Worksheets are labeled consecutively, beginning with the letter A (see the next section for more info on worksheet labels). So the complete address for the current cell shown in the figure is A:B4 (the second cell in the fourth row of the first worksheet).

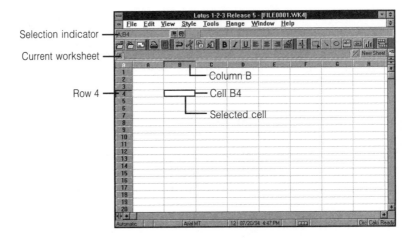

Complete cell address = worksheet name + column + row

A cell is often referred to by a shortened form of its cell address, which is made up of its column letter and row number only. (The cell in the sample figure could be referred to as simply cell B4, although that's not as precise.) If you do not use the worksheet name in the cell address, 1-2-3 automatically assumes that you mean the current worksheet.

The current cell's address is displayed in the *selection indicator*. Here, the worksheet name is always included as part of the cell's address.

Beyond Survival

Worksheet Files

A worksheet file originally contains only one worksheet, but you can add 255 more worksheets, for a total of 256 in one worksheet file. For example, you might want to place each month's budget on a separate worksheet to make them easier to work with. Worksheets are labeled with letters, beginning with A. You can change a worksheet's name to be more meaningful, such as Qtr 1, Qtr 2, Qtr 3, Qtr 4. (You learn how to add worksheets and change their names in Chapter 18.) You select a worksheet by clicking on its tab; it becomes the current worksheet. The tab for the *current worksheet* looks as if it's in front of the other tabs.

Current worksheet ——

Worksheet tabs ——

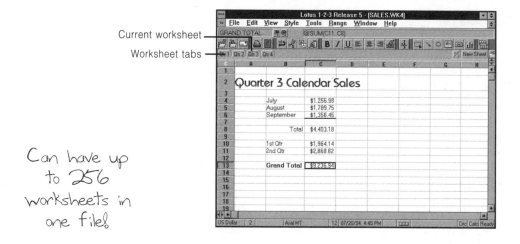

Can have up to 256 worksheets in one file!

Cheat Sheet

Mousing Around

Click   Position the mouse pointer over an object, then press the left mouse button once.

Double-click   Press the left mouse button twice in quick succession.

Drag   Move the mouse pointer to the starting position, press and hold down the left mouse button, and drag the mouse pointer to the ending position. Release the mouse button.

Basic Windows Concepts

To *maximize* a window, click on the maximize button ▲.

To *minimize* a window, click on the minimize button ▼. To maximize the window again, double-click its icon.

To *restore* a window, click on the restore button ⬍.

Resizing Windows

1. If your window is maximized, click on the Restore button first.
2. Move the mouse pointer over the window border. To resize a window horizontally and vertically at the same time, move to one of the corners.
3. Drag the border to a new location.
4. Release the mouse button.

Moving a Window Around

1. If your window is maximized, click on the Restore button first.
2. Move the mouse pointer to the window's title bar.
3. Drag the title bar to a new location.
4. Release the mouse button.

4

The Wonderful World of Windows

All Windows programs share a set of common rules under which they work. What that means to you is that you don't have to start over every time you learn a new Windows program. Instead, you can build on your existing knowledge. That makes it easy to learn how to use lots of Windows programs.

In this chapter, you learn the basic skills you use in all Windows programs: how to use a mouse and the parts of a basic window and what they do. If you hang in there for the Beyond Survival part, you even learn how to move and resize windows so they're exactly where you want them.

Basic Survival

Mousing Around

Trying to use Windows without a mouse is like trying to cut a lawn with a pair of scissors. You can do it, but it will take a long time. Thankfully, learning to use a mouse is easy. There are only three things you need to know how to do:

Click The most common mouse task, clicking usually selects something, such as a menu command or a particular cell. When you click on a cell, the cell pointer highlights that cell. That cell is now the active cell, and you can enter data into it.

To click, you move the mouse so that the mouse pointer (an arrow) is over the item you want to select. Then you press the mouse button one time. Always click with the left mouse button unless you are specifically told to use the right.

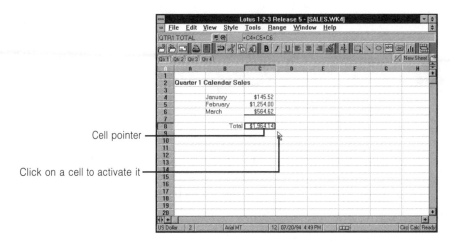

Cell pointer

Click on a cell to activate it

Important!

Double-click Double-clicking performs actions: it starts programs, closes programs and windows, and enables you to edit the contents of a cell, among other things. To double-click, quickly press the left button two times without moving the mouse.

Drag Dragging selects a group of cells so you can perform one operation on all of them. It also enables you to move things around on-screen.

To drag, position the mouse pointer over an item, press and hold the left mouse button, move the mouse pointer to a new location, then release the mouse button.

Basic Windows Concepts

Windows are the most basic element of all Windows programs. When you start Lotus 1-2-3 for Windows, the program opens in its own *window*, a resizeable on-screen box. Initially, that window (box) fills the entire screen, but it can be resized or moved around to suit your taste.

Inside the 1-2-3 program window is another window called the document window. If you want, you can resize the document window so you can view more than one file at a time in 1-2-3.

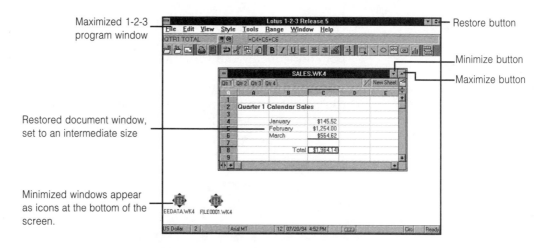

Maximized 1-2-3 program window

Restore button

Minimize button

Maximize button

Restored document window, set to an intermediate size

Minimized windows appear as icons at the bottom of the screen.

A window can exist in one of three forms:

Maximized   A maximized window fills the entire screen. To maximize a window, click once on the maximize button ▲.

Minimized   A minimized window is represented by a tiny icon at the bottom of the screen. To minimize a window, click on the Minimize button ▼. To maximize the window again, double-click on the icon.

Restored   Returned to some intermediate size. To restore a window to its previous intermediate size, click on the Restore button ⬍. When a window is restored, you can resize it to any shape or size or move it around; see the Beyond Survival section.

Beyond Survival

Resizing Windows

If window = max, restore before sizing/moving.

Instead of just minimizing, maximizing, and restoring a window, you can size a window to any shape you want. To resize a window:

1. Start with an intermediate-sized window. (When you first start 1-2-3, the 1-2-3 program and document windows are maximized.) If your window is maximized, click on the Restore button first ⬍.

To resize, drag
from a side or
a corner.

2. Move the mouse pointer over the window border. The mouse
pointer will change to a two-headed arrow. To resize a window
both horizontally and vertically at the same time, move to one of
the corners.

3. Click and hold down the mouse button as you drag the border to
a new location. Stretch the border out to make the window
bigger, or bring it in to make the window smaller. As you drag,
you see a ghostly outline that represents the new window.

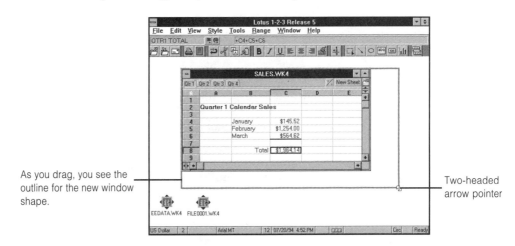

As you drag, you see the
outline for the new window
shape.

Two-headed
arrow pointer

4. Release the mouse button.

Moving a Window Around

If you don't like the location of a window on your screen, you're not
stuck. You can move windows around to place them where you want
them on-screen. To move a window:

1. Start with an intermediate-sized window. (When you first start
1-2-3, the 1-2-3 program and document windows are maximized.)
If your window is maximized, click on the Restore button ⬍ first.

To move, drag
the title bar.

2. Move the mouse pointer to the window's title bar.

3. Click and hold the mouse button as you drag the title bar to a new
location. As you drag, you see a ghostly outline that represents the
new window.

To move a window, drag it by its title bar.

As you move a window, you see its outline.

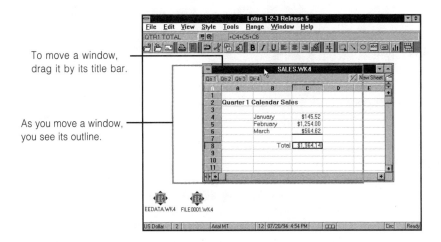

4. Release the mouse button.

25

Cheat Sheet

Selecting Commands from a Menu

1. Click on a menu name to open the pull-down menu.

2. Click on a command.

3. If a cascading menu appears, click on a selection.

Dealing with Dialog Boxes

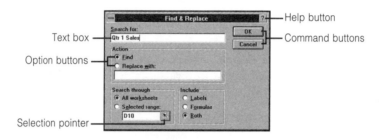

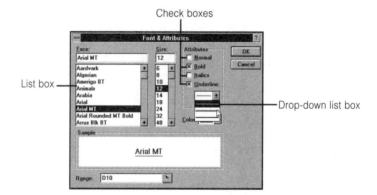

- Click on an option to select it.
- Click on the up or down arrows to scroll through a list box.
- Click on the selection pointer to select a range of cells.
- Click on ? to get help.
- Click on OK to execute the command, or click on Cancel to exit without executing.

5

Selecting Commands

Before you can get Lotus 1-2-3 to do most anything, you must give it a *command*. That means dealing with *menus* and *dialog boxes*. Thankfully, working with menus and dialog boxes is the same with all Windows programs, so you only have to learn the stuff in this chapter once. You can then apply these same techniques to take "command" of any Windows program.

Basic Survival

Selecting Commands from a Menu

A *menu bar* is displayed at the top of the 1-2-3 screen (below the title bar). Associated with each command on the menu bar is a *pull-down menu* that contains commands you select to tell 1-2-3 what to do.

Sometimes when you select a command from a menu, another menu called a *cascading menu* appears. The cascading menu appears next to the original menu in a kind of cascade effect. This menu provides additional selections from which you can choose.

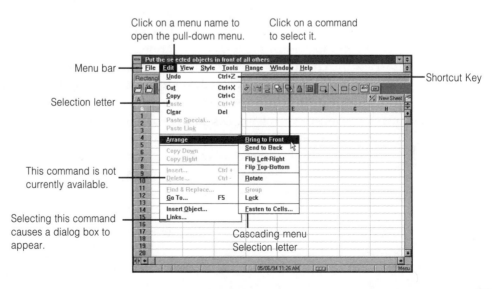

Click on a menu name to open the pull-down menu.

Click on a command to select it.

Menu bar

Selection letter

This command is not currently available.

Selecting this command causes a dialog box to appear.

Shortcut Key

Cascading menu
Selection letter

All commands follow the same set of conventions:

If a command is grayed, it's not currently available for you to select. This means that the command is not applicable at the moment; it's grayed out so you don't try to select it.

If a command appears with an arrow after it, a cascading menu appears when you select that command. You simply select a command from the cascading menu, and you're done!

If a command appears with three dots after it (an *ellipsis*), a dialog box appears when you select the command. You learn how to deal with dialog boxes in a minute.

All commands have one letter that's underlined. Instead of clicking on the command to select it, you can press the underlined letter. By the way, the underlined letter is called the *selection letter*.

To select a menu command:

1. Click on the menu name on the menu bar. For example, click on Edit to open the Edit menu.

2. Click on the command you want to select. For example, click on Arrange.

3. If a cascading menu appears, click on a selection.

Press Esc to close a menu

You can also select a command by clicking to open the menu, dragging the mouse pointer down to the command you want to choose, then releasing the mouse button. If a cascading menu appears, drag the pointer over to that menu and release when the mouse pointer is over the command you want. To close a menu you've opened by mistake, click inside the document somewhere or press the Esc key.

Dealing with Dialog Boxes

Sometimes 1-2-3 needs additional information in order to carry out a command. An ellipsis (three dots) next to a menu command indicates that 1-2-3 will need more information for that command. To get the additional information, 1-2-3 displays a *dialog box*.

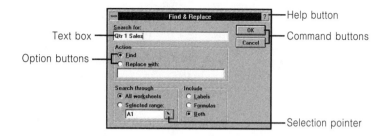

Text box

Option buttons

Help button

Command buttons

Selection pointer

Check boxes

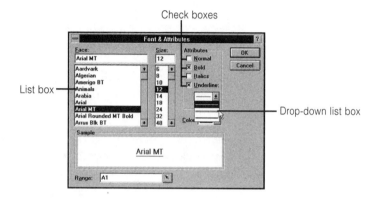

List box

Drop-down list box

Within a dialog box, there are several elements you use to select options:

List boxes present a list of choices. To scroll through the list, click on the up or down arrow of the scroll bar, then click on your choice.

Drop-down list boxes also present a list of choices. To open the drop-down list, click on the down arrow, then click on your choice.

Option buttons enable you to select one of a group of mutually exclusive options, such as left or right alignment. Click on the option you want. The selected option in the group appears with a solid dot.

Check boxes enable you to turn options (such as bold or italic) on or off. You can select multiple check boxes in a group. For example, you could select both the Bold and Underline check boxes if you wanted. Click on a check box to select the option or turn it on. Selected check boxes appear with an "X." Click on a check box that already contains an "X" to remove the "X" and turn the option off.

Text boxes are boxes in which you can type a unique selection, such as a file name.

Selection pointer enables you to select a *range* (group) of cells. You learn more about ranges and how to use the selection pointer in Chapter 12.

*Help = ?
button*

Help button enables you to access specific help on this dialog box. Simply click on the question mark in the dialog box's title bar, and you are taken directly to the appropriate section in Help.

*Wrong dialog
box? Press
Esc.*

Command buttons enable you to give 1-2-3 a direct command. Typical ones include OK, which tells 1-2-3 to accept the selections in the dialog box and to execute the command; Cancel, which tells 1-2-3 to cancel the selections and return to the document; and Close, which tells 1-2-3 to accept the selections and return to the worksheet without actually executing the command right now.

When you're presented with a dialog box, select the options you want, then click OK to execute them. To exit the dialog box without executing a command, click on Cancel or press Esc.

Beyond Survival

Using Quick Menus

For the quickest access to common commands, use a *quick menu*. Quick menus are *context-sensitive*, which means that the quick menu that appears corresponds to whatever is currently selected. For example, if you have selected a chart and you display a quick menu, only chart commands will be displayed on the quick menu.

To access a quick menu:

*Right-click
for quick
menu*

1. Select an object, such as a cell, a range of cells, or a chart.

2. Click the right mouse button. A quick menu appears.

3. Click on a command.

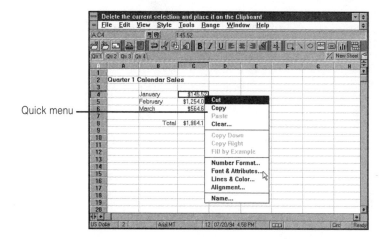

Quick menu ⎯

Using Shortcut Keys

Shortcut keys enable you to select a command without opening a menu. By memorizing popular shortcut keys, you can perform a variety of tasks simply by pressing a few keys. The shortcut key for a specific command appears to the right of that command on the menu. For example, the shortcut key for saving a file is Ctrl+S. So you can select the Save command by pressing Ctrl+S, without even opening the File menu.

To use a shortcut key:

1. Press and hold the first key (for example, Ctrl).

2. Press the second key (for example, S).

3. Release both keys.

Here's a listing of the most popular shortcut key combinations:

Command	Shortcut Key
File Open	Ctrl+O
File Save	Ctrl+S
File Print	Ctrl+P
File Close	Ctrl+F4
File Exit	Alt+F4

continues

Command	Shortcut Key
Insert Row/Column	Ctrl++
Delete Row/Column	Ctrl+−
Goto	F5
Undo	Ctrl+Z
Clear	Delete
Cut	Ctrl+X
Copy	Ctrl+C
Paste	Ctrl+V
Help	F1

Undoing Your Last Few Changes

Everyone makes mistakes. With a click of a mouse button or the press of a key, you could accidentally change—or even delete—important data. If this happens to you, follow these steps to undo your mistake:

1. Don't make any more changes to the worksheet until you undo your mistake.

2. Click on the Undo button ⤺ or open the Edit menu and select the Undo command.

Important!

Normally, Undo is enabled (turned on). But if someone has turned it off, the Undo process will not reverse your action. (Sorry, if Undo was not on when you made your mistake, you won't be able to use it to undo the mistake.) However, you'll want to enable it for later use. To turn Undo on:

1. Click on the Tools menu.

2. Select the User Setup command. The User Setup dialog box appears.

3. Select Undo.

4. Click OK.

There are some things you just can't undo, no matter what. These things include:

- Changes already saved to a file

- Changes caused by forced recalculation (in other words, you pressed F9 to recalculate the formulas in your worksheet)

- Changes caused by a previous Undo

- Cell pointer movement

- Printer activity. (There is a way to stop the printer, but this isn't it; see Chapter 35 for help.)

Cheat Sheet

Selecting a SmartIcon

1. If necessary, select cell(s) that you want the SmartIcon to affect.
2. Click on the SmartIcon.

Identifying a SmartIcon

1. Move the mouse cursor over the icon.
2. Read a description of the icon in the balloon that appears near the cursor.

Switching Between SmartIcon Sets

1. Click on the SmartIcon Selector on the status bar.
2. Select a SmartIcon set from the list.

Putting SmartIcons Where You Want Them

1. Open the Tools menu.
2. Select SmartIcons.
3. From the Position drop-down list box, select an option.
4. Click OK.

Moving a Floating SmartIcon Set

1. Follow the steps above and select the Floating position option.
2. Click on the title bar of the SmartIcon set and hold down the mouse button.
3. Drag the SmartIcon set where you want it, then release the mouse button.

Resizing a Floating SmartIcon Set

1. Move the mouse pointer to the corner of the SmartIcon set.
2. Click and hold the mouse button.
3. Drag the edge to resize the set, then release the mouse button.

Working the Smart Way with SmartIcons

SmartIcons are small pictures (icons) arranged in a row located at the top of the 1-2-3 screen, just under the menu bar and the edit line. You use SmartIcons to perform common tasks more quickly than you could with the menus. For example, instead of opening the File menu and selecting the Save command to save your worksheet file, you could simply select the File Save SmartIcon. To use SmartIcons, you must have a mouse.

When the 1-2-3 window first appears, the Default Sheet set of SmartIcons is usually displayed. However, there are many other sets to which you can switch, depending on the tasks you feel you're going to perform the most often. For example, if you're in the process of making your worksheet look pretty, you could switch to the Formatting SmartIcon set. There are eight sets in all, but only one is displayed at a time. You can customize each set to your taste by removing or inserting new SmartIcons; you can even create your own set from scratch. You learn all this and more in this chapter.

Basic Survival

Selecting a SmartIcon

There are many sets of SmartIcons from which you can choose. The set that is usually displayed at the top of the program window is called the Default Sheet. It includes these icons:

File Open	Opens a previously saved worksheet.
File Save	Saves the current worksheet.
Send Mail	Sends a worksheet file to another person on your network via electronic mail.

	Print	Prints the current worksheet.
	Preview	Previews the current worksheet before printing.
	Undo	Undoes the last change to the worksheet.
	Cut	Removes the current selection to the Clipboard in preparation for moving it.
	Copy	Copies the current selection to the Clipboard.
	Paste	Pastes the contents of the Clipboard into the worksheet.
	Bold	Bolds the current selection.
	Italics	Italicizes the current selection.
	Underline	Underlines the current selection.
	Left Align	Aligns data to the left.
	Center Align	Centers data.
	Right Align	Aligns data to the right.
	Fast Format	Copies formatting from one range to another.
	Sum	Adds the numbers above or to the left of the current cell.
	Select	Selects several objects.
	Arrow	Draws an arrow.
	Ellipse	Draws an ellipse.
	Text Box	Creates a text box.
	Button	Draws a button to which you can attach a macro.
	Chart	Creates a chart from a selected range.
	Next Set	Displays the next set of SmartIcons.

To select a SmartIcon:

1. If necessary, select a cell or a group of cells that you want the SmartIcon to affect.

To ID icon, point at it

2. Click on the SmartIcon you want to select.

You can identify a SmartIcon before you select it by moving the mouse cursor over the icon and resting it there briefly. A description of the icon appears in balloon near the cursor.

SmartIcon set or palette

A description of a SmartIcon appears in a balloon when you point at the SmartIcon with the mouse.

SmartIcons

Switching Between SmartIcon Sets

1-2-3 for Windows comes with several SmartIcon sets, but only one can be displayed at a time. So choose the set that fits the task you want to accomplish (editing, formatting, preparing to print, and so on). Some SmartIcon sets automatically appear when you select certain items (such as a chart or a drawn object). However, you can choose a different set manually at any time.

To manually switch to a different SmartIcon set:

Switch SmartIcon sets with selector on status bar

1. Click on the SmartIcon Selector on the status bar.

2. Select a SmartIcon set from the list that appears. The Hide SmartIcons option enables you to hide the SmartIcons (not display them). To redisplay them when they are hidden, follow these steps and select Show SmartIcons from the list.

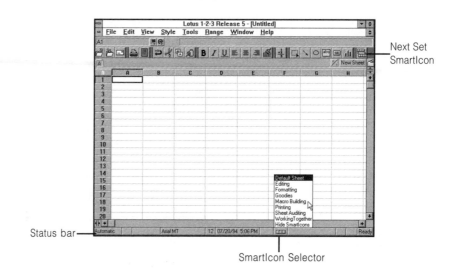

Next Set
SmartIcon

Status bar

SmartIcon Selector

You can also click on the Next Set SmartIcon 🔲 to switch to the next SmartIcon set in the list. Whatever SmartIcon set is displayed when you exit 1-2-3 is redisplayed when you start 1-2-3 the next time.

Beyond Survival

Putting SmartIcons Where You Want Them

You may find it more convenient to bring the SmartIcon set down from the top of the screen, closer to where you're working. This reduces wear and tear on your nerves, as well as your mouse. Here's how you move the SmartIcon set:

1. Open the Tools menu.

Change SmartIcon location with Tools/ SmartIcons/ Position

2. Select SmartIcons. The SmartIcons dialog box appears.

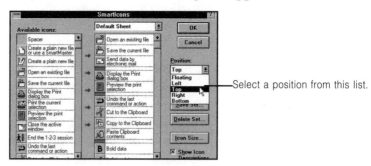

Select a position from this list.

3. Click on the Position drop-down list box and select a position option. If you choose the Floating option, you can drag the SmartIcon set to any location on-screen.

4. Click OK.

Using the Floating option, you can drag your SmartIcon set anywhere you want it. Simply click on the title bar and hold down the mouse button. Then drag the SmartIcon set where you want it and release the mouse button.

Resizing the SmartIcon Set

If you're using a floating SmartIcon set, you can reposition it anywhere you want on-screen by dragging it by its title bar. In addition, you can also resize the SmartIcon set:

1. Move the mouse pointer to the corner of the SmartIcon set; the pointer changes to a two-headed arrow.

2. Click and hold the mouse button.

3. Drag the edge to resize the set, then release the mouse button. You see a ghostly outline of the new size as you drag.

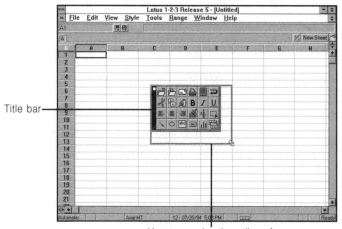

Title bar

You see a ghostly outline of
the new size as you drag.

Making SmartIcons Bigger

If you have one of those newer Super VGA monitors, or if you simply have trouble seeing those tiny icons at the top of your screen, make them bigger.

1. Open the Tools menu.

2. Select SmartIcons. The SmartIcons dialog box appears.

3. Click on the Icon Size button. The Icon Size dialog box appears.

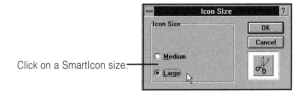

Click on a SmartIcon size.

4. Click on the option button next to the size you want.

5. Click OK.

6. Click OK again.

To return the SmartIcons to their default size, repeat these steps and select Medium.

Customizing Your SmartIcons

There are many SmartIcon sets, each of which is designed for a specific task. However, the creators of 1-2-3 recognized that *only you* can know how the SmartIcons should best be grouped and organized for your work. So Lotus left you a way to customize your own SmartIcon palette. You can add specific SmartIcons to the default set (or any other one for that matter), or you can create your own palette based on an existing SmartIcon set.

1. Open the Tools menu.

Cool ideas

2. Select SmartIcons. The SmartIcons dialog box appears.

Drag an icon from this list
to the other list to add it.

Select the set you
want to modify.

Spacer icon

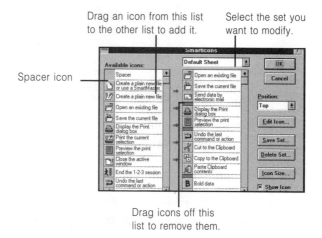

Drag icons off this
list to remove them.

3. Select the set you want to modify (or the one you want to use as a basis for a new set) from the drop-down list box.

4. The list on the left contains all of the SmartIcons currently available. The list on the right contains only the SmartIcons in the set you selected. Modify the selected list using these methods:

   To add a SmartIcon to the set, drag it from the list on the left onto the list on the right.

   To remove a SmartIcon from the set, drag it off the list.

   To move a SmartIcon to a different position in the set, drag it to where you want it and release the mouse button.

   To create groups of SmartIcons, drag the Spacer icon onto the list, creating spaces where you want them.

5. Click on the Save Set button. The Save Set of SmartIcons dialog box appears.

6. In the Name of set text box, type a name (such as Special) for your new SmartIcon set. If you want to modify the existing set, skip this step and go to step 8.

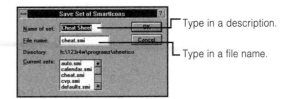

Type in a description.

Type in a file name.

7. In the File name text box, type a name (up to 8 characters) such as SPECIAL or MINE.

8. Click OK.

Lotus 1-2-3 automatically switches you to the new set. To switch to other sets, select them from the SmartIcon Selector on the status bar. If you are using this SmartIcon set when you exit 1-2-3, it is displayed anytime you restart 1-2-3 until you change it again.

Cheat Sheet

When in Trouble, Call for Help

To access Help:

>Press F1.

or

>Open the Help menu and select a topic.

or

>Click on the ? button in the upper right-hand corner of a dialog box.

Press Esc to exit Help.

Moving Around the Help System

Click **Contents** to see a table of contents.

Click **Search** to search for a particular topic.

Click **Back** to view the previous topic.

Click **History** to view any previously viewed topic.

Click the arrows to move back and forth through the Help system.

Click on an underlined word to jump to that topic.

Click on a dotted word to see a definition.

Searching for Specific Help

1. Select Search from the Help menu, or click on the Search button at the top of any Help screen.
2. Type the word you want to look up.
3. Click on Show Topics.
4. Scroll through the list of topics.
5. Double-click on the topic you want.

7

Getting Help

The Lotus 1-2-3 Help system is there to help you whenever you have a question, need clarification, or encounter a problem. The Help system is *context-sensitive*, which means that when you activate it, it knows what you are doing and takes you to an appropriate spot within the Help system. For example, if you were attempting to save your worksheet for the first time and accessed the Help system, 1-2-3 would display information on saving a worksheet. You get both guidance and step-by-step instructions in the Help system.

In this chapter, you learn how to call for help when you need it, how to use the tutorials, how to search for help on a specific topic, and more.

Basic Survival

When in Trouble, Call for Help

Getting into the Help system is easy: simply press F1. You are taken to an appropriate section of the Help system, based on whatever task you were attempting at the time. You can also access the various parts of the Help system through the Help menu:

Help = F1

Contents   Displays a table of contents for Help.

Search   Enables you to search for a topic within the Help system by typing in a key word such as "Save" or "SmartIcons."

Using Help   Explains how to navigate through the Help system.

Keyboard   Describes the keys that work with 1-2-3 and their functions.

How Do I?   Provides fast access to the most common questions users have.

For Upgraders   Describes features new to Lotus 1-2-3 version 5.0.

Tutorial   Accesses an animated tutorial that leads you through the most common tasks. Great for beginners or for a quick refresher.

About 1-2-3   Displays the program's version number and copyright information.

To use the Help menu:

1. Click on the Help menu to open it.

2. Click on the command you want to use.

To exit Help, press Esc.

To get help when you're in a dialog box, click on the question mark in the upper right-hand corner. You are taken to the area in help that discusses the current dialog box and its options.

Moving Around the Help System

When you select Contents from the Help menu, you see a window similar to this:

In dialog boxes, click ? for help

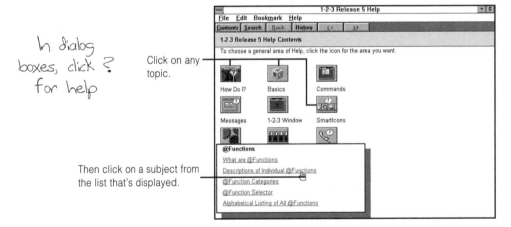

Click on any topic.

Then click on a subject from the list that's displayed.

Click on a topic (for example, How Do I?), and a list of subjects appears. Then click on a subject that interests you. Once you've looked at your topic, there are many ways to navigate around the Help system. For example, there's a row of buttons at the top of the Help window with which you can jump back and forth through the Help screens. Embedded in the text are dotted words, which display pop-up definitions when you click on them. In addition, there are underlined words, called *cross-references*, with which you jump right to a specific topic within Help.

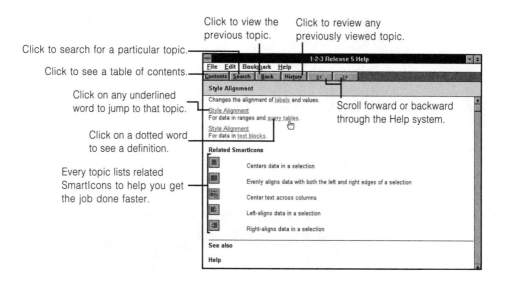

Click to view the previous topic.

Click to review any previously viewed topic.

Click to search for a particular topic.

Click to see a table of contents.

Click on any underlined word to jump to that topic.

Click on a dotted word to see a definition.

Every topic lists related SmartIcons to help you get the job done faster.

Scroll forward or backward through the Help system.

Beyond Survival

Searching for Specific Help

If you know what you're looking for, you can search for that specific topic, rather than wading through the Help system. Here's how:

1. Select Search from the Help menu, or click on the Search button at the top of any Help screen. The Search dialog box appears.

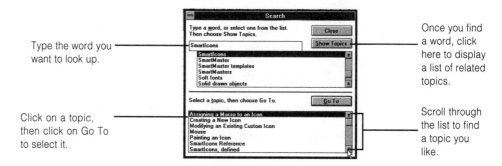

Type the word you want to look up.

Click on a topic, then click on Go To to select it.

Once you find a word, click here to display a list of related topics.

Scroll through the list to find a topic you like.

2. Type the word you want to look up. When you find something you like, click on Show Topics. A listing of related topics appears at the bottom of the Search window.

3. Scroll through the list of topics by clicking the up or down arrows on the scroll bar.

4. Click on a topic, then click on Go To. Or, you can simply double-click on the topic you want. The Help information on the topic you selected is displayed.

Taking a Tutorial

The 1-2-3 tutorials take you step by step through various common tasks. Using the tutorials, you can learn how to use 1-2-3 at your own speed. The 1-2-3 tutorials are highly recommended for new users.

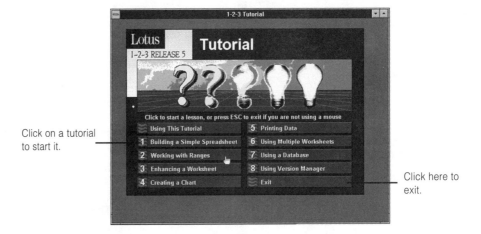

Click on a tutorial to start it.

Click here to exit.

To begin a tutorial:

1. Open the Help menu.

2. Select Tutorial. The 1-2-3 Tutorial window appears.

3. Click on a tutorial to start it.

When the tutorial begins, it opens a worksheet for you to work on so you don't have to worry about making mistakes in a real worksheet. Just read the instructions and follow the steps. (You may have to scroll down through the Tutorial window to view all of the steps. Just click on the down arrow of the scroll bar.)

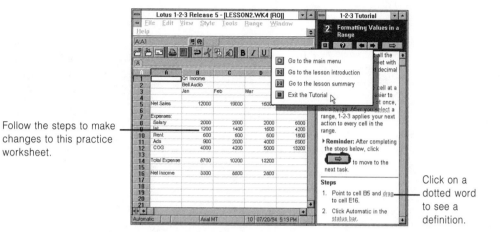

Follow the steps to make changes to this practice worksheet.

Click on a dotted word to see a definition.

You can navigate back and forth through the tutorial by using the following buttons:

Button	Description
	Click to view a menu from which you can exit or return to the table of contents.
	Click for a description of each button.
	Click to view a previous screen in the tutorial.
	Click to have the tutorial complete the steps for you.
	Click after you complete the steps.

When you complete the tutorial, you see a summary screen similar to this one.

Click here to view a menu from which you
can exit or return to the table of contents.

Click here to
continue to
the next
tutorial.

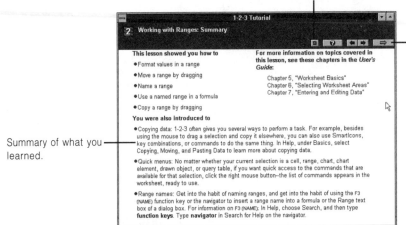

Summary of what you
learned.

1-2-3 Tutorial

2 **Working with Ranges: Summary**

This lesson showed you how to

● Format values in a range

● Move a range by dragging

● Name a range

● Use a named range in a formula

● Copy a range by dragging

You were also introduced to

● Copying data: 1-2-3 often gives you several ways to perform a task. For example, besides
using the mouse to drag a selection and copy it elsewhere, you can also use SmartIcons,
key combinations, or commands to do the same thing. In Help, under Basics, select
Copying, Moving, and Pasting Data to learn more about copying data.

● Quick menus: No matter whether your current selection is a cell, range, chart, chart
element, drawn object, or query table, if you want quick access to the commands that are
available for that selection, click the right mouse button--the list of commands appears in the
worksheet, ready to use.

● Range names: Get into the habit of naming ranges, and get into the habit of using the F3
(NAME) function key or the navigator to insert a range name into a formula or the Range text
box of a dialog box. For information on F3 (NAME): In Help, choose Search, and then type
function keys. Type **navigator** in Search for Help on the navigator.

**For more information on topics covered in
this lesson, see these chapters in the** *User's
Guide*:

Chapter 5, "Worksheet Basics"
Chapter 6, "Selecting Worksheet Areas"
Chapter 7, "Entering and Editing Data"

Cheat Sheet

Exit Lotus 1-2-3, Stage Right

1. Open the File menu.
2. Select Exit.
3. If you have forgotten to save your work, a dialog box appears. Just click on Yes and type a file name if prompted.

Closing a Worksheet File and Continuing to Work

1. Open the File menu.
2. Select Close.
3. If you have forgotten to save your work, a dialog box appears. Just click on Yes and type a file name if prompted.
4. Begin work on a new worksheet or open an existing worksheet.

Closing Down Windows Itself

1. Exit all programs first.
2. Open Program Manager's File menu.
3. Select Exit Windows. A dialog box appears, asking you if you really want to leave Windows.
4. Click on OK. When you see a DOS prompt (like **C:\>**), you can turn off your PC.

Exiting Lotus 1-2-3 for Windows

8

When you are through working in Lotus 1-2-3 for Windows, you should save all of your worksheets before you exit. (You learn how to save your worksheets in Chapter 15.) Once you've exited 1-2-3, you can start another program or exit Windows altogether.

In this chapter, you learn how to exit 1-2-3 safely, and the Beyond Survival section even teaches you how to exit Windows itself.

Basic Survival

Exit Lotus 1-2-3, Stage Right

Before you exit Lotus 1-2-3 for Windows, you must save all of your worksheets. If you don't, the changes you made to them will not be saved, and all of your work is lost. So jump to Chapter 15 to learn how to save your worksheets before you attempt to exit 1-2-3.

To exit Lotus 1-2-3 for Windows:

1. Open the File menu.

2. Select Exit.

3. If you have forgotten to save your work, the Exit dialog box appears. Just click on Yes and type a file name if prompted. Click on Save All to save all open worksheet files. For more info on how to save your work, see Chapter 15.

When you exit Lotus 1-2-3 for Windows, you return to Program Manager. From Program Manager, you can start another program or exit Windows.

Double-click Control-menu box to exit

If you're in a hurry, you can double-click the Program Control-menu box ▭ to exit Lotus 1-2-3 for Windows. The Program Control-menu box is located at the top left-hand corner of the 1-2-3 window, just above a similar (smaller) Control-menu box, called the Document Control-menu box ▭.

Beyond Survival

Closing a Worksheet File and Continuing to Work

If you're done with the Expenses worksheet and you want to open the Budget worksheet, you don't have to exit 1-2-3. You can simply close the file you're working on, then open another worksheet or start a new one. Closing a worksheet file puts it out of your way so you can work faster.

Again, before you close a worksheet file, you must save it. (See Chapter 15 for details on saving your work.) To close a worksheet file:

1. Open the File menu.

2. Select Close.

3. If you have forgotten to save your work, the Close dialog box appearss. Just click on Yes and type a file name if prompted. (For more info on how to save your work, see Chapter 15.)

Close docs when done with them

If you're in a hurry, you can double-click the Document Control-menu box ▭ to close the current worksheet file. The Document Control-menu box is located at the top left-hand corner of the window, just below a similar (bigger) Control-menu box, called the Program Control-menu box ▭.

Once you've closed a worksheet file, you can start a new worksheet or open an existing one. For information on opening an existing worksheet, see Chapter 17.

Closing Down Windows Itself

After you've safely exited Lotus 1-2-3 for Windows and all your other programs, you can safely exit Windows itself. Here's what you do:

1. Exit all programs first.

2. Open Program Manager's File menu.

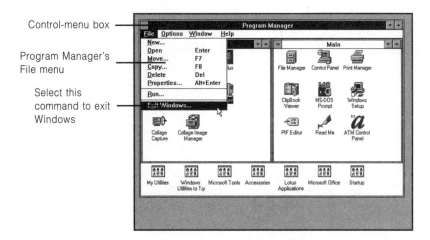

Control-menu box

Program Manager's File menu

Select this command to exit Windows

3. Select Exit Windows. The Exit Windows dialog box appears, asking you if you really want to leave Windows.

4. Click on OK. (Or, click Cancel to return to Windows unscathed.) When you see a DOS prompt (like **C:\>**), you can turn off your PC.

If you're in a hurry, you can double-click Program Manager's Control-menu box to exit Windows. It's located at the top left-hand corner of the Program Manager window.

PART 2

Creating Your First Worksheet

By now, you've learned a little about 1-2-3 and something about worksheets. In this section, you'll learn how to put it all together by creating your first worksheet. Along the way, you'll learn some pretty useful skills such as:

- Moving Around
- Entering Data
- Changing Data
- Selecting a Range
- Copying and Moving Data
- Naming a Range
- Saving Your Work

Cheat Sheet

Moving Around with the Mouse

Click to move the cell pointer.   Drag the scroll box to move a variable amount.

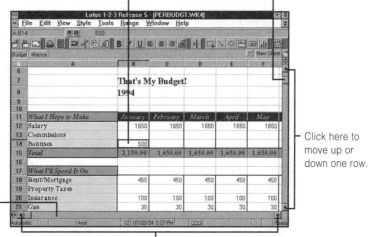

Click here to move up or down one row.

Click between arrows to move a whole screen.

Click here to move left or right one column.

Moving from Cell to Cell with the Keyboard

To move here:	Press this:
One cell in any direction	Arrow key
One whole screen up or down	PgUp or PgDn keys
One whole screen left or right	Ctrl+arrow key
To cell A1 of the current worksheet	Home
To cell A1 of the first worksheet	Ctrl+Home
To the last cell with data	End, then Home
To the last cell with data in the indicated direction	End, then arrow key

Moving to a Specific Cell

1. Press F5 (Go To).
2. (Optional) Select an object type from the Type of item list.
3. Type the address of the cell to move to, or select a name from those listed.
4. Click OK.

Moving Around

9

The active cell is marked by the cell pointer, a dark outline around the borders of the cell. To enter data in cells, you move the cell pointer to the appropriate cell and type your data. You can move the cell pointer with the mouse or the keyboard, whichever you prefer.

In this chapter, you'll learn how to move through your worksheet quickly and easily. In the Beyond Survival section, you'll learn how to move to a specific cell, and how to "freeze" certain cells so they always remain on-screen, even as you move through the worksheet.

Basic Survival

Moving Around with the Mouse

To move the cell pointer with the mouse, simply click on a visible cell. If the cell you want to move to is not visible, you'll need to use the scroll bars to see it.

There are two scroll bars: the horizontal scroll bar (located at the bottom of the screen) and the vertical scroll bar (located to the right side of the screen). With the scroll bars you can view parts of the worksheet that are not currently visible on-screen. For example, using the vertical scroll bar, you can move up or down to view rows above or

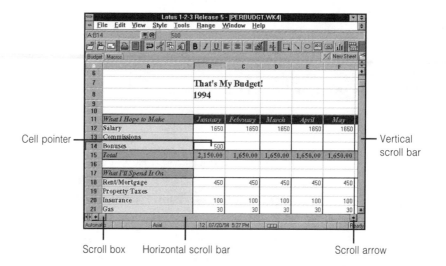

Cell pointer

Vertical scroll bar

Scroll box   Horizontal scroll bar   Scroll arrow

below the current viewing area.

Here's how to use a scroll bar:

To Move...	Click
One column or row	Click on a scroll arrow.
One whole screen	Click between the scroll arrows.
A variable amount	Click on the scroll box, drag it a variable amount, and then release.

Scrolling DOES NOT MOVE cell pointer

As you scroll, the cell pointer does *not* move. Once you've scrolled enough so that the cell you want to move to is visible, you must click on that cell to make it active (so move the cell pointer there). Once a cell is active, you can enter data into it.

Beyond Survival

Moving from Cell to Cell with the Keyboard

Sometimes it's faster to press a key to move to the cell you want than to fuss with the mouse. Here's a listing of 1-2-3's cell movement keys:

To move here:	Press this:
One cell in any direction	Arrow key
One whole screen up or down	PgUp or PgDn keys
One whole screen left or right	Ctrl+arrow key
To cell A1 of the current worksheet	Home
To cell A1 of the first worksheet	Ctrl+Home
To the last cell with data	End, then Home
To the last cell with data in the indicated direction	End, then arrow key

Cell A1 =
Home

Unlike scrolling with the mouse, pressing one of these keys or key combinations actually moves the cell pointer. For example, if you were to press Home, cell A1 would become the current cell.

Moving to a Specific Cell

Go To = F5

You can quickly move to any cell in the worksheet if you know its address or its name. (You'll learn how to name cells or ranges in Chapter 14.)

Select a range name from this list.

Or, type in a cell address.

1. Press F5 (Go To). The Go To dialog box appears.

2. (Optional) If you want to go to a named chart or other object, select it from the Type of item list.

3. Type the address of the cell to which you want to move, or select a name from those listed.

4. Click OK.

If you often move to certain cells in a worksheet, you can give those cells a name and then select them with the Navigator, located on the Control Panel. For example, if you are always moving to cell G6 because it contains the sales total for May, you could name cell G6 MAY_TOTALS. You could then select MAY_TOTALS from the Navigator list to go directly to cell G6. Again, you'll learn how to name cells and ranges in Chapter 14.

Freezing Titles As You Move

If you have a large worksheet and you scroll to see data outside the normal viewing range, it's easy to lose track of what you're doing because the row and column titles that help you identify things may no longer be visible. It's possible to "freeze" row and/or column titles before you scroll. Freezing the titles ensures that they remain on-screen as reference points—no matter how far you scroll. Here's what you do to freeze titles:

1. Move the cell pointer to a cell *below* any rows and/or to the *right* of any columns you want to freeze. For example, to freeze rows 1 and 2, move the cell pointer to row 3. To freeze column A, move the cell pointer to column B.

2. Open the View menu.

3. Select Freeze titles. The Freeze Titles dialog box appears.

4. Select Rows, Columns, or Both.

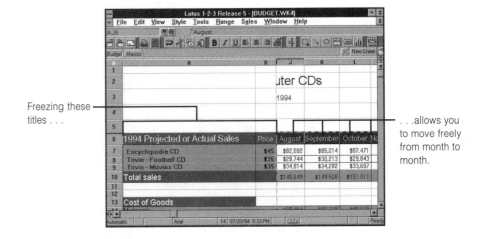

Freezing these titles . . .

. . .allows you to move freely from month to month.

5. Click OK.

You can now move the cell pointer to view other parts of the worksheet, without losing the titles that explain what that data represents. However, you won't be able to move to a frozen cell, unless you use the Go To command (F5), as explained in the previous section, or unless you "unfreeze" the titles. To unfreeze the rows and/or columns, follow these steps:

1. Open the View menu.

2. Select Clear Titles.

Cheat Sheet

Entering Values, Labels, or Dates

Cancel button ─┐ ┌─ Confirm button   Data is displayed in the
                                       contents box and in the cell.

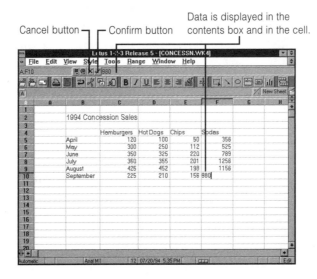

1. Move to the cell in which you want to enter your data.
2. Type the value, label, or date (see examples).
3. Click on the Confirm button or press Enter.

Examples

Value	Label	Date	Time
−199	Mrs. Jones	04/08/94	2:30 PM
.567	12 West Washington	8-Apr-94	2:30:15 PM
$24.98	278-1345	8-Apr	14:30:15
(98.12)	Qtr 1		14:30

Entering a Series of Years, Months, and Other Data

1. Enter the first two values of a series into adjoining cells.
2. Select the two cells.
3. Slide the mouse pointer to the right-hand corner of the second cell.
4. Click and drag over cells you want to fill, and then release the mouse button.

10

Entering Data

Data is information you type into your 1-2-3 worksheet. Data takes one of three forms: a value, a label, or a formula. A value is a number, something that can be used in a calculation, such as $1,200, −10, or .567. A label is anything else, such as Expenses, January '94, or 578-0921. You'll learn more about formulas in Chapter 29.

When you enter data into a cell, it overlays whatever is already in the cell (if there is anything). So if you make a mistake while entering data, you can simply select the cell again and retype it. Or you can edit a cell's contents instead of typing it over; see Chapter 11 for details.

In this chapter, you'll learn all the ins and outs of entering data correctly. When you are entering data, the mode indicator on the status bar changes to Value or Label. As you enter data, check the mode indicator on the status bar to ensure that 1-2-3 has correctly identified your entry. The data you enter appears in both the contents box and the cell.

Basic Survival

Entering Numbers (Values)

Values (numbers) begin with one of these:

0, 1, 2, 3, 4, 5, 6, 7, 8, or 9

+ (plus), − (minus), ((left parenthesis), . (period), or a currency symbol such as $.

When you enter a value beginning with one of the characters listed above, 1-2-3 identifies it as such and automatically right-justifies it (moves it to the right within the cell). To enter a value (number):

Important!

1. Move to the cell in which you want to enter a number.

2. Type the number. You enter negative numbers by pressing – first and then typing the number. If you make a mistake, press Backspace to erase it, and then retype. If you don't want to make the entry at all, click on the Cancel button or press Esc.

3. Confirm the entry by either clicking on the Confirm button or by pressing Enter. You can also confirm an entry by moving the cell pointer (by pressing an arrow key or clicking in another cell). To cancel the entry, click on the Cancel button or press Esc. If you enter a value that is wider than the cell, you'll see ********. Refer to Chapter 22 for help on widening the column so you can see the actual number in the cell.

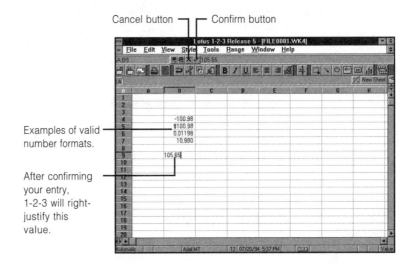

Cancel button ⎤ ⎡ Confirm button

Examples of valid number formats.

After confirming your entry, 1-2-3 will right-justify this value.

Press Esc to cancel.

How the value appears in the cell depends on how 1-2-3 is set up. Usually, numbers appear with one decimal place. To change the way numbers appear, you *format* them. Formatting saves you the time and trouble of entering extra zeroes, commas, or dollar signs. With the touch of a button, you can decide exactly how all your numbers should look. For example, you can make negative numbers appear within parentheses or in red if you want. You'll learn how to format numbers in Chapter 24. So for the greatest speed and accuracy, just enter the value as is, without trailing zeros, commas, or currency symbols.

Entering Labels

When you enter something that is not a number (label), 1-2-3 identifies it and automatically left-justifies it (moves it to the left edge of the cell). You can override this and center or even right-align labels if you want.

When you enter a label, 1-2-3 inserts a *label prefix* at the beginning of the label. The prefix tells 1-2-3 how to align the label. For example, the prefix ' tells 1-2-3 to automatically align the label to the left. You can right-align and even center labels if you want, either by typing a prefix or by selecting the proper commands and letting 1-2-3 insert the correct prefix for you. You'll learn how to align labels in Chapter 25.

To enter a label:

1. Move to the cell in which you want to enter a label.

Type ' in front of ZIP codes and phone #'s

2. Type the label. If you need to enter a label that is all numbers, such as a ZIP code or a phone number, type the ' prefix before you type the label. 1-2-3 understands that you're entering a label, and aligns the label to the left. If you make a mistake, press Backspace to erase it, and then retype. If you don't want to make the entry at all, click on the Cancel button or press Esc.

3. Confirm the entry by either clicking on the Confirm button or by pressing Enter. You can also confirm an entry by moving the cell pointer (by pressing an arrow key or clicking in another cell).

Type ' in front of any label that 1-2-3 would normally treat as a number.

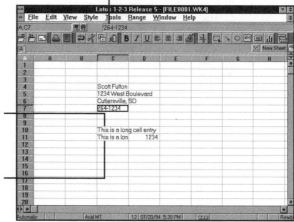

Labels that are too big for their cells are displayed in adjacent cells if those cells are empty.

If the adjacent cell contains data, labels that are too long for their cells are not fully displayed.

Remember this!

If you enter a label that is wider than the cell, it is displayed over top of the cells to the right if those cells are empty. If those cells aren't empty, you'll only see whatever can be displayed in the cell's regular space. What you actually type still remains, even though the entire label is not displayed until you select that cell.

Entering Dates and Times

Dates and times must be entered in a special format so 1-2-3 can recognize them and act accordingly. If you don't use one of these formats, the dates and times will not be identified properly, and you won't be able to sort by those dates or times or use them to perform calculations (such as calculating age, years of service, and so on). Here is a list of the standard date and time formats:

Format	Example
Day-month-year	16-Oct-93
Day-month	16-Oct
Long international	10/16/93
Long AM/PM	2:25:59 PM
Short AM/PM	2:25 PM
Long 24-hour	14:25:59
Short 24-hour	14:25

If one of these formats doesn't suit you, don't worry. You can reformat dates in a variety of ways after you enter them. See Chapter 24 for more information.

To enter a date or time:

1. Move to the cell in which you want to enter a date or time.

2. Type the date or time using one of the above formats. If you make a mistake, press Backspace to erase it, and then retype. If you don't want to make the entry at all, click on the Cancel button or press Esc.

3. Confirm the entry either by clicking on the Confirm button or by pressing Enter. You can also confirm an entry by moving the cell pointer (by pressing an arrow key or clicking in another cell).

If you enter a date any other way, 1-2-3 treats it as a label.

Valid date formats ——

Beyond Survival

Entering a Series of Years, Months, and Other Data

1-2-3 can help you quickly enter data in a series, such as a series of months, days, years, quarters, or even a range of numbers such as 1–10 or 5%–25%.

To enter data in a series:

1. In a cell, enter the first value in the series.

2. In an adjoining cell, enter the next value in the series. (The two cells must be right next to each other.)

3. Drag the mouse over the first cell and then the second cell to select both cells.

4. Release the mouse button and slide the mouse pointer to the right-hand corner of the second cell. (The first two cells remain selected.) The pointer changes to 🖑.

5. Click the mouse button and stretch the selection by dragging over additional cells you want to fill with your series. (For example, if you're filling in the days of the week and you entered Monday and Tuesday in the first two cells, drag over the next five cells to fill the whole week.)

6. Release the mouse button, and 1-2-3 fills the selected cells with your data series. (For example, Wednesday through Sunday would appear in the next five cells.)

Select the first two cells in the series, and then drag.

Data series examples

1-2-3 fills the selected cells with your data series.

You can skip the part about entering data in the second cell (step 2 above) if your series is common and uses an increment of 1, as in these series, for example:

Monday, Tuesday, Wednesday . . .

January, February, March . . .

1, 2, 3 . . .

1994, 1995, 1996 . . .

If 1-2-3 does not fill the series correctly, click the Undo button. Repeat the steps with data in the second cell.

Cheat Sheet

In-Cell Editing of Data

1. Double-click on the cell you want to edit.
2. Click at the spot where you want to begin editing, or use any of these keys:

Arrow keys	Move the cursor left or right one character.
Home	Moves cursor to the first character in the cell.
End	Moves cursor to the last character in the cell.

3. You can delete characters with these keys:

Delete	Deletes the character to the *right* of cursor.
Backspace	Deletes the character to the *left* of cursor.

4. Click on the Confirm button or press Enter.

Updating Old Data with New Data

1. Click on the cell whose contents you want to replace.
2. Type your new entry.
3. Click on the Confirm button or press Enter.

Deleting Data

1. Click on the cell or range of cells whose contents you want to delete.
2. Press Delete.

Changing Data

11

After you've entered and confirmed your data, you may decide that the data needs to be changed. For example, facts and figures may have changed, or you may have made a mistake in data entry. Whatever the reason for the change, 1-2-3 makes it easy to change the contents of a cell. You can retype the cell's contents, but in some cases (such as a forgotten decimal point or parenthesis), it's simply easier to edit the contents of the cell. You can also erase the contents of a cell completely if you want to. In this chapter, you'll learn how to do all this and more. In the Beyond Survival section, you'll even learn how to undo your changes and how to delete the contents of cells quickly with the mouse.

Basic Survival

In-Cell Editing of Data

The easiest way to change the data in a cell is with in-cell editing:

1. **Double-click on the cell** you want to edit, or move the cell pointer to that cell and **press F2.**

To edit, double-click or press F2

2. **Click at the area in the cell where you want to begin editing,** or use any of these keys to move the cursor (the blinking vertical line):

   ← or →   Moves the cursor left or right one character.

   Home   Moves the cursor to the first character in the cell.

   End   Moves the cursor to the last character in the cell.

3. If you begin typing, **what you type is inserted** (added) to the right of the cursor. You can delete characters with one of these keys:

   Delete   Deletes the character to the *right* of the cursor.

   Backspace   Deletes the character to the *left* of the cursor.

4. When the entry is correct, click on the Confirm button or press Enter. If you don't want to edit the entry and you want it to stay as it was, click on the Cancel button or press Esc.

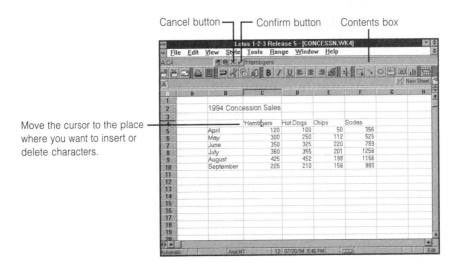

Cancel button ⎯⎯ ⎯ Confirm button ⎯⎯ Contents box

Move the cursor to the place where you want to insert or delete characters.

If you've used older versions of 1-2-3, you're probably used to editing a cell's contents with the contents box. You can still do that if you want by clicking on the cell you want to edit, clicking in the contents box, and then making your changes. However, you'll probably find that in-cell editing is more convenient than using the contents box.

Updating Old Data with New Data

If you need to make extensive changes to a cell's contents, it may be easier to simply replace its contents with something else than to edit. This is often the case when figures are updated from last month or last year.

To replace a cell's contents with new data:

1. Click on the cell whose contents you want to replace, or use the arrow keys to move the cell pointer to that cell.

2. Type your new entry. What you type completely replaces the current contents of the cell.

3. Click on the Confirm button or press Enter.

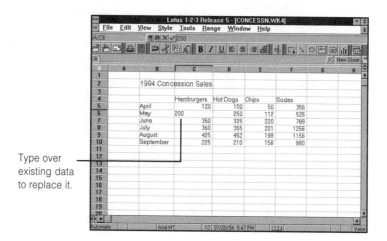

Type over existing data to replace it.

Deleting Data

You can delete the contents of a cell, its style, or both. The *style* or format of a cell's data controls how it looks. When you erase the style, the data remains but it is changed to a generic format. You'll learn more about styles and how to format data in Chapters 23–28. You'll learn how to remove style formatting in Chapter 28.

To delete the contents of a cell:

1. Click on the cell whose contents you want to delete, or use the arrow keys to move the cell pointer to that cell.

2. Press Delete.

Select cell & press Delete

To delete the contents of several adjacent cells (a range of cells):

1. Click on the first cell in the range whose contents you want to delete.

2. Continue to hold down the mouse button as you drag downward or to the right, over the adjacent cells you want to select. The cells you select are highlighted.

3. Press Delete.

Click on the first cell in the range. ──

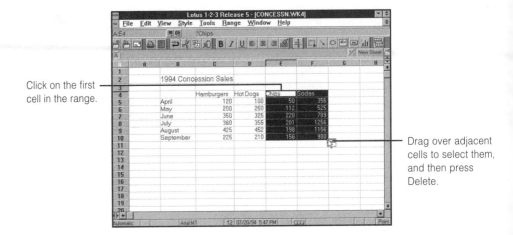

── Drag over adjacent cells to select them, and then press Delete.

Beyond Survival

Undoing Your Edits

Don't forget this. Very Important!

If you've accidentally deleted or edited a cell's valuable data and confirmed the change, it's not too late to get back the cell's original contents. To restore the cell's contents, follow these steps:

1. Don't make any additional changes to the worksheet.

2. Click on the Undo button ⮌. Your editing change is undone, and the contents of the cell returns to what it was.

Clicking the Undo button restores the last change made to the worksheet, so if you've made additional changes after the one you want to undo, Undo won't be able to help you. Instead you must re-enter the contents of the cell. If you don't know what that data originally was, refer to a recent printout.

If all else fails, you can close the worksheet without saving your changes, but that means you'll lose all changes that have not yet been saved, not just the one you want to undo. To close the worksheet without saving changes, just open the File menu and select Close. Click on No when it asks you if you want to save changes. Reopen the worksheet file, and you'll be back to where you were before you made any changes. (See Chapter 17 for information on opening a worksheet file.)

Deleting Cells with Drag and Clear

Deleting the contents of a range of cells couldn't be any easier than with Drag and Clear. (Clear is another word 1-2-3 uses for delete.) As you learned earlier in this chapter, you can delete the contents of range of cells by selecting them and then pressing Delete. However, that method involves both the mouse (for selecting the cells) and the keyboard (for pressing the Delete key). Drag and Clear is a method of deletion which involves only the mouse:

1. Click on the first cell in the range whose contents you want to delete.

2. Continue to hold down the mouse button as you drag downward or to the right over the adjacent cells you want to select. The cells you select are highlighted.

3. Release the mouse button. Move the mouse pointer to the right-hand corner of the last cell in the range. The mouse pointer changes to 🔳.

Click on the first cell in the range, and then drag over adjacent cells to select them.

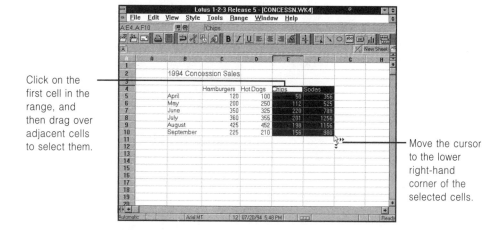

Move the cursor to the lower right-hand corner of the selected cells.

4. Press and hold down the mouse button. Drag upwards, over the top of the cells you originally selected.

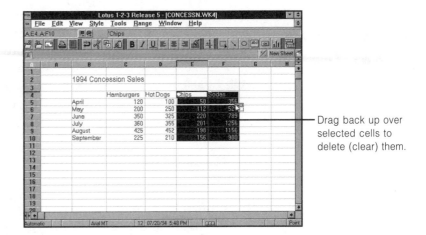

Drag back up over
selected cells to
delete (clear) them.

5. Release the mouse button, and 1-2-3 deletes the contents of all
the cells you selected, except for the first cell in the range.

Cheat Sheet

Selecting a Range with the Mouse

1. Click on the upper left-hand cell in the range.
2. Press and hold the left mouse button.
3. Drag down and/or to the right to select additional cells.

Selecting a Range with the Keyboard

1. Using the arrow keys, move the cell pointer to the upper left-hand cell in the range.
2. Press and hold the Shift key.
3. Use the arrow keys to highlight the range.

Selecting a Noncontiguous Range (Collection)

1. Select the first range in the collection.
2. Press and hold down the Ctrl key.
3. Select additional ranges.

Selecting a 3-D Range

1. Select the range within the first worksheet.
2. Press and hold the Shift key.
3. Click on the tab of the last worksheet in the range.

12

Selecting a Range

A *range* can be a single cell, but most often a range refers to a collection of *connected* cells. The cells in a range may all be in one column or one row, or in a combination of columns and rows that form a rectangle. A range is defined by its anchor points: the upper left and lower right-hand cells of the range. The figure here shows the ranges C4..E6, B9..E9, and D12.

A range is any combination of cells that form a rectangle.

A range can also be a single cell.

Range = connected cells

You can select a single range as shown, or a 3-D range, which includes the *same cells* in multiple worksheets. You can also select a group of noncontiguous cells (a *collection*). Once you've selected a range or collection, you can format, copy, move, or delete the range, or use the range in a formula. In this chapter, you'll learn how to select ranges in various ways.

Basic Survival

Selecting a Range with the Mouse

Selecting a range with the mouse is probably the most common method. If the range is named, you can use the mouse to select it from the Navigator, located in the Control Panel at the top of the 1-2-3 window. You'll learn how to name ranges in Chapter 14.

To select a unnamed range with the mouse:

1. Click on the upper left-hand cell in the range.

2. Press and hold the left mouse button.

Drag from upper left to lower right

3. Drag down and/or to the right to select additional cells.

You can actually drag from any corner to select a range, but dragging from the upper left to the lower right corner of a range is by far the most common method.

To select a range, click on the upper left-hand cell and drag to the lower right-hand cell.

Click on a worksheet label to select an entire worksheet.

Click on a column label to select an entire column.

Click on a row label to select an entire row.

Lotus 1-2-3 Release 5 - [REVBYPER.WK4]

File Edit View Style Tools Range Window Help

Revenue by Sales Person

	Jane	Joe	Scott
Whatsits	$325,025	$260,596	$259,489
Widgets	$299,360	$369,125	$298,745
Total Revenue	$624,385	$649,721	$558,234
Percentage of Projected	107.65%	112.02%	96.25%
Projected Sales Per Person		$580,000	

If you select the wrong range, simply repeat these steps. To deselect a range, click anywhere in the worksheet. Here are some tips for selecting ranges quickly:

- To select an entire column or row, click on the column or row label.

- To select multiple columns or rows, drag over the column/row labels.

- To select an entire worksheet, click on the worksheet label (the button in the upper left-hand corner of the worksheet).

- To select more than one worksheet, press Ctrl and click on each worksheet label. To quickly select a group of worksheets, click on the first worksheet's label, press Shift, and click on the label of the last worksheet in the group.

- You can quickly select a range by clicking on the upper left-hand cell, holding the Shift key, and then clicking the lower right-hand cell.

- To reshape a range, press and hold the Shift key as you drag the lower right-hand corner to its new location.

Selecting a Range with the Keyboard

Although selecting a range with the mouse is much easier, you can also select a range with the keyboard:

1. Use the arrow keys to move the cell pointer to the upper left-hand cell in the range.

2. Press and hold the Shift key.

3. Use the arrow keys to highlight the range. Again, you can select a range beginning from any corner, but selecting a range from its upper left to its lower right corner is the most common method.

Start at the upper left-hand cell.

Then extend the selection to the lower right-hand cell.

You can also select a range by pressing F4 and then using the arrow keys to highlight the range. You don't have to hold the F4 key down as you do the Shift key, because F4 "anchors" the left-hand corner of the range for you.

If you select the wrong range, simply repeat these steps. Deselect a range by pressing Esc or any arrow key.

Selecting a Range from Within a Dialog Box

Some commands allow you to select a range from within a dialog box, instead of selecting the range before you issue the command. Follow these steps to select the range from within a dialog box:

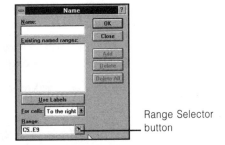

Range Selector button

1. In a dialog box in which you are asked to select a range (such as the Name dialog box), click on the Range Selector button, or press Tab until it's highlighted and then press an arrow key.

2. Select the range with the mouse as usual. Or, to select the range with the keyboard, press Esc if necessary to free the anchor cell. Then use the arrow keys to relocate it and press period (.) to reanchor the range. Use the arrow keys to extend the range. When the range you want is selected, press Enter.

3. Make any additional selections in the dialog box, and then click OK or press Enter.

Beyond Survival

Typing in a Range Address

Remember this!

In a dialog box or in a formula, you can type a range address instead of selecting the range with the mouse or the keyboard. A range is defined by its anchor points: the upper left and lower right-hand cells of the range. A *range address* uses these two anchor points, separated by two dots. The ranges shown in the next figure have these addresses:

B5..B6

D4..E6

B9..E9

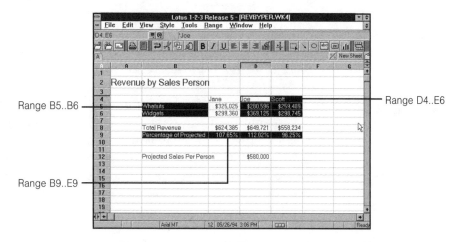

3-D ranges include the same cells in adjacent worksheets and are written by including the worksheet name as part of the address, as in A:D4..C:E6. The 3-D range A:D4..C:E6 includes the range of cells from D4..E6 in worksheets A, B, and C.

Selecting a Noncontiguous Range (Collection)

Noncontiguous = Ctrl + mouse

Sometimes the cells you want to work with are not connected to each other (they are *noncontiguous*). You can select a noncontiguous range (called a *collection* in 1-2-3), but you must use a mouse:

1. Select the first range in the collection.

2. Press and hold down the Ctrl key.

3. Select additional ranges, including entire columns or rows if you like. You can switch to other worksheets too; simply continue to hold down the Ctrl key as you make your selections.

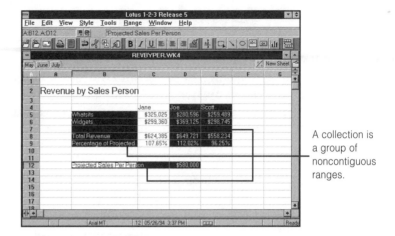

A collection is a group of noncontiguous ranges.

The range address for a collection consists of the addresses of each range, *separated by commas*. The address of the collection pictured here is B5..B9, D4..E9, B12..D12.

Selecting 3-D Ranges

A 3-D range is a collection of the same group of cells within several contiguous worksheets. For example, the 3-D range shown in the figure includes the cells C4..E6 within three adjacent worksheets, worksheets A, B, and C. If you wanted to select the range C4..E6 in worksheets A and C, that would be a collection—and not a 3-D range. To select the collection instead, you should follow the directions in the previous section. To select a 3-D range:

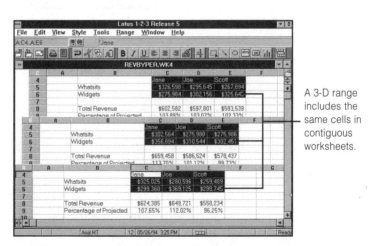

A 3-D range includes the same cells in contiguous worksheets.

1. Select the range within the first worksheet. For example, select the range C5..E6.

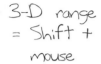
3-D range
= Shift +
mouse

2. Press and hold the Shift key.

3. Extend the selection to include these same cells in additional worksheets by clicking on the tab of the last worksheet in the range. For example, holding down the Shift key, click on the tabs A, B, and C. (Remember, in a 3-D range, the worksheets are contiguous, as in A, B, C.)

Cheat Sheet

Copying Data

1. Click on the first cell you want to copy.
2. Drag down and/or to the right to select additional cells.
3. Click on the Copy button .
4. Click in the first cell of the new location.
5. Click on the Paste button .

Moving Data

1. Click on the first cell you want to move.
2. Drag down and/or to the right to select additional cells.
3. Click on the Cut button or press Ctrl+X.
4. Click in the first cell of the new location.
5. Click on the Paste button or press Ctrl+V.

Copying the Same Data to a Range of Cells

1. Click on the cell you want to copy.
2. Drag down and/or to the right to select the cells to which you want to copy.
3. Click the right mouse button and select Copy Down or Copy Right.

Copying or Moving Data Using Drag and Drop

1. Select the cells you want to copy or move.
2. Move the mouse pointer to the left-hand edge of the range, until it appears as a hand.
3. To copy the cells, press and hold the Ctrl key. If you're moving the cells, skip this step.
4. Drag the cells to the new location and release the mouse button.

Copying and Moving Data

Being able to copy and move data makes it easier for you to construct your worksheet. Rather than use up valuable time retyping data, you can copy it or move it wherever you like—all with a few keystrokes. You can copy or move data within a single worksheet, from one worksheet to another, and even between files.

When you copy or move data, it is placed temporarily in a storage area called the *Clipboard*. You can paste the data from the Clipboard to your current cell location at any time. The Clipboard is a common area that all Windows programs share. Thus, while the Clipboard makes it easy to copy or move data within a 1-2-3 worksheet, it also makes it easy to copy or move data between Lotus 1-2-3 and other Windows programs.

You should also know that the contents of the Clipboard is never erased (unless you exit Windows altogether). Instead, it is replaced with new data each time you use the Copy or Cut commands. That means you can copy the same piece of data over and over again, until you replace the data on the Clipboard with something else (that is, until you use the Copy or Cut commands again).

Basic Survival

Copying Data

When you copy data, the original data remains in place, and 1-2-3 places a copy on the Clipboard. When you paste the data to a new location, that data exists in *two places*—the original location and the new location. If you want to actually relocate data, you should use the Move command (see steps later in this chapter).

To copy the contents of a cell:

1. Click on the cell whose contents you want to copy.

2. Click on the Copy button or press Ctrl+C.

3. Click in the new location, or use the arrow keys to move the cell pointer.

$Ctrl+C = Copy$

4. Click on the Paste button 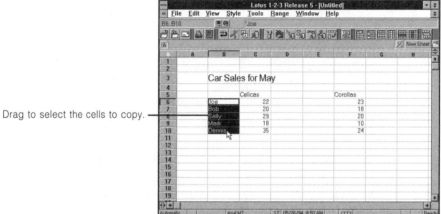 or press Ctrl+V. The data is copied to the new location.

$Ctrl+V = Paste$

To copy the contents of a range of cells:

1. Click on the first cell whose contents you want to copy.

2. Press and hold the left mouse button. Drag down and/or to the right to select additional cells.

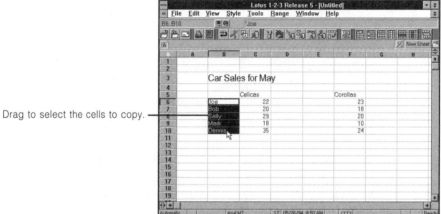

Drag to select the cells to copy.

3. Click on the Copy button or press Ctrl+C.

4. Click in the first cell of the new location, or use the arrow keys to move the cell pointer.

5. Click on the Paste button or press Ctrl+V. The data is copied to the new location, beginning at the cell you selected in step 4.

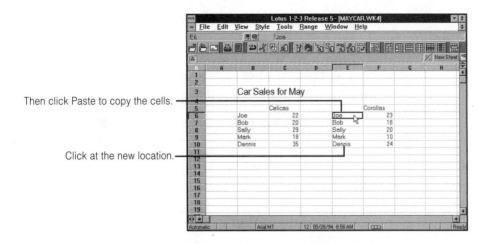

Then click Paste to copy the cells.

Click at the new location.

Copying data overlays the contents of the cells in the new location. If you accidentally overwrite data, click on the Undo button ![undo]. If you want to insert the copied data between existing cells, you must first insert a range of cells to which you can copy. See Chapter 21 for help on inserting cells.

Moving Data

When you move data, the data is removed from its original place and placed on the Clipboard. Later, when you paste the data, it is copied from the Clipboard into the new location. Unlike data that is copied, data that is moved exists in the new location only. If you want data to exist in both the original and the new location, you should use the Copy command discussed earlier in this chapter.

To move the contents of a cell:

1. Click on the cell whose contents you want to move, or use the arrow keys to move the cell pointer.

2. Click on the Cut button ![cut] or press Ctrl+X.

Ctrl+X = Cut

3. Click in the new location, or use the arrow keys to move the cell pointer.

Ctrl+V = Paste

4. Click on the Paste button ![paste] or press Ctrl+V. The data is moved to the new location.

91

To move the contents of a range of cells:

1. Click on the first cell whose contents you want to move.

2. Press and hold the left mouse button. Drag down and/or to the right to select additional cells.

Select the range of cells to move. —

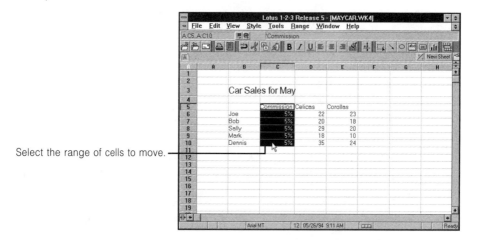

3. Click on the Cut button or press Ctrl+X.

4. Click in the first cell of the new location, or use the arrow keys to move the cell pointer.

5. Click on the Paste button or press Ctrl+V. The data is moved to the new location, beginning at the cell you selected in step 4.

Click at the new location. —

Then click Paste to move the cells. —

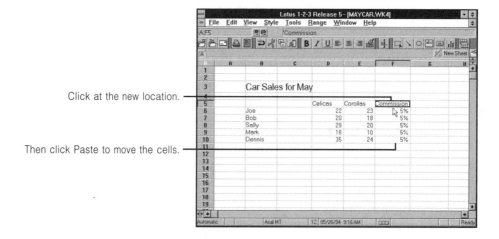

Moving data also overlays the contents of the cells in the new location. If you accidentally overwrite data, click on the Undo button 🔄. If you want to insert the data between existing cells, you must first insert a range of cells into which you can then paste the data. (See Chapter 21 for details on inserting cells.)

Beyond Survival

Copying the Same Data to a Range of Cells

You can copy the contents of a cell so that it fills a range of cells. This is especially useful for copying formulas (such as copying a formula that computes a total from one column to other columns). Here's what to do.

1. Click on the cell whose contents you want to copy.

2. Press and hold the left mouse button. Drag down and/or to the right to select the cells to which you want to copy.

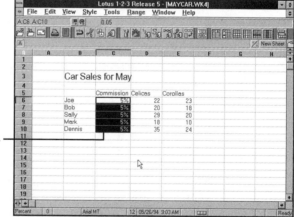

Copy the same data down a range of cells.

3. Click the right mouse button and select Copy Down or Copy Right. The contents of the first cell is copied to the other cells you selected.

In step 3, you can click the Copy Right ⊞ or Copy Down ⊞ buttons instead of selecting the commands from the quick menu. You'll find these buttons on the Editing SmartIcon set.

Copying Data Using Drag and Drop

Probably the easiest way to copy data is with 1-2-3's drag and drop feature.

1. Click on the first cell whose contents you want to copy.

2. Press and hold the left mouse button. Drag down and/or to the right to select additional cells.

3. Move the mouse pointer to the left-hand edge of the range, until it changes into a hand.

Select the cells you want to copy.

Move the mouse pointer to the left until it changes to a hand.

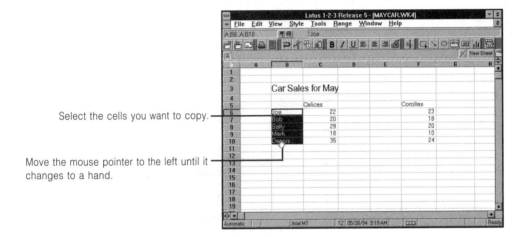

4. Press and hold the Ctrl key.

5. Drag the cells to the new location. The pointer changes to a fist with a plus sign.

6. The selected cells appear with a dotted outline to help you mark their location as you drag. Release the mouse button, and the cells are copied to the new location.

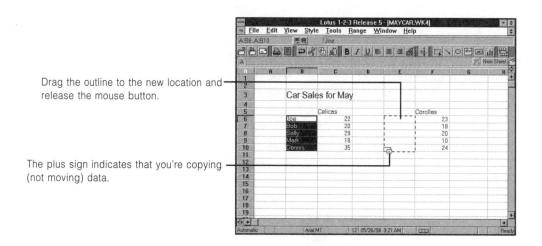

Drag the outline to the new location and release the mouse button.

The plus sign indicates that you're copying (not moving) data.

Moving Data Using Drag and Drop

Drag and drop is even easier to do when you're moving data than when you're copying it.

1. **Click on the first cell** whose contents you want to move, or use the arrow keys to move the cell pointer.

2. Press and **hold the left mouse button.** Drag down and/or to the right to select additional cells.

3. Move the mouse pointer to the **left-hand edge of the range,** until it changes into a hand.

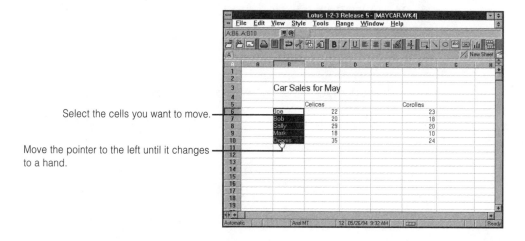

Select the cells you want to move.

Move the pointer to the left until it changes to a hand.

95

4. Drag the cells to the new location. The pointer changes to a fist.

5. The selected cells appear with a dotted outline to help you mark their location as you drag. Release the mouse button, and the cells are copied to the new location.

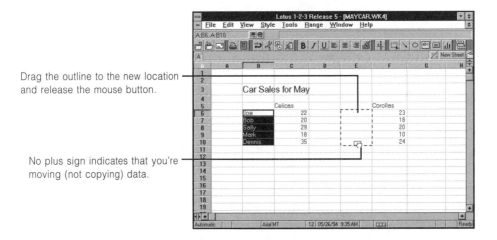

Drag the outline to the new location and release the mouse button.

No plus sign indicates that you're moving (not copying) data.

Copying a 3-D Range

If you have more than one worksheet in your file, you may need to copy data from one worksheet to adjacent (contiguous) worksheets in the file. Luckily enough, 1-2-3 provides an easy way to do just that. (If you need to review how to select 3-D ranges, see Chapter 12.)

To copy a range from one worksheet to adjacent worksheets:

1. Select the range you want to copy in the first worksheet.

2. Press and hold the Shift key.

3. Click on the tab of the last worksheet to which you want to copy.

4. Now that you have your 3-D range selected, press the Ctrl key.

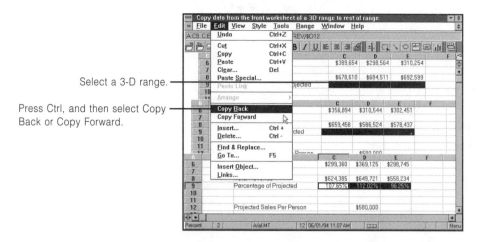

Select a 3-D range.

Press Ctrl, and then select Copy Back or Copy Forward.

5. Open the Edit menu and select Copy Back. The data from the first worksheet is copied to later worksheets in the group.

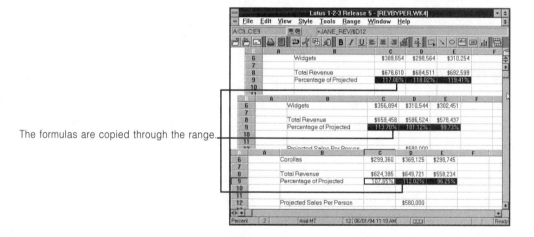

The formulas are copied through the range.

You can copy forward from the last worksheet in the group (such as E) to the first worksheet in the group (such as B) by selecting Copy Forward instead.

Cheat Sheet

Naming a Range

1. Select the range you want to name.
2. Open the Range menu.
3. Select Name.
4. Type a range name.
5. Click on the Add button.
6. Click OK.

Deleting a Range Name

1. Open the Range menu.
2. Select Name.
3. Select a range name from the list.
4. Click on the Delete button.
5. Click OK.

Selecting and Going to a Named Range

1. Click on the Navigator.
2. Select a range name from the list.

14

Naming a Range

When you're working in a large worksheet, it's easier to name areas of the worksheet and use these names than to have to remember actual cell addresses. You can use range names anywhere you'd normally use a cell address (for example, in a formula or in a command, such as Copy or Print). You can use range names to quickly select a group of cells, or to move to that area of the worksheet.

Basic Survival

Naming a Range

Naming a range is fairly easy, but there are a few things you need to remember:

Range names can contain up to 15 characters.

Don't use these characters: ! , ; . + − * / & > < @ # {

Don't use a space between words. Instead, use an underscore, as in Qtr_1 or Sales_94.

Don't use anything that looks like a cell address (for example, don't use Q4 to stand for quarter 4).

Don't use anything that looks like the name of a keyboard key, such as Home, End, or Delete.

To create a range name:

1. Select the range you want to name.

2. Open the Range menu.

3. Select Name. The Name dialog box appears.

Type your range name here

Range selector

4. Type a range name in the Name text box.

5. Click on the Add button.

6. Click OK.

Instead of following steps 2 and 3, you can right-click and select Name from the quick menu. Also, you don't have to select your range in step 1; instead, you can select it in step 5 using the Range Selector in the dialog box.

Once you've created a range name, you can use it instead of the range address. In dialog boxes that call for a range, you can type the range name in the Range text box, or you can press F3 and select the range name from a list. You can also go to a named range by clicking on the Navigator at the top of the 1-2-3 window, and selecting it from the list (see later section in this chapter for details).

Deleting a Range Name

When you delete a range name, the data in that range is unaffected—in other words, the data itself is not deleted, only the range name. If you were using the range name in a formula, 1-2-3 automatically substitutes the proper range address.

To delete a range name:

1. Open the Range menu.

2. Select Name. The Name dialog box appears.

3. Select the range name you want to delete from the Existing named ranges list.

Select a range name from the list.

Then click Delete.

4. Click on the Delete button.

5. Click OK.

You can delete all range names in a file by clicking on the Delete All button in the Name dialog box.

Beyond Survival

Selecting and Going to a Named Range

Use Navigator to go to a named range

Once a range is named, you can use the Navigator to quickly select that range and move the cell pointer to it. The Navigator is a button located at the top of the 1-2-3 window. When you click on the Navigator, 1-2-3 displays a list of range names for the current worksheet file. Here's what you do:

1. Click on the Navigator.

2. Select a range name from the list that appears.

Click on the Navigator and select a range name.

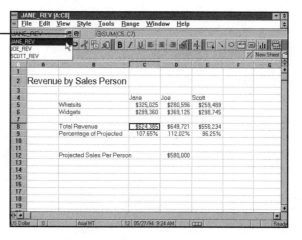

Cheat Sheet

Saving a Worksheet for the First Time

1. Click on the File Save button 🖫.
2. Type a name for your worksheet using up to 8 characters.
3. Click OK.

Saving That Worksheet Again

Click on the File Save button 🖫.

Saving to a Different Drive or Directory

1. Open the File menu and select Save As.
2. To change the file name, type in a new one. Otherwise, skip this step.
3. To save to a different directory, double-click on the directory name.
4. To save to a diskette, click on the down arrow under Drives, and select either A: or B:.
5. Click OK.

Saving Automatically As You Work

1. Open the Tools menu and select User Setup.
2. Click on the Save files every... option.
3. Type the number of minutes you want 1-2-3 to wait between automatic saves.
4. Click OK.

Saving Your File with a Password

1. Open the File menu and select Save As.
2. Select the With password option and click OK.
3. Type in your password.
4. Press Tab to move to the Verify text box, and type the same password again.
5. Click OK.

15

Saving Your Work

The work you create is held temporarily in the computer's memory. If you shut off the power to the computer or exit the 1-2-3 program without first saving your work, this data is erased. To retain a permanent copy of the work you do, you need to save it to disk.

Save at least every 10 minutes

You should save frequently throughout a work session, so that the permanent copy on disk is updated. Save your work every time you make any major changes or at least every 10 minutes. That way, should something happen (such as an unexpected power failure), you won't lose very many of the changes you've made because you'll have a fairly recent copy of your work saved safely to disk.

Saving a worksheet file saves all of the worksheets in that file. So if you have a big file with multiple worksheets, such as January, February, March, and so on, you save it all in one step. (See Chapter 18 for information on adding worksheets to a file.) In this chapter, you learn how to save your work in various ways and how to automate the process so you can't forget!

Basic Survival

Saving a Worksheet for the First Time

When you save a worksheet file for the first time, you must give it a name. That name can be up to eight characters long, and it can include letters and numbers but no spaces (use an underscore instead). For example, here are four valid names: SALES_94, FY94INCM, MAY_PROJ, and HOMEBGT. All file names have an *extension* (a last name), which helps programs identify them. Lotus 1-2-3 automatically adds the extension .WK5 to all worksheets. So the worksheet file names above become: SALES_94.WK5, MAY_PROJ.WK5, and so on.

To save your worksheet for the first time:

1. Click on the File Save button 📁. You can also open the File menu and select the Save command, or press Ctrl+S to save. The Save As dialog box appears.

Type your filename here.————

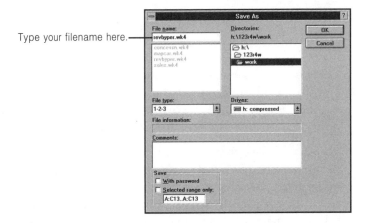

2. In the File name text box, type a name for your worksheet using up to 8 characters. Don't worry about the .WK5 extension; 1-2-3 will add that for you.

3. Click OK.

If a file already exists with the same name, you should select Cancel, then repeat these steps using a different file name. If you want to save your file to a different directory or onto a diskette, or if you want to protect your file with a password, see the appropriate sections later in this chapter for more information.

Saving That Worksheet Again

Once your worksheet file has been saved, it's a simple procedure to save it again. Since 1-2-3 already knows the name of the file, you won't need to enter it again:

1. Click on the File Save button 📁, or open the File menu and select the Save command, or press Ctrl+S to resave your file.

2. That's it! (It just can't get any easier than this.)

If you want to save your file with a new name, to a different directory, or to a diskette, you use the File Save As command, explained later in this chapter.

Beyond Survival

Saving to a Different Drive or Directory

Sometimes you may want to save your worksheet file to a diskette (to take home with you) or to your own directory. A directory is like a separate "room" on your hard disk where you store the same kind of files. All of the files that 1-2-3 uses are stored in the \123r5w directory. By default, 1-2-3 stores the files you create in a subdirectory off of the main directory, called \123r5w\WORK. However, you don't have to use the WORK directory; instead, you can create your own directory for storing special projects, and so on. Then you can save your 1-2-3 files to that directory if you want. This is a really good idea if you're sharing 1-2-3 with other people on a network. Why store your files with theirs in the same directory? Just create your own directory and use it instead. (If you don't know how to create a directory, get someone to help you.)

Use File Save As to save to a diskette

Here's how to save your files to a different directory, or to a diskette:

1. Open the File menu.

2. Select Save As. The Save As dialog box appears.

Type in a new file name if you like.

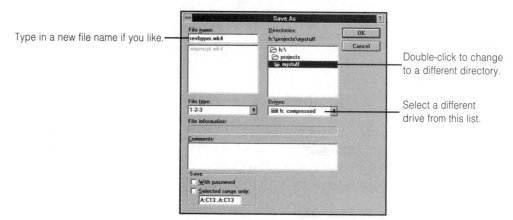

Double-click to change to a different directory.

Select a different drive from this list.

3. If you need to change the file name, go ahead and type in a new one in the File name text box. Otherwise, skip this step.

4. To save your file to a different directory, scroll through the Directories list and double-click on the directory name in which you want to save your file.

5. To save your file to a diskette, click on the down arrow under Drives and select either A: or B:.

6. Click OK.

Saving Automatically As You Work

While you're working, your changes are saved in a temporary place. To store those changes permanently, you have to resave your file. Instead of relying on your memory to remind you to save your worksheet off and on as you're working, why not set it up so 1-2-3 does the remembering for you? Just follow these steps to set 1-2-3 to save automatically:

1. Open the Tools menu.

Reminder: Set up 1-2-3 to save automatically

2. Select User Setup. The User Setup dialog box appears.

Click on this option.

Enter the number of minutes you want 1-2-3 to wait between saves.

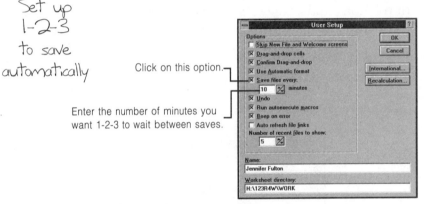

3. Click on the Save files every: checkbox.

4. In the minutes text box under Save files every, type the number of minutes you want 1-2-3 to wait between automatic saves. (Actually, I usually don't type anything, because I like my program set to save every 10 minutes, which is the default.)

5. Click OK.

After the appropriate interval, 1-2-3 will automatically save all the files you have open. If they have not yet been saved, the Save dialog box appears, in which you can give them a name. If they have already been saved, they are resaved under that same name automatically.

Saving Your File with a Password

If you work with confidential data, it might be a good idea to protect it with a password. If someone tries to open the file, he won't be able to unless he can type in your password. Of course, that means that *you* won't be able to open the file either if you can't remember the password, so make it something simple or write it down in a secure place.

Write down that password!

To save a file with a password:

1. Open the File menu.

2. Select Save As. The Save As dialog box appears.

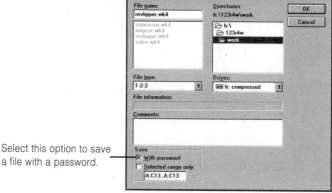

Select this option to save a file with a password.

3. Select the With password option.

4. Click OK. The Set Password dialog box appears.

5. In the Password text box, type in your password. (You won't see it displayed, but that's okay.)

Your password is not displayed on-screen.

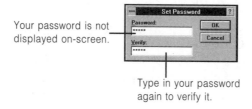

Type in your password again to verify it.

6. Press Tab to move to the Verify text box, and type the password again. Make sure you type the password exactly the way you did in the Password text box—for example, if you typed SECRET in all caps, type it again in all caps now.

7. Click OK.

Your file is now saved with a password. You can continue working. When you reopen the file later on, the Get Password dialog box appears. Type the password you assigned to this file and click OK.

Type in your password to open the file.

If you decide to remove the password later on, follow these steps:

1. Open the file as usual and select the File Save As command.

2. Click on the With password option again to deselect password protection.

3. Click OK.

4. Click on Replace. The file is saved without a password.

Saving a Worksheet to Use with Another Program

If you need to share your data with other people who use an earlier version of Lotus 1-2-3 or some other program (such as Microsoft Excel, Paradox, and so on), you must save your file in a way that the other program can understand. To do so, perform the following steps:

1. Open the File menu.

2. Select Save As. The Save As dialog box appears.

1-2-3 automatically changes the extension to match the file type you choose.

Select a file type from this list.

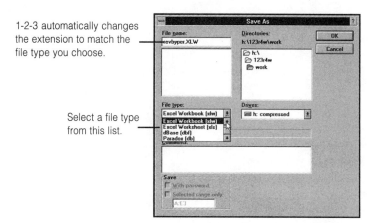

3. Click on the down arrow in the File type box and click on the program type to save your worksheet. You can save your file for use in Excel, Paradox, and dBASE, as well as earlier versions of 1-2-3.

4. If you want to save this file to a diskette, click on the down arrow under Drives and select either A: or B:.

5. Click OK.

PART 3

Working with Worksheets

Now that you've created your first 1-2-3 worksheet, how can you rearrange and manipulate its contents so that your data is more clear to you? In this section, you'll learn useful techniques for manipulating worksheets, such as:

- Starting a New Worksheet File
- Opening an Existing Worksheet File
- Adding More Worksheets
- Changing Your Point of View
- Working with Multiple Worksheets

Cheat Sheet

Starting a Plain Worksheet When You Start 1-2-3

1. Start 1-2-3 as usual.
2. Click on the Create a new worksheet option button.
3. Click OK.
4. Select the Create a plain worksheet option.
5. Click OK.

Starting a Plain Worksheet from 1-2-3

1. Open the File menu.
2. Select New.
3. Select the Create a plain worksheet option.
4. Click OK.

Using a SmartMaster to Create a New Worksheet

1. Open the File menu.
2. Select New.
3. Select a SmartMaster from the list.
4. Click OK.

Adding Document Information

1. Open your worksheet file.
2. Open the File menu.
3. Select Doc Info.
4. Enter your document information.
5. Click OK.

16

Starting a New Worksheet File

When you start a new worksheet file, you can begin from scratch with a plain worksheet or you can use a SmartMaster. *SmartMasters* are templates for common business tasks, such as budgeting, financing, and forecasting. SmartMasters contain sample data that you can analyze to determine how the SmartMaster works. After you understand how the SmartMaster is set up, you remove the sample data and replace it with your own. With a SmartMaster, most of the work is done for you.

In this chapter, you'll learn how to start a plain worksheet. And if you continue to the Beyond Survival section, you'll learn how to start a worksheet using a SmartMaster.

Basic Survival

Starting a Plain Worksheet When You Start 1-2-3

There will not be a SmartMaster for every situation, so you may want to start from scratch, building a worksheet with your own formulas and labels. To start a plain worksheet at the same time you start 1-2-3:

1. Start 1-2-3 as usual. The Welcome to 1-2-3 dialog box appears.

2. Click on the Create a new worksheet option button.

Click here to create a new worksheet.

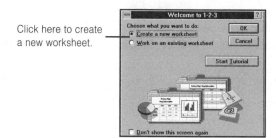

3. Click OK. The New File dialog box appears.

4. Select the Create a plain worksheet option.

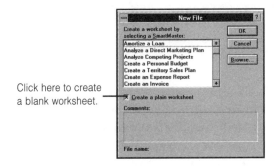

Click here to create
a blank worksheet.

5. Click OK.

Starting a Plain Worksheet from 1-2-3

If you have finished with one worksheet and would like to begin another, save the first worksheet. Then, to begin a new plain worksheet, follow these steps:

1. Open the File menu.

2. Select New. The New File dialog box appears.

File New = new worksheet file

3. Select the Create a plain worksheet option.

4. Click OK.

You may want to add one of the SmartIcons below to one of your sets because they make the process of creating a new worksheet so much easier. (To learn how to customize your SmartIcon sets, see Chapter 6.)

Icon	Icon Name	Description
🗋	File New	Allows you to create a plain worksheet or to use a SmartMaster. (Same as selecting the File New command.)
📄	Quick File New	Creates a plain worksheet.

114

Beyond Survival

Using a SmartMaster to Create a New Worksheet

SmartMasters provide a template for building a worksheet specialized to some common business task, such as financial reporting, managing expenses, or project evaluation. To use a SmartMaster to create a new worksheet:

1. Open the File menu.

2. Select New. The New File dialog box appears.

3. Select a SmartMaster from the list.

Select the SmartMaster you want to use from this list.

4. Click OK. You can also select a SmartMaster when you start 1-2-3 by choosing the Create a new worksheet option from the Welcome to 1-2-3 dialog box and selecting a SmartMaster from the New File dialog box that appears.

The SmartMaster opens, complete with sample data and instructions. You'll find buttons that take you from sheet to sheet and buttons that enable you to fill the worksheets with sample data so that you can analyze how the SmartMaster works. You can later clear this sample data out, and fill the SmartMaster with your own data.

Click here to fill this SmartMaster with sample data.

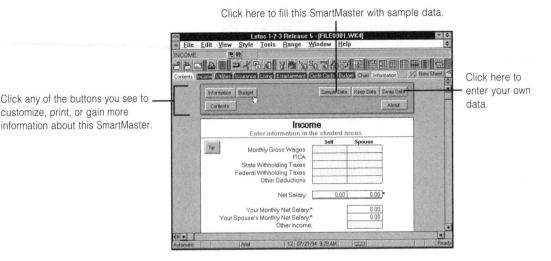

Click any of the buttons you see to customize, print, or gain more information about this SmartMaster.

Click here to enter your own data.

Adding Document Information

Remember to add doc info to each worksheet file.

To help you identify your worksheets when you need to open them, you can add some descriptions to an area of your worksheet file called document information. So instead of trying to identify the worksheet you want by just its file name, you can include comments in the document information area that actually describe the worksheet and its purpose in detail. Some of this information is displayed later in the File Open dialog box—other pieces, such as revision dates and original author, can be viewed in the Doc Info dialog box. This information also becomes useful in identifying data shared with Lotus Notes.

Follow these steps to enter document information:

1. Open your worksheet file.

2. Open the File menu.

3. Select Doc Info. The Doc Info dialog box appears.

4. Enter your document information (such as the title, subject, comments, and so on). Within the comments section, press Ctrl+Enter to move to the next line.

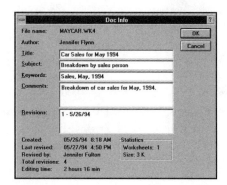

5. Click OK. When you open the file later, the document information you entered helps you to identify it.

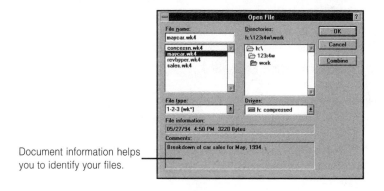

Document information helps you to identify your files.

117

Cheat Sheet

Opening a Worksheet

1. Click on the Open File button 📂.
2. If necessary, change to a different drive by clicking on the down arrow under Drives and selecting a drive letter.
3. If necessary, change to a different directory by double-clicking on it.
4. Click on the file you want to open in the file list.
5. Click OK.

Opening a Recent Worksheet

1. Open the File menu.
2. Click on the name of a recent worksheet.

Opening a Worksheet with a Password

1. Click on the Open File button 📂.
2. Click on the file you want to open in the file list.
3. Click OK.
4. In the Get Password dialog box, type your password.
5. Click OK.

Opening Multiple Worksheets at One Time

1. Click on the Open File button 📂.
2. Click on the first file you want to open in the file list.
3. Press and hold the Ctrl key.
4. Click on the additional files you want to open.
5. Click OK.

17

Opening an Existing Worksheet File

Before you can begin working again on a previously saved worksheet file, you must *open* it. Once the file is opened, you can make changes to it as necessary. You can open one file or several files at the same time, as you'll discover in the Beyond Survival section. To open a worksheet file when you start Lotus 1-2-3, see Chapter 1.

Basic Survival

Opening a Worksheet

When you open a worksheet file, the contents of that file are read and then displayed on your screen. Once the data is displayed on-screen, you can begin making changes to it. To open a worksheet file, follow these steps:

1. Click on the Open File button ![button]. You can also open the File menu and select Open, or press Ctrl+O to open a file. The Open File dialog box appears.

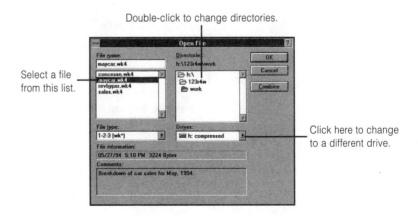

Double-click to change directories.

Select a file from this list.

Click here to change to a different drive.

2. If necessary, change to a different drive by clicking on the down arrow under Drives and selecting a drive letter (such as A:, B:, or D:).

3. If necessary, change to a different directory by double-clicking on it in the Directories list.

4. Click on the file you want to open in the file list.

5. Click OK. The selected file opens, filling the worksheet window.

If you were already working on another file, it's still open, and you can flip between the two worksheet files if you like. See Chapter 19 for tips on moving between open worksheets.

Opening a Recent Worksheet

To save time in opening worksheets, the File menu contains a list of recently opened worksheets. You can use this list to open a worksheet that you have used recently.

1. Open the File menu.

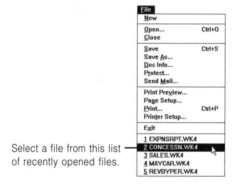

Select a file from this list of recently opened files.

2. Click on the name of a recent worksheet.

File menu = list of recently opened files

The File menu lists the five most recent worksheets. You can increase or decrease this number by making a change in the User Setup dialog box. To do so, follow these steps:

1. Open the Tools menu.

2. Select User Setup. The User Setup dialog box appears.

3. Click on the up or down arrow under Number of recent files to show.

4. Click OK.

Beyond Survival

Opening a Worksheet with a Password

To restrict access to confidential data, you can password protect your files (see Chapter 15 for information on saving files with a password). To open a password-protected file, you must type the correct password. Begin by following the same steps you would to open any other file:

1. Click on the Open File button 📂 . The Open File dialog box appears.

Select your password-protected file.

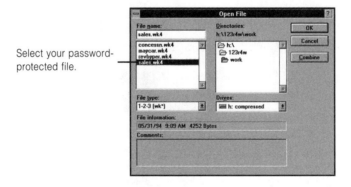

2. Click on the file you want to open in the file list.

3. Click OK.

4. The Get Password dialog box appears. Type your password.

Type your password to open the file.

5. Click OK, and the file opens.

Opening Multiple Worksheets at One Time

You can open multiple worksheets in one step, provided all of the worksheets you want to open are located in the same directory. Here's how:

1. Click on the Open File button. The Open File dialog box appears.

Select multiple files to open.

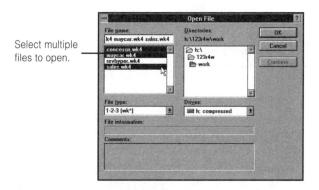

2. Click on the first file you want to open in the file list.

Ctrl and click each file

3. Press and hold the Ctrl key.

4. Click on the additional files you want to open.

5. Click OK.

The selected files are opened alphabetically, one at a time. The last worksheet opened becomes the current worksheet—the one that contains the cell pointer. You can begin making changes to the current worksheet right away. For information about switching between open worksheets, see Chapter 19.

Shift and click first/ last files

You can select a list of *contiguous* files (files listed consecutively) by holding the Shift key and clicking on the first and last files you want to open. This method is quicker than clicking on each file name individually.

Opening a Worksheet Created in Another Program

In 1-2-3, you're not restricted to using just 1-2-3 files. You can open files created in such programs as Symphony, Excel, dBASE, and Paradox and use them in 1-2-3. The file is translated into 1-2-3 format and then saved as a separate file; the original file is left unchanged. That means that if the person who created the Excel file still wants to use it in Excel, he can because the original file is left alone and is not changed by 1-2-3. However, there may be some elements (for example, unusual formatting, charts, and drawn objects) that 1-2-3 cannot translate. If so, those elements would have to be recreated in the 1-2-3 file.

To open a worksheet created in another program:

1. Click on the Open File button [button]. The Open File dialog box appears.

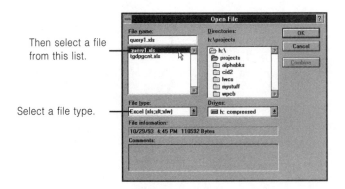

Then select a file from this list.

Select a file type.

2. Click on the File type down arrow and select a type from the list. For example, select Excel.

3. If necessary, change to a different drive by clicking on the Drives down arrow and selecting a drive letter (such as A:, B:, or D:).

4. If necessary, change to a different directory by double-clicking on it in the Directories list. For example, switch to the Excel directory by double-clicking on it.

5. Click on the file you want to open in the file list.

6. Click OK.

Once you make changes to the file, you may want to save it again in its original format. (Remember that when the file was opened, it was converted into 1-2-3 format.) For example, you may want to save your file in Excel format. You can do that, but keep in mind that the process is not perfect; as before, certain elements such as charts, might not translate back into the other format. To save your file in another format, see Chapter 15.

Cheat Sheet

Adding a Worksheet

1. Click on the tab of the worksheet you want to add the new worksheet.
2. Click on the New Sheet button New Sheet .

Adding Multiple Worksheets at One Time

1. Open the Edit menu.
2. Select Insert.
3. Select Sheet.
4. Select Before or After.
5. Select the number of worksheets to insert.
6. Click OK.

Copying a Worksheet

1. Switch to the worksheet whose contents you want to copy.
2. Click on the Worksheet Label.
3. Click on the Copy button .
4. Switch to the worksheet to which you want to copy.
5. Click in cell A1.
6. Click on the Paste button .

Renaming a Worksheet

1. Double-click on the tab of the worksheet whose name you want to change.
2. Type the new name.
3. Press Enter.

18

Adding More Worksheets

When you start a new worksheet file, it contains one worksheet (worksheet A). However, you are not limited to only one worksheet in a file. You can add additional worksheets to organize your data. For example, you could add three more worksheets, designating the first worksheet as Qtr 1 and the additional worksheets Qtrs 2, 3, and 4. You could then place an entire year's worth of data in the file and have easy access to each quarter's information. Each file can contain up to 255 worksheets.

In this chapter, you learn how to add worksheets to a file. In the Beyond Survival section, you find out how to rename these new worksheets to whatever you like (such as Qtr1, Qtr2, and so on).

Basic Survival

Adding a Worksheet

Adding one worksheet to the current file is fairly simple:

1. Click on the tab of the worksheet after which you want to add the new worksheet. Worksheets are inserted after the current worksheet, not before it. For example, if you click on worksheet B, the new worksheet is added *after* worksheet B and is called C.

2. Click on the New Sheet button New Sheet .

Use New Sheet button to add worksheets

The new worksheet takes its name based on the current worksheet. For example, if you clicked on worksheet C and then clicked on the New Sheet button, worksheet D would be added after C. This naming business also extends to worksheets you've named yourself. For example, if (in step 1) you opted to add a new worksheet after a worksheet named July, the new worksheet would be named August. (To learn how to name your worksheets, see the section later in this chapter.)

If you want to add multiple worksheets in one step, follow these directions:

1. Open the Edit menu.

2. Select Insert. The Insert dialog box appears.

Select whether to insert the new worksheets before or after the current worksheet.

Select the number of worksheets to insert.

3. Click on Sheet.

4. Select Before or After. Using this method you can insert worksheets before or after the current worksheet (unlike when you use the New Sheet button).

5. Click on the up or down arrows under Quantity to select the number of worksheets to insert.

6. Click OK.

You can also insert multiple worksheets by selecting a group of worksheets and then clicking the Insert Worksheets SmartIcon ▦. When you do so, the number of worksheets you selected is inserted after the last worksheet in the group. (The Insert Worksheets SmartIcon does not appear on any of the SmartIcon sets, but you can add it to any set with the instructions for customizing SmartIcon sets in Chapter 6.) To select a group of worksheets, click on the worksheet letter (the gray rectangle in the upper left corner of the worksheet) of the first worksheet in the group. Press and hold the Shift key. Then click on the tab of the last worksheet you want to select.

Naming a Worksheet

When you start a new worksheet file, the worksheet in the file is simply called "A." You can rename your worksheets to help you identify them. For example, you could call a worksheet Income, or Expenses, or Budget 1995. Naming a worksheet helps you identify its purpose.

There are some things you should keep in mind when naming a worksheet:

- Worksheet names can be up to 15 characters long.

- Avoid using characters such as ! , ; . + – * / ? _ < > @ # { and &.

- Don't use names that look like cell addresses, as in Q3.

- Avoid beginning names with a number and using spaces in worksheet names if you can. Although it's permitted, macros (automated tasks) that use these worksheets might get confused.

- You can use upper- or lowercase letters in a name.

To rename a worksheet:

Double-click on tab to change worksheet name

1. Double-click on the tab of the worksheet whose name you want to change. The tab expands, allowing you to type in your new name for the worksheet.

Double-click to change a worksheet name.

2. Type the new name onto the worksheet tab.

3. Press Enter.

To remove a worksheet name (and have it revert back to its original letter name):

1. Double-click on the tab of the worksheet whose name you want to change. Again, the tab expands, and the existing name is selected.

2. Press Backspace or Delete. The existing name is deleted, and the tab is now blank.

3. Press Enter. The tab reverts to its original name, such as B. (You cannot have a worksheet that is not named.)

Keep in mind that when a new worksheet is inserted, 1-2-3 names it based on the name of the current worksheet. For example, if the current worksheet is called 1994 and you insert a new worksheet after it, the inserted worksheet will be named 1995 automatically. So renaming your first worksheet before you add additional ones can often save you the trouble of having to rename worksheets after you insert them.

Beyond Survival

Copying a Worksheet

After inserting a new worksheet, you may want to copy the contents of an existing worksheet to save yourself some time in setup. For example, if you just added a worksheet called NW Sales, you could copy the SW Sales sheet onto it to create the same headings and totals. You could then update the new worksheet with the Northwest sales data. If you don't want to copy an entire worksheet onto another, you can copy a selected range instead.

To copy the contents of one worksheet onto another:

1. Switch to the worksheet whose contents you want to copy.

2. Click on the worksheet letter (the button in the upper left-hand corner of the worksheet).

Click on the worksheet letter to select the entire worksheet.

3. Click on the Copy button 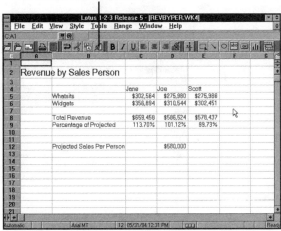.

4. Switch to the worksheet to which you want to copy the data. If you need to insert a worksheet, click on the New Sheet button.

5. Click in cell A1 to position the cell pointer there.

6. Click on the Paste button. The contents of the first worksheet are copied onto the worksheet selected in step 4. This will overwrite any data in the second worksheet, so be careful!

Click on the Paste button to copy the other worksheet onto this worksheet.

To copy a range of cells from one worksheet onto another:

1. Switch to the worksheet whose contents you want to copy.

2. Select the range you want to copy.

3. Click on the Copy button.

4. Switch to the worksheet to which you want to copy the data. If you need to insert a worksheet, click on the New Sheet button.

5. Click in the cell to which you want to copy the range.

6. Click on the Paste button.

As you may have noticed, these instructions copy everything (numbers, labels, formulas, and formatting) from one worksheet to another. If you want to copy just the style (formatting) of the first worksheet to all the others in a worksheet file, you don't have to use the techniques discussed here. Instead, you can group your worksheets and format them in one step. (This process copies the formatting, such as bold, underline, or borders, but it does not copy the data.) See Chapter 20 for instructions on how to group worksheets.

Hiding Worksheet Tabs

If you want, you can hide the worksheet tabs and not display them. This might be convenient when you're working in a file that contains only one worksheet.

To hide worksheet tabs, simply click on the Tab button [icon]. To redisplay the worksheet tabs, click on the Tab button again.

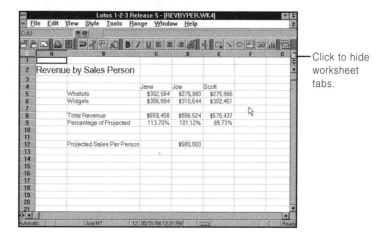

Click to hide worksheet tabs.

Cheat Sheet

Moving from One Worksheet to the Next

Click on the tab of the worksheet to which you want to move.

Moving from One Worksheet File to the Next

1. Open the Window menu.
2. Select the file to which you want to move.

Viewing Multiple Worksheets at the Same Time

1. Open the View menu.
2. Select Split.
3. Select Perspective.
4. If you want, select Synchronize scrolling.
5. Click OK.

Viewing Multiple Worksheet Files

1. Open the Window menu.
2. Select either Tile or Cascade.

Splitting a Worksheet into Two Viewing Panes

1. Move the mouse pointer over the horizontal or vertical splitter.
2. Drag the splitter into the window and release the mouse button.

19

Changing Your Point of View

Having more than one worksheet in a worksheet file makes it easy to organize data. Within a multiple worksheet file, data is separated into logical units: months, quarters, and sales divisions are placed on separate worksheets. You can analyze your data by viewing these separate worksheets one at a time or all at once, depending on your needs. In this chapter, you learn how to do this and more.

Basic Survival

Moving from One Worksheet to the Next

To move to another worksheet, click on tab

In this section, you learn how to move from one worksheet to another within the same worksheet file. If you want to move *between* worksheet files, see the next section.

To move from worksheet to worksheet with the mouse, click on the tab of the worksheet to which you want to move.

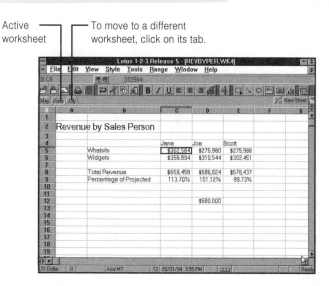

Active worksheet

To move to a different worksheet, click on its tab.

Moving from One Worksheet File to the Next

You can easily move between worksheet files. For example, if you're working in your revenue worksheet and you want to view figures in the unit sales worksheet, you can quickly flip over to the unit sales worksheet and then flip back again. Of course, these worksheet files have to already be open for you to be able to move between them. If you need a review on opening worksheets, see Chapter 17. With several worksheet files open, move between them using these steps:

1. Open the Window menu. At the bottom of the menu, 1-2-3 displays a list of all open worksheet files.

2. Select the file to which you want to move.

To move to other worksheet files, use Window menu

Select a file to move to from this list.

If more than one worksheet file is visible in the window, you can switch between files by simply clicking inside the windows. See the section later in this chapter for information on arranging your worksheet files so you can see more than one at a time and move between them more easily.

Viewing Multiple Worksheets at the Same Time

Although your data may be organized into separate worksheets in a single worksheet file for logical reasons, you may need to look at several worksheets at the same time in order to compare their data. For example, you might need to compare worksheet A with worksheet C. While viewing multiple worksheets, you can synchronize the scrolling within all the sheets so that when you move the cell pointer in one sheet, the same rows and columns appear in the other sheets. Follow these steps to view multiple worksheets:

1. Click on the View menu.

2. Select Split. The Split dialog box appears.

3. Select the Perspective option button.

4. If you want, select the Synchronize scrolling check box.

5. Click OK.

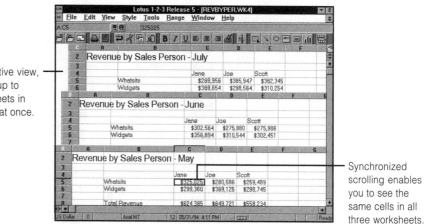

With Perspective view, you can see up to three worksheets in the same file at once.

Synchronized scrolling enables you to see the same cells in all three worksheets.

In Perspective view, you can view up to three worksheets from the same file. To return to normal view:

1. Click on the View menu.

2. Select Clear Split.

To view multiple worksheets in the same file, use View Split Perspective

Beyond Survival

Viewing Multiple Worksheet Files

If you have more than one worksheet file open, you can view all of your open files at the same time if you want. This makes it easy to switch between multiple files and to compare their data. However, this is different than Perspective view, which allows you to view multiple worksheets in *the same file*. To view *multiple files* at the same time, you use Tile or Cascade view. When you tile windows, the screen is split into vertical panes, each of which displays a view of an open file. When you cascade windows, open files are arranged in windows that overlap each other.

To view open worksheet files:

1. Open the Window menu.

2. Select the Tile command or the Cascade command.

Tiled windows

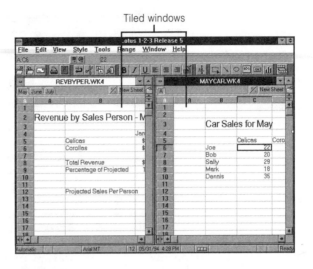

Cascaded windows

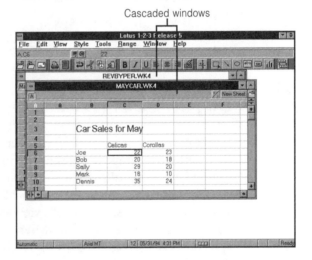

Remember, to switch between files displayed in either a tile or cascade pattern, simply click inside the window of the file to which you want to switch. You can also change the worksheet shown in each file window by clicking on its tab.

Splitting a Worksheet into Two Viewing Panes

Sometimes you may want to view different parts of the same worksheet. For example, suppose you had a really long worksheet, and you were trying to compare some data at the top to some formulas at the bottom. Scrolling back and forth between the two cells could be quite a nuisance. Instead, you accomplish this by splitting the window into two viewing panes. In one pane you could look at cells at the top of your worksheet, and in the other, you could look at the cells at the bottom, enabling you to perform your comparison. You can split the window either horizontally or vertically, whichever you prefer.

To split a window, you use a button called a *splitter*. There's one located on the horizontal scroll bar and one on the vertical scroll bar. By dragging the appropriate splitter along the scroll bar, you divide the window at that point either horizontally or vertically.

To split the window:

1. Move the mouse pointer over the horizontal or vertical splitter. The mouse pointer changes to a two-headed arrow.

2. Click on the splitter and drag along the scroll bar. Release the mouse button. The window is divided at the point on the scroll bar where you released the splitter.

Splitting a window enables you to see two parts of the same worksheet.

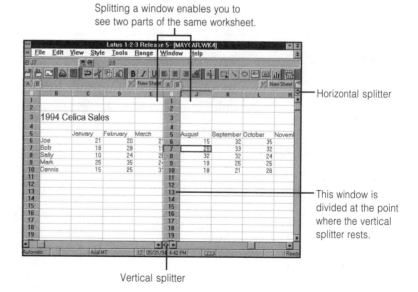

Horizontal splitter

This window is divided at the point where the vertical splitter rests.

Vertical splitter

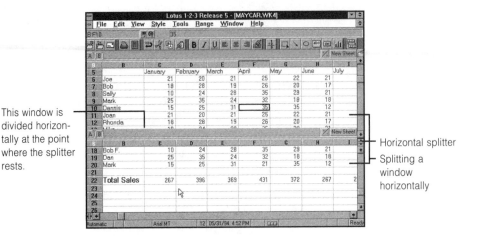

This window is divided horizontally at the point where the splitter rests.

Horizontal splitter

Splitting a window horizontally

Important!

To move from pane to pane, simply click in a pane to make it active, or press F6 to switch back and forth. There is one important thing you need to know about using split windows. If you make any changes to column width, row height, or worksheet titles, make those changes in the upper or left window. Why? Because that's the window in which 1-2-3 keeps track of changes; any changes you make in the lower or right window are ignored when the normal view of your worksheet is restored.

To return to normal view, either drag the splitter back to its original position, or open the View menu and select Clear Split.

Zooming In or Out

You can increase or decrease the magnification of the viewing window in order to "zoom out" and view a larger portion of the worksheet, or "zoom in" and examine it in detail. Each time you use the Zoom command, the view is increased or decreased by 10%.

To zoom in or out:

1. Open the View menu.

2. Select either Zoom In or Zoom Out.

3. Repeat as necessary to increase or decrease the zoom percentage.

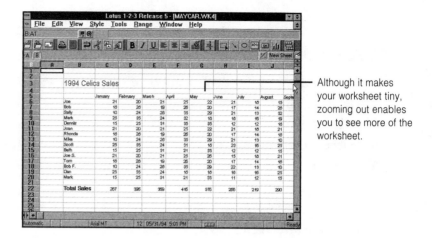

Although it makes your worksheet tiny, zooming out enables you to see more of the worksheet.

You can zoom more quickly with the Zoom In ⊕ and Zoom Out ⊖ buttons, located on the Sheet Auditing SmartIcon set.

To return to normal view:

1. Open the View menu.

2. Select Custom.

You can change the percentage of the normal view (called "Custom" view on the menu because you can customize the setting) by opening the View menu and selecting Set View Preferences. Click the up or down arrows under Custom view % to change the normal viewing percentage. Click OK. (The normal viewing percentage, by the way, is 87%.)

You can also zoom while previewing a worksheet just prior to printing it. See Chapter 36 for details.

Cheat Sheet

Deleting a Worksheet

1. Move to the worksheet you want to delete.
2. Open the Edit menu.
3. Select Delete.
4. Select Sheet.
5. Click OK.

Grouping Worksheets

1. Open the Style menu.
2. Select Worksheet Defaults.
3. Click on the Group mode check box.
4. Click OK.

Selecting a Group of Worksheets

To select a group of contiguous (adjacent) worksheets:

1. Select the first worksheet by clicking on its letter.
2. Press and hold the Shift key.
3. Click on the tab of the last worksheet you want to select.

To select a group of noncontiguous worksheets:

1. Select the first worksheet by clicking on its letter.
2. Press and hold the Ctrl key.
3. Click on the letters of the other worksheets you want in the group.

Adding Color to Tabs to Identify Worksheet Groups

1. Move to the worksheet whose tab you want to change.
2. Open the Style menu.
3. Select Worksheet Defaults.
4. Click on the down arrow under Worksheet tab and select a color.
5. Click OK. Repeat for additional tabs.

20

Working with Multiple Worksheets

Adding extra worksheets to a file allows you to keep your data in one place while organizing it into logical units such as months, years, or business locations. However, working with multiple worksheet files requires some additional skills, which you will learn in this chapter.

Basic Survival

Cell Addresses in Multi-Worksheet Files

Each cell has its own address, or location, within the worksheet. A cell's address is made up of its column letter followed by its row number. The sample here shows cell C5.

The complete cell address shows in the Selection Indicator.

Cell C5

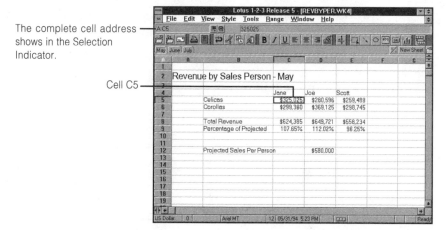

In a multiple worksheet file, the cell address includes the name of its worksheet. So the complete address for the current cell shown here is A:C5, or the third cell in the fifth row of the first worksheet. If you've named a worksheet, you can use that name in the cell address instead, as in MAY:C5.

When a file contains more than one worksheet, it's possible to define *3-D ranges* and use them in formulas. A 3-D range includes the same cells in several contiguous (adjacent) worksheets, such as A, B, and C. The 3-D range shown here is A:A5..C:E6, which means the range A5..E6 in worksheets A through C.

A 3-D range includes the same cells in adjacent worksheets.

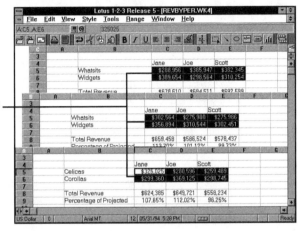

Deleting a Worksheet

If you decide after adding a worksheet that you no longer need that worksheet, you can delete it. Of course, when you delete a worksheet, you delete all the data on it. Here's how to delete a worksheet:

1. Move to the worksheet you want to delete.

2. Open the Edit menu.

3. Select Delete. The Delete dialog box appears.

Edit Delete
to delete
worksheet

4. Click on the Sheet option button.

5. Click OK.

To delete multiple worksheets at the same time, select a cell in each worksheet you want to delete. Click on the first cell, press Ctrl, and then click on a cell within each of the other worksheets you want to delete. Then follow the steps above.

You can also delete multiple worksheets by selecting a group of worksheets and then clicking the Delete Worksheet's SmartIcon . The Delete Worksheet's SmartIcon does not appear on any of the SmartIcon sets, but you can add it to any set with the instructions in Chapter 6.

When you delete a worksheet, all remaining worksheets are renamed and formulas are automatically adjusted.

Beyond Survival

Grouping Worksheets

Grouping worksheets is an easy way to make a set of worksheets all look alike. When worksheets are grouped, 1-2-3 applies the current *style settings* of the first worksheet to the others in the group. Changes to the first worksheet are also applied to each of the others in turn. The style settings include number formats, fonts, text attributes (such as bold or italic), colors and borders, alignment, row height, column width, protection settings, and page breaks.

Careful when grouping

Although grouping is convenient, you do have to be careful when you group worksheets. When you delete a column in the first worksheet of a group, for example, it's deleted in the other worksheets automatically. The best way to use grouping is to style one worksheet, group the worksheets so the styles are copied, and then ungroup them before you start entering data.

To group worksheets:

1. Open the Style menu.

2. Select Worksheet Defaults. The Worksheet Defaults dialog box appears.

3. Click on the Group mode check box to activate it.

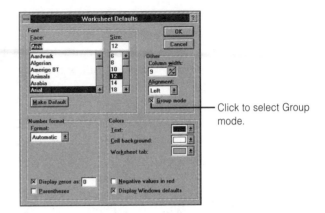

Click to select Group mode.

4. Click OK.

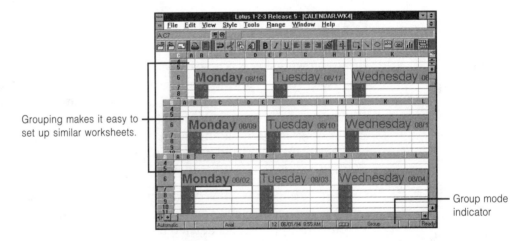

Grouping makes it easy to set up similar worksheets.

Group mode indicator

The Group mode indicator appears in the status bar to remind you that worksheets are currently grouped. To ungroup worksheets:

1. Open the Style menu.

2. Select Worksheet Defaults. The Worksheet Defaults dialog box appears.

3. Deselect the Group mode option button by clicking on it.

4. Click OK.

At this point, the Group mode indicator disappears from the status bar. You can now make changes to each worksheet without affecting the others.

Selecting a Group of Worksheets

Just as you can select a group of cells and format them all in one step, you can also select a group of worksheets. This procedure is different from grouping worksheets, which requires that all the worksheets in the group be contiguous. Also, grouping is active until you turn it off. With this technique, you can select contiguous or non-contiguous worksheets and do whatever you want with your selection (not just formatting). Selecting a worksheet selects all the cells in that worksheet, so make sure that what you want to do should affect all the cells.

To select a group of contiguous (adjacent) worksheets:

1. Select the first worksheet by clicking on its worksheet letter or name.

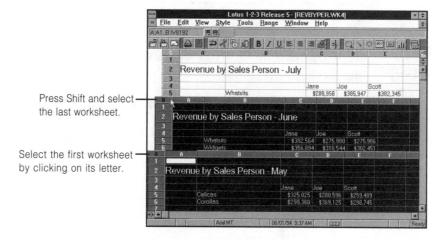

Press Shift and select the last worksheet.

Select the first worksheet by clicking on its letter.

Adjacent worksheets — use Shift

2. Press and hold the Shift key.

3. Click on the tab of the last worksheet you want to select. All of the worksheets between the two chosen worksheets are selected.

To select a group of non-contiguous worksheets:

1. Select the first worksheet by clicking on its worksheet letter or name.

Non-adjacent worksheets — use Ctrl

2. Click and hold the Ctrl key.

3. Click on the letters of the other worksheets you want in the group. Each worksheet you click on will be selected.

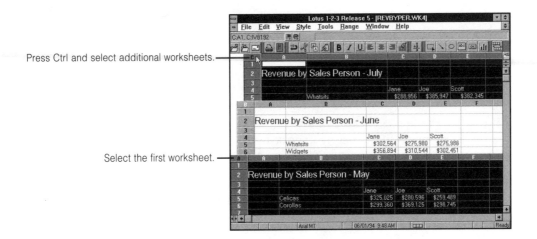

Press Ctrl and select additional worksheets.

Select the first worksheet.

Adding Color to Tabs to Identify Worksheet Groups

Beginning with version 5, Lotus 1-2-3 enables you to change the color of the worksheet tabs. This is a simple feature with powerful results: by changing the color of worksheet tabs, you can easily organize a large file into logical sections.

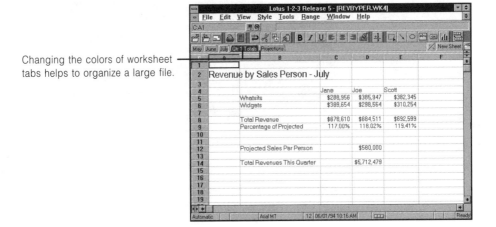

Changing the colors of worksheet tabs helps to organize a large file.

To change the color of a worksheet tab:

1. Move to the worksheet whose tab you want to change.

2. Open the Style menu.

3. Select Worksheet Defaults. The Worksheet Defaults dialog box appears.

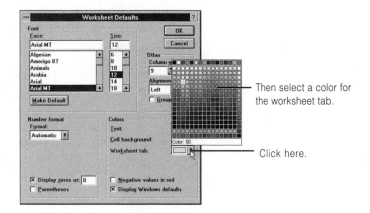

Then select a color for
the worksheet tab.

Click here.

4. Click on the down arrow under Worksheet tab and select a color
from the color palette that appears.

5. Click OK.

6. Repeat for additional tabs.

Experiment until you find colors you like. The color of any given tab
appears darker when that tab is selected, so keep that in mind.

Formatting Your Worksheet

An ordinary worksheet is full of black lines, white space, and a somewhat lackluster appearance. This is okay for everyday use, but if you're going to share your worksheet with co-workers (or your boss), you'll want to dress it up. Even if you're the only one who will ever see your worksheet, you'll want it to look good. With just a little effort, you can make it much easier to read and to use. In this section, you'll learn useful skills such as:

- Adding Columns and Rows

- Changing the Size of Cells

- Playing with Fonts

- Changing How Numbers Look

- Changing the Alignment of Data

- Protecting Your Data

- Adding Borders, Fills, and Frames

- Fancy Free Formatting

Cheat Sheet

Inserting Columns and Rows

1. Select as many columns or rows as you'd like to insert.
2. Open the Edit menu.
3. Select Insert.

Deleting Columns and Rows

1. Select the columns or rows you want to delete.
2. Open the Edit menu.
3. Select Delete.

Inserting a Range of Cells

1. Select a range of cells equal to what you want to insert.
2. Open the Edit menu.
3. Select Insert.
4. To shift the selected cells to the right, select Columns. To shift the selected cells downward, select Rows.
5. Choose Insert selection.
6. Click OK.

Deleting a Range of Cells

1. Select a range to delete.
2. Open the Edit menu.
3. Select Insert.
4. To shift adjacent cells to the left, select Columns. To shift the adjacent cells upward, select Rows.
5. Choose Delete selection.
6. Click OK.

21

Adding Columns and Rows

With 1-2-3, you can insert or delete entire columns and rows from a worksheet. For example, if you've already typed data into two columns only to discover that you need to insert a new column between them, you can do it without losing what you've already entered. However, you should be careful when deleting (removing) columns, because data contained in the columns or rows you delete is deleted also. In addition, if the worksheets are grouped (see Chapter 20 for details), inserting or deleting a column or a row in the first worksheet causes the same thing to happen to all of the worksheets.

Basic Survival

Inserting Columns and Rows

You can insert a single column or row, or multiple columns or rows at one time. When you insert a column, the new column is placed to the left of the column you select, in essence shifting all of the existing columns to the right. For example, if you select column D and then insert a column following these instructions, the new column becomes column E, and the old column E becomes column F, and so on. When you insert a row, the new row is placed above the row you select, shifting all existing rows down.

1. Select as many columns or rows as you'd like to insert. For example, select two existing columns if you want to insert two new columns. To select a column or row, click on the column/row marker. For example, click on the letter E at the top of column E. Drag to select additional columns or rows.

Select the number of columns
equal to what you want to insert.

To select multiple columns, drag
across the column markers.

Column marker

Row marker

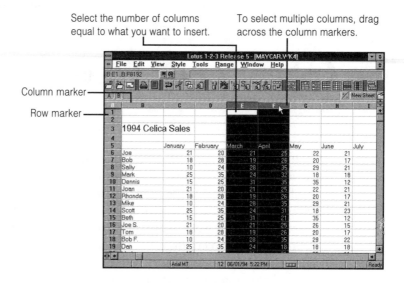

2. Open the Edit menu.

3. Select Insert.

Inserted
columns

Existing
columns are
shifted to the
right.

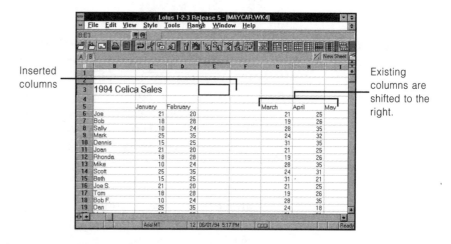

Ctrl and +
to insert

You can also press Ctrl and the + key or select Insert from the quick
menu to insert columns or rows. In addition, you can click on the
Insert Columns ▦ or Insert Rows ▦ buttons, located on the Editing
SmartIcon set.

Deleting Columns and Rows

When you delete a column or row, 1-2-3 deletes the data in that column or row along with it (if there is any). Deleting a column causes the data in columns to the right to be shifted over. For example, if you delete column B, column C is renamed B, and so on. Deleting a row causes data in lower rows to be shifted up.

Careful when deleting columns/rows

1. Select the columns or rows that you want to delete. To select a column or row, click on the column/row marker. Drag to select additional columns or rows.

Select the rows to delete.

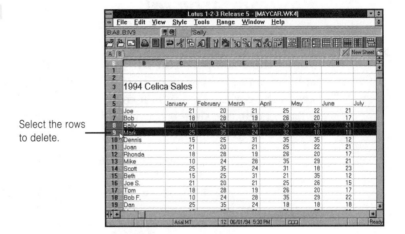

2. Open the Edit menu.

3. Select Delete.

The rows beneath the deleted rows are moved up.

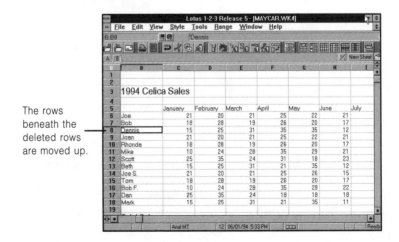

Ctrl + – to delete

You can also press Ctrl and the – key or select Delete from the quick menu to delete columns or rows. In addition, you can click on the Delete Columns ▦ or Delete Rows ▦ buttons, located on the Editing SmartIcon set.

If you've accidentally deleted the wrong columns or rows, click on the Undo button ↵.

Beyond Survival

Inserting a Range of Cells

Instead of inserting columns or rows, you can insert a range of cells. For example, suppose you started keying in data in the wrong row or column, and now you need to shift that data over or down so you can key in the correct data. When you insert a range, an equal number of adjacent cells are shifted downward or to the left to make room for the inserted range. To insert a range:

1. Select a range equal to the number of cells you want to insert.

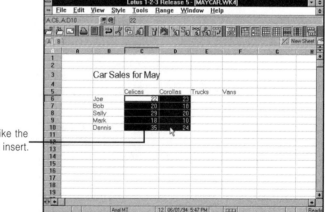

Select a range like the one you want to insert.

2. Open the Edit menu.

3. Select Insert. The Insert dialog box appears.

4. To shift the selected cells to the right, select the Column option button. To shift the selected cells downward, select the Row option button.

5. Choose the Insert selection check box.

6. Click OK. The new range of cells is inserted, and existing data moves in the direction you indicated to make room.

If you select Columns, cells are shifted to the right.

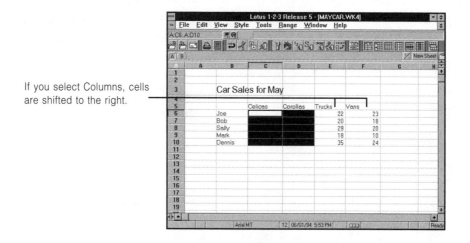

If you select Rows, cells are shifted downward.

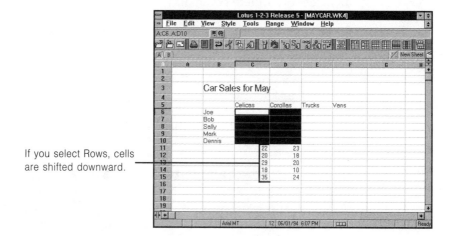

Deleting a Range of Cells

You can delete a range of cells, but the effect may not be what you think. When you delete a range of cells, adjacent cells are shifted upwards or to the right, filling the "hole" left by the deleted range. This is completely different from simply deleting the contents of a range of cells (which you can do by selecting those cells and pressing Delete).

To delete a range of cells:

1. Select the range you want to delete.

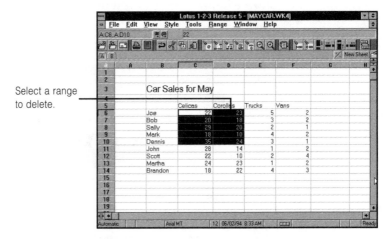

Select a range to delete.

2. Open the Edit menu.

3. Select the Delete command. The Delete dialog box appears.

4. To shift adjacent cells to the left, select the Column option button. To shift the adjacent cells upward, select the Row option button.

5. Choose Delete selection.

6. Click OK. The selected range is deleted, and that area is filled in with data according to your selections.

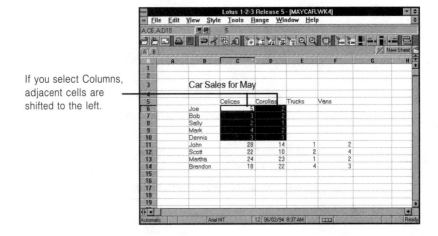

If you select Columns, adjacent cells are shifted to the left.

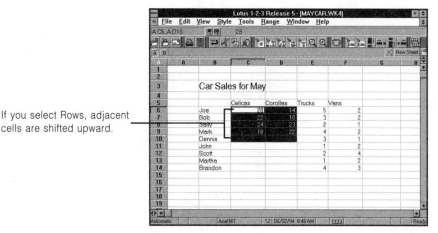

If you select Rows, adjacent cells are shifted upward.

If deleting this range of cells produces the wrong effect, click on the Undo button .

Hiding Columns, Rows, or Worksheets

Hide columns to prevent printing them.

Instead of deleting columns or rows, you can hide them. (You can even hide entire worksheets if you want!) Hiding columns and rows enables you to keep them in your worksheet without being distracted by their contents when analyzing data. It also prevents others from seeing their contents.

For example, in a budget worksheet you might have a description column that explains miscellaneous expenses, but since it doesn't contain values, you may not want it displayed all the time. So you hide the column but keep it in your worksheet. By doing so, you can also print the worksheet without printing that column because hidden columns and rows *do not print*. Note, however, that formulas within hidden cells work as usual.

To hide columns or worksheets:

1. Select a cell in each of the columns or worksheets you want to hide.

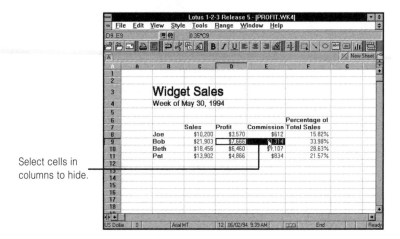

Select cells in
columns to hide.

2. Open the Style menu.

3. Select Hide. The Hide dialog box appears.

4. Select Column or Sheet.

5. Click OK. The selected columns are hidden. (You can tell a
worksheet contains hidden columns or rows if there are column
letters or row numbers missing.)

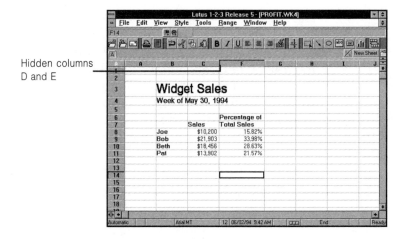

Hidden columns
D and E

To unhide columns or worksheets:

1. Select the cells or worksheets surrounding the hidden area.

2. Open the Style menu.

3. Select Hide. The Hide dialog box appears.

4. Select Column or Sheet.

5. Click on Show.

To hide rows:

1. Select the entire row(s) you want to hide.

2. Drag the bottom edge of the selection to the top edge. The row(s) are hidden from view.

To unhide the rows, simply drag the bottom edge back to its original position.

Cheat Sheet

Changing Column Width and Row Height

1. Select the columns or rows whose width you want to change.
2. Move the mouse pointer to the border of a row or column.
3. Drag the border to its new location and release the mouse button.

Adjusting Columns and Rows to Fit Their Data

1. Select the columns or rows whose width you want to change.
2. Move the mouse pointer to a border of a column or row.
3. Double-click on the border.

Setting Columns to a Specific Width

1. Select the columns you want to adjust.
2. Open the Style menu.
3. Select Column Width.
4. Enter a number under Set width to *xxxx* characters. You can reset the column width by selecting Reset to worksheet default instead.
5. Click OK.

Setting Rows to a Specific Height

1. Select the rows you want to adjust.
2. Open the Style menu.
3. Select Row Height.
4. Select Set height to *xxxx* points, and then enter a number. You can reset the row height by selecting Fit largest font instead.
5. Click OK.

Changing the Default Column Width

1. Open the Style menu.
2. Select Worksheet Defaults.
3. Click on the up or down arrow under Default column width to change its value.
4. Click OK.

22

Changing the Size of Cells

When you enter data into the worksheet, the cells do not automatically change to fit the size of that data. As a result, the data sometimes appears to be cut off (as in the case of long labels) or is displayed as a row of asterisks (as in the case of large numbers). When this happens, you can adjust the width of the columns so that the data is displayed properly.

When values are too large, they appear as asterisks.

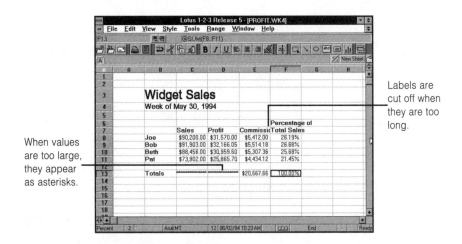

Labels are cut off when they are too long.

When you choose large text, the row height is automatically adjusted to fit it. So it is rare that you might need to adjust the height of a row. However, there may be times when you want to manually adjust row height to provide additional visual space between rows of data.

Basic Survival

Changing Column Width and Row Height

You can easily change the width of a column or the height of a row with the mouse:

1. Move the mouse pointer to the right edge of the column or the bottom border of the row whose width you want to change. The mouse pointer changes to a two-headed arrow.

2. Drag the border to its new location and release the mouse button.

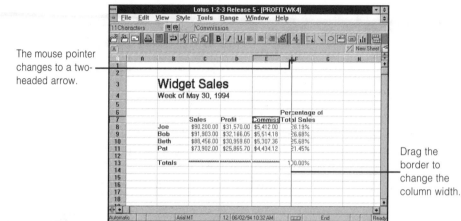

The mouse pointer changes to a two-headed arrow.

Drag border to change the width & height of columns or rows

Drag the border to change the column width.

You can change multiple columns or rows at one time, if you want. This technique is great when you want to make the columns or rows a uniform size. Just follow these steps:

1. Select the columns or rows whose width you want to change.

2. Move the mouse pointer to the border of any column (or row).

3. Drag the border to its new location and release the mouse button. All of the selected columns or rows are adjusted accordingly.

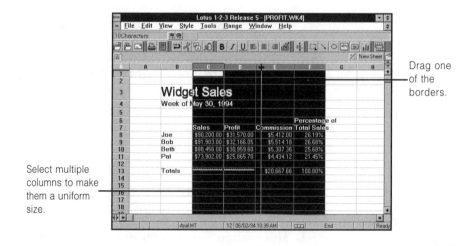

Drag one of the borders.

Select multiple columns to make them a uniform size.

Adjusting Columns and Rows to Fit Their Data

You can automatically adjust the width of a column or the height of a row to exactly fit the data it contains. This method is more convenient than adjusting columns or rows manually. To have 1-2-3 adjust a column or row to fit its data:

1. Move the mouse pointer to the *right* edge of the column or the *bottom* edge of the row whose width you want to change. The mouse pointer changes to a two-headed arrow.

Move the mouse pointer to the column's edge and double-click.

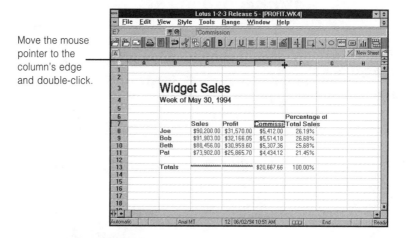

Double-click to fit data.

2. Double-click on the edge. 1-2-3 adjusts the row or column to fit the size of its data.

The column is automatically adjusted to fit the size of its data.

You can adjust multiple columns or rows to fit their data at one time, if you want:

1. Select the columns or rows whose width you want to change.

2. Move the mouse pointer to an inner edge.

3. Double-click on the edge.

Beyond Survival

Setting Columns and Rows to a Specific Size

Instead of adjusting columns and rows manually, you can set them to a specific size if you like. This is useful for creating forms or databases in which data of a specific length is used. To set column width:

1. Select the columns you want to adjust.

2. Open the Style menu.

3. Select the Column Width command. The Column Width dialog box appears.

Click here to reset the column width.

Type a number.

4. Enter a number under Set width to *xxxx* characters. You can reset the column width by selecting Reset to worksheet default instead.

5. Click OK.

Row height is automatically adjusted to fit the height of text, but you can set the height to a specific value if you want. This value is measured in *points* (a typographical standard); there are 72 points in an inch. To set row height:

1. Select the rows you want to adjust.

2. Open the Style menu.

3. Select the Row Height command. The Row Height dialog box appears.

Click here to change row height.— —Then enter a number.

Click here to reset row height.—

4. Select Set height to *xxxx* points and enter a number. You can reset the row height by selecting Fit largest font instead.

5. Click OK.

Changing the Default Column Width

By default, **all columns are 9 characters wide.** When you insert a new column, its width is set to 9 characters, regardless of the size of the columns surrounding it. If you want to, you can change this default value. However, if you change the default, 1-2-3 changes all existing columns in the current worksheet that have not already been adjusted manually. To change the default column width:

1. Open the Style menu.

2. Select the Worksheet Defaults command. The Worksheet Defaults dialog box appears.

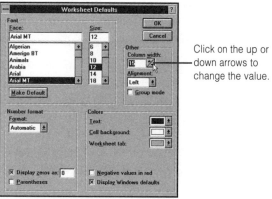

Click on the up or down arrows to change the value.

3. Click on the up or down arrow under Default column width to change its value.

4. Click OK. 1-2-3 changes all columns in the worksheet to the width you specified (except those that have already been changed manually).

By the way, using this option affects *only* the current worksheet. Repeat for additional worksheets.

Default changes affect the current worksheets only

Cheat Sheet

Changing How Text Looks

1. Select the cells you want to change.
2. Click on the Font selector on the status bar.
3. Click on a desired font.

Changing Point Size

1. Select the cells you want to change.
2. Click on the Point-Size selector on the status bar.
3. Click on a desired font size.

Adding Attributes

1. Select the cells you want to change.
2. Click on the appropriate SmartIcon:

   B   Bold

   I   Italics

   U   Underline

   U   Double underline

   N   Normal

Changing Font Formatting in One Step

1. Select the cells you want to change.
2. Open the Style menu and select Font & Attributes, or click on the Font & Attributes SmartIcon.

3. Select the font, size, and attributes you desire.
4. Click OK.

Playing with Fonts

A *font* is a set of characters with a similar style. Each font has its own name, such as Arial, Times New Roman, or Bodini. Fonts come in a variety of sizes and attributes, such as bold, italic, or underline. With the proper use of fonts, you can emphasize important data and add sophistication to your worksheets. (Although some fonts change the style of numbers, you probably won't want to change them in order to keep them legible. To change the way numbers appear, you add a number format such as US Dollar or Comma. See Chapter 24.)

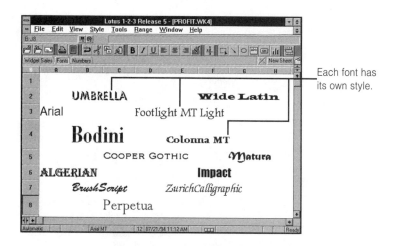

Each font has its own style.

Certain fonts come with Windows and with your Lotus 1-2-3 program. Each additional Windows program you install adds more fonts to this list, so the list of fonts on your system will vary from those shown here. You can choose any font that appears on your font list.

Once you've applied your font to a cell, you can copy that font (along with other attributes such as bold or color) to other cells if you want. See Chapter 28 for more information.

Basic Survival

Changing How Text Looks

To change how your text looks, change the font. After changing the font, you can add text attributes such as bold or underline, or change the text's size (see upcoming sections in this chapter). You can make these changes individually, or in one step. For example, you can change the font and make text bold at the same time if you want. (You can change the font of your number cells too, although in order to keep them legible, you'll probably want to stick to Arial MT, which is the default font.)

To change the font:

1. Select the cells you want to change.

2. Click on the Font selector on the status bar. A list of available fonts appears.

Select a font from the list.

First, select the cells you want to change.

Font selector

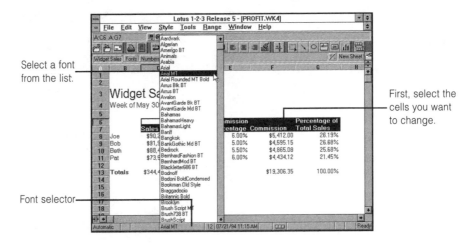

3. Click on a font to select it. Use the scroll bar to scroll through this list.

By default, all text you type into a worksheet is formatted with the Arial MT font. You can change the font of individual cells as described here. If you want to change the default, use the Style Worksheet Defaults command and select a new font. When you change the default, any text you enter from that point on is set in the font you select. In addition, any cells that you have not already modified are also changed to this new default font. Changing the default font affects the current worksheet only.

Changing Point Size

To make important information stand out, increase its size. Text size is measured by *points*, an old typographical term. There are 72 points in an inch. By default, the text (and numbers) you type into your worksheet are set to 12 points. You can change the point size of individual cells, or change the default with the Style Worksheet Defaults command. When you change the default, any data you enter from that point on is set to the size you select. In addition, any cells that have not been modified are changed. Changes to the default affect the current worksheet only.

To change the point size:

1. Select the cells you want to change.

2. Click on the Point-Size selector on the status bar. A list of point sizes appears.

Use status bar to change font and point size

3. Click on a size to select it.

First, select the cells you want to change.

Select a size from the list.

Point-size selector.

You can change a font to a point size that is not on the list with the Font & Attributes command, explained later in this chapter.

Adding Attributes

You can add many attributes, such as bold or italics, to data. Changing attributes affects text and numbers equally. For example, you can easily make both your text headings and your number totals bold. In addition, 1-2-3 offers a variety of underline styles, including single, bold, and double-underline. Adding any of these attributes can help you

171

emphasize or draw attention to certain data in your worksheet. To remove these attributes, you select Normal.

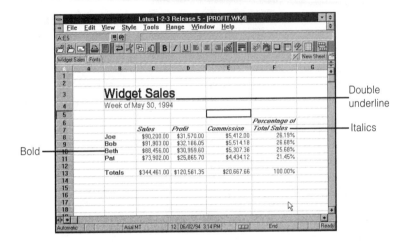

To add bold, italics, and so on:

1. Select the cells you want to change.

2. Open the Style menu.

3. Select Font & Attributes. The Font & Attributes dialog box appears.

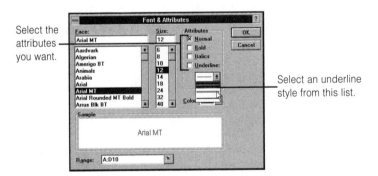

4. Select the attributes you want to apply by clicking in the attributes check box. (Remember that an "X" indicates an attribute is turned on.) You can select more than one attribute; for example, choose Bold and Italics. To remove attributes, select Normal.

5. If you selected Underline, choose an underline style, such as double-underline, from the drop-down list box.

6. Click OK.

You can quickly change attributes with these SmartIcons, found on the Default Sheet and Formatting SmartIcon sets:

B   Bold

I   Italics

U   Underline

In addition, these buttons can be added to any SmartIcon set (see Chapter 6):

U   Double-underline

N   Normal

Beyond Survival

Changing Font Formatting in One Step

If you need to change the font, the size, and the attributes of a cell or group of cells, you can do that in one step instead of using each selector on the status bar or using SmartIcons. Here's what to do:

1. Select the cells you want to change.

2. Open the Style menu.

3. Select Font & Attributes. The Font & Attributes dialog box appears.

Select the font, size, and attributes you desire.

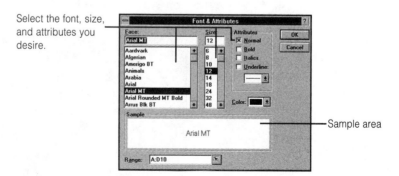

Sample area

4. Select the font, size, and attributes you desire in the dialog box. The sample area shows what your selections look like.

173

5. Click OK.

You can format text quickly by selecting the Font & Attributes command from the quick menu. Just select the cells you want to change, right-click, and then select the Font & Attributes command.

You can also change font attributes by selecting the desired cells and then clicking the Font & Attributes SmartIcon 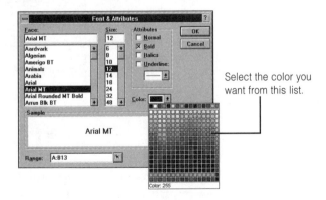 found on the Formatting SmartIcon set.

Adding Color to Data

In 1-2-3, you can add color to text or numbers, which often makes it easier for you to analyze complex worksheets on-screen. You can also change the color of the cell background to create even greater contrast (see Chapter 27 for more details). In addition, if you have a color printer, you can print your worksheets in color.

If you want to display all negative numbers in red, you don't have to go through your worksheet and manually change the data color. Instead, you can have 1-2-3 change any negative numbers automatically. See Chapter 24 instead of following the directions in this section.

To change the color of text or numbers:

1. Select the cells you want to change.

2. Open the Style menu.

3. Select Font & Attributes. The Font & Attributes dialog box appears.

4. Click on the Color drop-down list. A palette of colors appears.

Select the color you want from this list.

5. Click on the desired color.

6. Click OK. The data in the cells you selected in step one is displayed in the selected color.

You can change the color of data more quickly by selecting the Font & Attributes command from the quick menu. Just select the cells you want to change, right-click, and then select the Font & Attributes command.

You can also change colors by selecting the desired cells and then clicking the Font & Attributes SmartIcon found on the Formatting SmartIcon set.

Cheat Sheet

Changing the Number Format with the Status Bar

1. Select the cells you want to change.
2. Click on the Format selector on the status bar.
3. Select a format.
4. If desired, click on the Decimal selector on the status bar and select the number of decimal places.

You can also use these SmartIcons to change the format of numbers:

Currency

Percentage

Comma

Changing the Format with the Number Format Command

1. Select the cells you want to change.
2. Open the Style menu and select Number Format.
3. Select a format from the list box.
4. Select a number of decimal places.
5. To have 1-2-3 display negative numbers in parentheses, select the Parens check box.
6. To reset numbers to the default format, click on Reset.
7. Click OK.

Making Negative Numbers Appear Red

1. Select the cells you want to change.
2. Open the Style menu and select Lines & Color.
3. Select Negative values in red.
4. Click OK.

24

Changing How Numbers Look

Whether we realize it or not, a number's appearance affects how it is interpreted. A number followed by a percent sign is seen as a percentage of something. That same number, preceded by a dollar sign, is seen as an amount of currency. By default, 1-2-3 automatically formats numbers based on the way you enter them. For example, if you enter a number followed by a percent sign, it's treated as a percentage. Dates and times are identified as such when you enter them in one of several set formats.

1-2-3 supports many numeric formats.

However, with the exception of dates and times (which must be entered in a specific format), it's much easier to enter your data and then format it with commas, dollar signs, or percent signs. This chapter will show you how.

Once you apply your formatting to a cell, you can copy that formatting to other cells if you want (see Chapter 28 for more information). You can also change the default format, which will automatically change the format of all unformatted cells. Just use the Style Worksheet Defaults command and select the number format you prefer.

Basic Survival

Changing the Number Format with the Status Bar

Probably the easiest way to change the format of a number is with the status bar:

1. Select the cells you want to change.

2. Click on the Format selector on the status bar. A list of formats appears.

Remember to use status bar to change numbers

First select the cells you want to change.

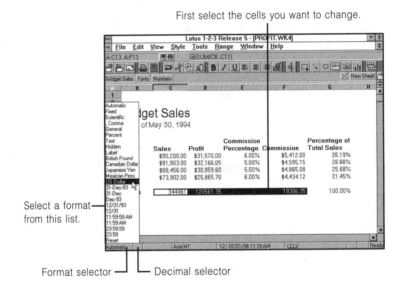

Select a format from this list.

Format selector — └ Decimal selector

3. Click on a format from the list.

4. If desired, click on the Decimal selector on the status bar and select the number of decimal places.

If you use the Currency, Percentage, or Comma formats often, you may want to consider adding these SmartIcons to a set (see Chapter 6 for details):

Currency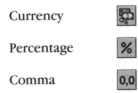

Percentage %

Comma 0,0

What to do
if you see
asterisks?

After you change the formatting of your numbers, you may see asterisks in some cells. That means that the cell is no longer wide enough to display the newly formatted number. Simply double-click on the border of a column to widen it (see Chapter 22 for more details).

Changing the Format with the Number Format Command

If you want to see what your number will look like before you actually assign it a particular format, use the Number Format command. With this command, you can change both the format and the number of decimal places in one step. In addition, you can use this command to reset a group of cells to the default format.

1. Select the cells you want to change.

2. Open the Style menu.

3. Select Number Format. The Number Format dialog box appears.

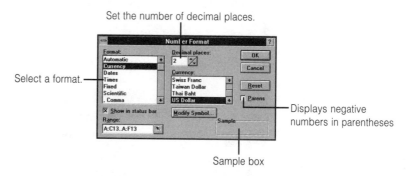

Set the number of decimal places.

Select a format.

Displays negative numbers in parentheses

Sample box

4. Select a format from the Format list box. A sample of your selection is displayed in the sample box.

5. Select a number of decimal places.

Can make
negative #'s
appear in
parens

6. If you want to display negative numbers in parentheses, select the Parens check box.

7. If you want to reset numbers to the default format, click on Reset.

8. Click OK.

You can format numbers quickly by selecting the Number Format command from the quick menu. Just select the cells you want to change, right-click, and then select the Number Format command.

179

Remember that after you change the formatting of your numbers, you may see asterisks. 1-2-3 displays a row of asterisks in a cell when the cell is no longer wide enough to display the newly formatted number. Simply double-click on the border of a column to widen it. See Chapter 22 for more information.

Beyond Survival

Making Negative Numbers Appear Red

If you prefer traditional accounting methods, you can make your negative numbers appear red. To do this, you must take the following additional steps after you've formatted your numbers. Negative numbers will then appear red on-screen; if you have a color printer, they will print in red also. That way, when you're "in the red," you'll really know it.

1. Select the cells you want to change.

2. Open the Style menu.

3. Select Lines & Color. The Lines & Color dialog box appears.

Click here to make negative numbers appear in red.

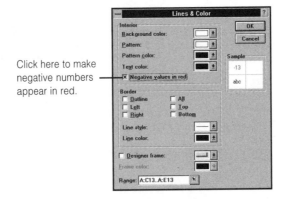

4. Click on the Negative values in red check box.

5. Click OK.

You can make this change quickly by selecting the Lines & Color command from the quick menu. Just select the cells you want to change, right-click, and then select the Lines & Color command.

If you want to change all the negative numbers in a worksheet to red without having to go through the trouble of selecting them first, open the Styles menu and select Worksheet Defaults. Select the Negative values in the red check box from the dialog box that appears, and then click OK.

Cheat Sheet

Changing Alignment

1. Select the cells you want to change.
2. Open the Style menu.
3. Select Alignment.
4. Under Horizontal or Vertical, select the desired option buttons.
5. Click OK.

You can also use these SmartIcons to align data:

Left Align		Right Align	
Center		Evenly spaced	

Centering Across Columns

1. Select the cells in which you want to center your title.
2. Open the Style menu.
3. Select Alignment.
4. Under Horizontal, select the Center option button.
5. Select Across columns.
6. Click OK.

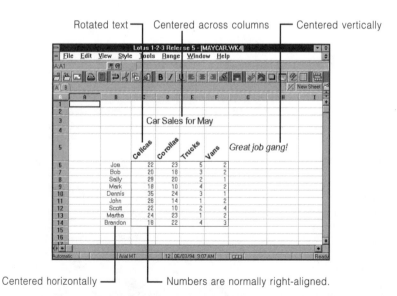

25

Changing the Alignment of Data

Normally, 1-2-3 aligns labels to the left and numbers to the right within a cell. You can override this arbitrary alignment whenever you want. In addition, you can center a title across several cells, instead of just within a single cell. You can even change the horizontal alignment of your data; by default, data is aligned at the bottom of a cell.

To create dramatic effects, you can rotate data and place it on a slant. This technique is particularly effective with titles.

Refer to the figure on the Cheat Sheet for examples of text alignment.

Basic Survival

Changing Alignment

Changing the alignment of data is simple:

1. Select the cells you want to change.

2. Open the Style menu.

3. Select Alignment. The Alignment dialog box appears.

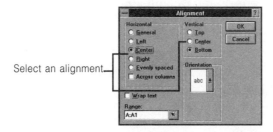

Select an alignment.

4. Under Horizontal, click on one of the following option buttons:

General   Returns the cells to the default alignment: left-
                 aligned labels and right-aligned numbers.

Left   Left-aligns data within the cell.

Center	Centers data within the cell.
Right	Right-aligns data within the cell.
Evenly spaced	Spaces data evenly within a cell.

5. Or under Vertical, click on one of the following option buttons:

Top	Aligns data at the top of the cell.
Center	Centers data vertically within a cell.
Bottom	Aligns data at the bottom of the cell. This is the default.

6. Click OK.

You can also change the alignment of data with the quick menu. Just select the cells you want to change, right-click, and select Alignment. You can also specify the alignment of data as you type, by inserting one of these *prefixes* in front of the data. For example, you could type ^ Sales to center the word "Sales" within a cell.

Prefix	What it does
'	Left-aligns
^	Centers
"	Right-aligns

In addition, you can change the alignment of data with these SmartIcons on the Default and Formatting SmartIcon sets:

Left Align	
Center	
Right Align	

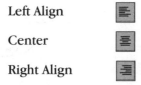

This SmartIcon does not appear on any SmartIcon set, but you can add it to a set with the instructions from Chapter 6:

| Evenly spaced | |

Centering Across Columns

Place title in first cell, then center across columns

Centering your title across the data columns is much easier than trying to use the Spacebar to align it properly. Follow these steps to center across columns:

1. Select the cells over which you want to center your title. The title itself should be in the first cell of this range.

2. Open the Style menu.

3. Select Alignment. The Alignment dialog box appears.

Select Center alignment ——
Select Across columns ——

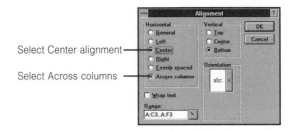

4. Under Horizontal, click on the Center option button.

5. Click on the Across columns check box.

6. Click OK. Your title is centered over the selected columns.

You can also center data across columns with the quick menu. Just select the cells you want to change, right-click, and select Alignment.

The Center Across Columns SmartIcon 🔲 does not appear on any SmartIcon set, but you can add it to a set with the instructions from Chapter 6.

Beyond Survival

Wrapping Text

If you type a large amount of text (such as a paragraph) into a cell, you may want to wrap text. *Text wrapping* is a feature you normally see in word processors. It's the feature that automatically moves text to the next line when it reaches the right margin; if a word is too long to fit on the current line, it's wrapped to the next line. In 1-2-3, this option expands the height of a cell to fit the text paragraph, wrapping the words between the edges of the cell. If this makes the cell too big, you can wrap text across many cells (across columns) too.

A long cell entry overflows into adjacent cells if they are empty.

Text wrapped in a single cell

Text wrapped across many cells

To wrap text in a cell:

1. Move to the cell whose contents you want to wrap. If you want to wrap the contents across several columns, select those cells too.

2. Open the Style menu.

3. Select Alignment. The Alignment dialog box appears.

4. Click on the Wrap text check box.

5. If you want the text to wrap across the selected columns, click on the Across columns check box.

6. Click OK.

You can also wrap text with the quick menu. Just select the cells in which you want to wrap text, right-click, and select Alignment.

Changing Orientation or Rotation of Data

You can change the orientation of text so that it reads downward or sideways in a cell instead of from left to right. When you do, the height of the cell is increased to hold the vertical data, so this is not a good technique to use when you have a large amount of text in a cell.

Use rotation
to save space
in wide
worksheets

Rotating data within a cell realigns that data at an angle. This is a nice technique to use when space is limited, as shown here. It's also a nice visual effect, calling attention to important data.

Rotating data saves space.

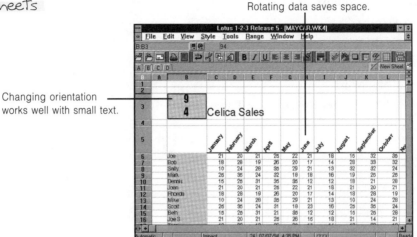

Changing orientation works well with small text.

To change the orientation or rotation of data:

1. Select the cells whose orientation or rotation you want to change.

2. Open the Style menu.

3. Select Alignment. The Alignment dialog box appears.

4. Select an orientation from the Orientation drop down list. To rotate text, be sure to select the rotation orientation (text shown at an angle).

5. If you are changing the rotation of data, select an angle of rotation.

6. Click OK. The orientation or rotation of the data is changed.

You can also change orientation or rotate text with the quick menu. Just select the cell whose orientation you want to change, right-click, and select Alignment.

You can also click on the Rotate Text SmartIcon, located on the Formatting SmartIcon set ![abc].

Cheat Sheet

Protecting a File Against Changes

1. Open the File menu.
2. Select Protect.
3. Select Seal file.
4. Click OK.
5. Enter a password.
6. Press Tab and enter the password again to verify it.
7. Click OK.

Unsealing a File

1. Open the File menu.
2. Select Protect.
3. Deselect the Seal file check box by clicking on it.
4. Click OK.
5. Enter your password as verification.
6. Click OK.

Unprotecting Some Cells to Allow Changes

1. Select the cells you want to unprotect.
2. Open the Style menu and select Protection.
3. Select Keep data unprotected after file is sealed.
4. Click OK. Repeat for additional cells you want to leave unprotected.
5. Seal the file with the File Protect command.

26

Protecting Your Data

If you work with confidential data, you might want to protect your files against unauthorized use. Thereafter, if anyone wants to use the file, he must supply a password in order to open it. If you don't give anyone the password, you are the only person who can open such a file, let alone make any changes to it. To learn how to save a file in this manner, don't follow the directions in this chapter; instead see Chapter 15.

Sometimes you have no choice: you must share certain files with co-workers. However, you can still place limits on what they can change by *sealing* a file rather than password-protecting it. In this chapter, you learn how to do just that.

In addition, if you are connected to a network and there is a possibility that more than one person might try to access the same file at the same time, you can *reserve* the file so that no one can make changes while you are using it. After you are done, you can release the file for others to use.

Basic Survival

Protecting a File Against Changes

When you seal a file, you tell 1-2-3 that it can only be viewed; no one can make changes to the file while it is sealed (not even you). A password is not used to open a sealed file. It is only used to change the protection level later on.

If you want to allow limited changes (changes to certain areas of the worksheet, but not to others), see the section under Beyond Survival.

To seal an entire file:

1. Open the File menu.

2. Select Protect. The Protect dialog box appears.

Select this
option to
seal the file.

3. Select the Seal file check box.

4. Click OK. The Set Password dialog box appears.

Write down
the pass-
word in a
safe place!

5. Enter a password in the Password text box. You must supply this
password if you want to unseal the file at a later time, so make
sure you write it down in a secure place.

Type your
password.

Verify your password
by typing it again.

6. Press Tab and enter the password again to verify it. Make sure you
type the password just as you did in the Password text box above.

7. Click OK. You're returned to the file, but you will no longer be
allowed to make changes to the file unless you unseal it.

Unsealing a File

When a file is sealed, all the cells are marked "protected." That means
that no one can make changes to the data in those cells. Anyone can
open the file without a password, but no one can make changes to the
file (except to cells that you manually change to "unprotected"—see
the next section). When the user clicks in a protected cell, the letters
"Pr" appear in the status bar to let him know that the cell is protected
against changes. If a user attempts to change data in a protected cell,
he sees this warning:

If you want to unseal the file so you can make changes to it:

1. Open the File menu.

2. Select Protect. The Protect dialog box appears.

3. Deselect the Seal file check box by clicking on it.

4. Click OK. The Get Password dialog box appears.

5. Enter your password as verification. (This is the password you typed in when you sealed the file in the first place.)

6. Click OK. You (and anyone else for that matter) can now enter changes to the file. To reseal it, follow the same steps you did before.

Beyond Survival

Unprotecting Some Cells to Allow Changes

When you seal a file, no one can make changes to any cell in the entire sealed file. If you want to allow limited changes, you can unprotect certain cells *before* you seal the file. Any cells you unprotect will be open for changes after the file is sealed. All other cells will be protected. For example, suppose you had a monthly sales sheet and you wanted to allow users to add the daily sales amounts, but you wanted to prevent them from changing the formulas or the previous month's amounts. You could unprotect this month's daily sales area and leave the rest of the worksheet protected.

Unprotect cells; then seal the file.

To unprotect cells:

1. Select the cells you want to unprotect.

2. Open the Style menu.

3. Select Protection. The Protection dialog box appears.

Select this option to unprotect cells.

4. Select Keep data unprotected after file is sealed check box.

5. Click OK.

6. Repeat for additional cells you want to leave unprotected.

7. Seal the file with the File Protect command. See the previous section for more details.

When a cell is unprotected, a "U" appears in the status bar when the cell pointer is in that cell. This lets you know that data in that cell can be changed. The letters "Pr" appear in the status bar when a protected cell is selected.

Unprotected cell ————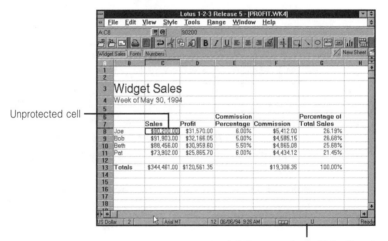

A "U" appears in the Status Bar when an unprotected cell is selected.

Cheat Sheet

Adding Borders to Cells

1. Select the cells in which you want to place a border.
2. Open the Style menu.
3. Select Lines & Color.
4. Click on the down arrow under Line style and make a selection.
5. Select a line color if you want.
6. Under Border, select one or more options.
7. Click OK.

Filling a Cell with a Pattern or a Color

1. Select the cells whose fill or data color you want to change.
2. Open the Style menu.
3. Select Lines & Color.
4. Select a background color.
5. Select a pattern if you want.
6. Select a pattern color if you want.
7. Select a data color if you want.
8. Click OK.

Adding a Frame

1. Select the cells you want to frame.
2. Open the Style menu.
3. Select Lines & Color.
4. Select a frame style.
5. Select a frame color if you want.
6. Click OK.

27

Adding Borders, Fills, and Frames

Add borders, fills, or frames to emphasize important areas of the worksheet. A *border* is a dark outline around some or all of the sides of a cell. A *frame* surrounds a group of cells with a fancy border. A *fill* controls the color inside a cell. By adding the right amount of contrast with borders, fills, and frames, you can make your worksheet more professional-looking and easier to read.

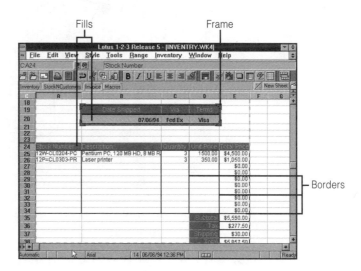

Fills   Frame   Borders

Basic Survival

Adding Borders to Cells

When you add data to a 1-2-3 worksheet, the individual cells are outlined by faint gray lines (called *gridlines*). These lines are provided so you can easily distinguish one cell from another; however, these lines are not normally printed when you print your worksheet. If you would like to print the cell gridlines, see Chapter 37.

Instead of printing gridlines around every cell, you can select certain cells for emphasis and place borders around them. A border can be placed along any side of a cell, or along all four sides. You can select a group of cells and add the same border to all of them at once; you can also place an outline around the entire group of cells if you want. To place a border around a cell or a group of cells:

1. Select the cells around which you want to place a border. If you only want to modify one cell, move the cell pointer there.

2. Open the Style menu.

3. Select Lines & Color. The Lines & Color dialog box appears.

Select a side.   Select a border style.

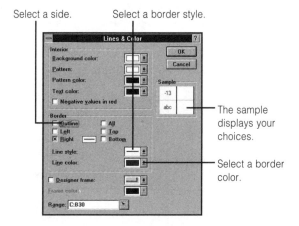

The sample displays your choices.

Select a border color.

4. Click on the down arrow for the Line style drop-down list and select the thickness of the line you want to use as a border.

5. If you want the border line to be displayed and printed in color, click on the down arrow for the Line color drop-down list and select a color for the border line.

6. Under Border, select one or more options. All places a border around all four sides of each cell; Outline places a border around the group of selected cells. Left, Right, Top, and Bottom each place a border along the corresponding side of each cell.

7. Click OK. The border you specified appears around selected cells.

Instead of selecting the Lines & Color command from the Style menu, you can right-click and select it from the quick menu. You can also click the Lines & Color SmartIcon, located on the Formatting SmartIcon set ▣ .

If you want a border to surround a given range, you can click on the Border Outline SmartIcon, also found on the Formatting SmartIcon set ▨ .

Filling a Cell with a Pattern or a Color

Fill = color of cell

To draw attention to a particular group of cells on-screen, fill them with a pattern and/or color. Or you can change the color of the data in your cells. If you have a color printer, these cells will print in color also.

The color that fills the cell is a blend of the background and pattern colors. The amount of "blending" that occurs depends on the pattern you select. For example, a blending of a white background and a black pattern color produces gray when you select the solid pattern. If you choose a striped pattern instead of a solid pattern, you'll get a white background with black stripes instead of a gray background. Select your background and pattern colors to create thousands of effects.

To fill a cell or a group of cells with a blended color or a pattern:

1. Select the cells whose fill or data color you want to change. If you want to change only one cell, move the cell pointer there.

2. Open the Style menu.

3. Select Lines & Color. The Lines & Color dialog box appears.

Select a
pattern if you want.

Select a
background color.

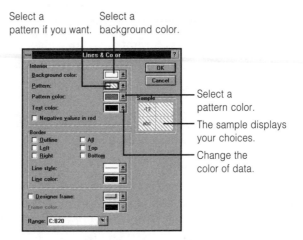

Select a
pattern color.

The sample displays
your choices.

Change the
color of data.

4. Click on the down arrow of the Background color drop-down list and make a selection.

5. If you want to change the color to a lighter shade or add a textured pattern (such as diagonal stripes or waves), click on the down arrow of the Pattern drop-down list and make a selection. If you don't select a pattern, you get a 50/50 blend of the background and pattern colors.

6. If you want to change the pattern color, click on the down arrow of the Pattern color drop-down list and make a selection.

7. If you want to change the color of the data in the selected cells, click on the down arrow of the Text color drop-down list and make a selection.

8. Click OK. The selected cells are displayed in the color and pattern you specified.

Instead of selecting the Lines & Color command from the Style menu, you can right-click and select it from the quick menu. You can also click the Lines & Color SmartIcon, located on the Formatting SmartIcon set ▦ .

Adding a Frame

A frame is a fancy type of outline border. Placing a frame around a title or an area containing instructions sets them off so they are noticed. There are many different types of frames from which you can choose— but be careful. Large frames can sometimes make data hard to read. To add a frame:

1. Select the cells you want to frame.

2. Open the Style menu.

3. Select Lines & Color. The Lines & Color dialog box appears.

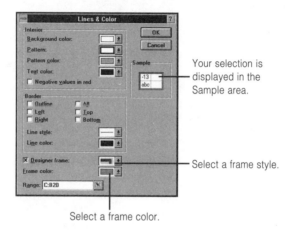

Your selection is displayed in the Sample area.

Select a frame style.

Select a frame color.

4. Click on the down arrow of the Designer frame drop-down list and make a selection.

5. If you want to change the frame color, click on the down arrow of the Frame color drop-down list and make a selection.

6. Click OK.

Instead of selecting the Lines & Color command from the Style menu, you can right-click and select it from the quick menu. You can also click the Lines & Color SmartIcon, located on the Formatting SmartIcon set.

Beyond Survival

Adding a Drop Shadow

A drop shadow creates the effect of "lifting" the cells it surrounds off the page. There is a drop shadow frame style, but it creates a simple drop shadow effect (not much shadow).

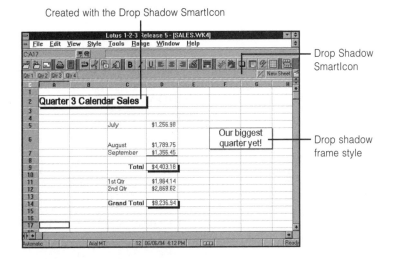

Created with the Drop Shadow SmartIcon

Drop Shadow SmartIcon

Drop shadow frame style

To create the drop shadow frame, follow the directions in the previous section. When the Lines & Shadows dialog box is displayed, just select the second frame style in the Designer frame palette, and then click OK. You'll get a shadow, as shown in the figure. For a more dramatic effect, try creating a shadow with the Drop Shadow SmartIcon instead.

1. Select the cells to which you want to add a drop shadow.

2. Click on the Drop Shadow SmartIcon located on the Formatting SmartIcon set ▣. A drop shadow is placed around the selected cells.

Cheat Sheet

Using the Style Gallery

1. Select the cells you want to format. If you want to select the entire worksheet, click on the worksheet letter.
2. Open the Style menu.
3. Select Gallery.
4. Select a style template you like.
5. Click OK.

Copying Formatting from One Cell to Another

1. Select the cell or cells whose format you want to copy.
2. Open the Style menu.
3. Select Fast Format.
4. Select the cell or cells to which you want to copy the formatting.
5. Repeat for additional cells or ranges.
6. When you're done, press Esc to turn fast formatting off.

Removing Formatting

1. Select the cells whose formatting you want to remove.
2. Open the Edit menu.
3. Select Clear.
4. Select Styles only or Both.
5. Click OK.

Creating Your Own Style

1. Format a cell or group of cells in the normal manner.
2. Select the cells whose style you want to save.
3. Open the Style menu.
4. Select Named Style.
5. Enter a style name using up to 32 characters, including spaces.
6. Click on Define.
7. Click on Close.

Once you have a named style, you can apply it to a cell by selecting that cell and selecting the style from the Style selector on the status bar.

28

Fancy Free Formatting

Because it's usually hard work, formatting can sometimes take all the fun out of creating a worksheet in the first place. But with the 1-2-3 Style Gallery, all of the hard work is done for you. Just select the style template you like, and 1-2-3 does all the rest. A style *template* is a collection of "styles" that can be applied to the selected range. A *style*, in this case, is the look of a cell—for example, the combination of specific color, font, and border selections. If you look at the example here, you see that 1-2-3 has taken the styles of various cells and combined them into a package it calls a style template. You select a style template, and these same styles are applied to your cells.

Common style templates

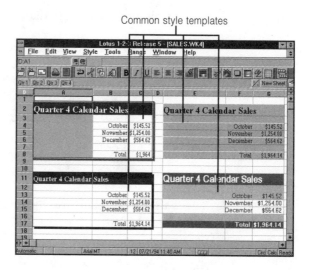

You can even modify the cells after a style template is applied in order to customize the look. If you like what you create, you can save it as your own style template and reuse it over and over. If you prefer to do your formatting from scratch, go ahead. Then use Fast Format to copy the formatting from one cell to another.

Basic Survival

Using the Style Gallery

The style gallery is a set of ready made *style templates* designed by the experts at Lotus. A style template is a collection of borders, fonts, and colors that is applied to your cells in a specific fashion. By selecting a style template you like and then applying it to your worksheet, you can achieve a professional look in no time.

You can apply the style template to the entire worksheet (which is the most common method) or to part of the worksheet if you want to create a customized look. All you have to do is choose the style template you like. Here's how:

1. Select the cells you want to format. If you want to select the entire worksheet, click on the worksheet letter. For example, click on the button marked "A," located in the upper left-hand corner of worksheet A.

2. Open the Style menu.

3. Select Gallery. The Gallery dialog box appears.

Select a style template.

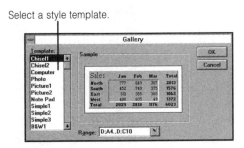

4. Select a style template you like from the Template list. A sample of the style template you select is displayed in the Sample area of the dialog box.

5. Click OK.

For quicker formatting, use the Style Gallery SmartIcon, found on the Formatting SmartIcon set ![icon].

Copying Formatting from One Cell to Another

If you decide you'd rather do the formatting yourself, that doesn't mean you have to go it alone. Just do a minimal amount of formatting (such as changing the font and font size, and adding borders, fills, or frames). Then simply copy that formatting from one cell to another.

Fast formatting copies all formatting, including the font, font size, alignment, number format, attributes (such as bold and italics), border styles, frames, and fills. To apply fast formatting:

1. Select the cell or cells whose format you want to copy.

2. Open the Style menu.

3. Select Fast Format. The mouse pointer changes into a little paint-brush.

Select a cell to copy.

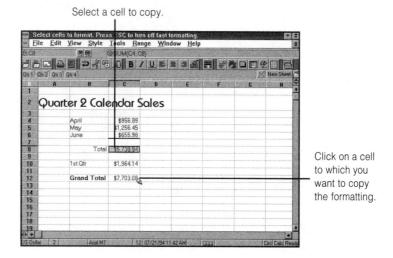

Click on a cell to which you want to copy the formatting.

4. Select the cell or cells to which you want to copy the formatting. The new cell will now have the formatting you copied.

5. Repeat for additional cells or ranges.

6. When you're done, press Esc to turn fast formatting off.

Press Esc to turn off fast formatting

You can also click the Fast Format SmartIcon to turn on fast formatting. It's located on the Default Sheet and Formatting SmartIcon sets. Drag the mouse over any cells you want to format. To turn fast formatting off, click on the Fast Format SmartIcon.

Beyond Survival

Removing Formatting

Removing formatting removes such things as alignment, attributes (such as bold or underline), borders, frames, and fills from the cells you select. It also resets the font to Arial MT 12-point and changes numbers to the default format. If you need to remove all formatting from a cell, it's fairly easy to do:

1. Select the cells whose formatting you want to remove.

2. Open the Edit menu.

3. Select Clear. The Clear dialog box appears.

Select Styles only.

4. Select the Styles only check box. Or select Both if you also want to clear data from the selected cells.

5. Click OK. The formatting and/or data is removed.

Use Edit Clear to remove formatting and clear data.

You can also remove formatting by selecting Clear from the quick menu. Or you can click on the Remove Formatting SmartIcon, located on the Formatting SmartIcon set.

Creating Your Own Style

After you do a lot of formatting, you start to think, "There has to be a better way." One better way is to use the Style Gallery, explained earlier in this chapter. Another way is to create your own styles and use them instead.

A *style* in this case is a collection of specific formats which are all applied to a cell or group of cells in one step. A style can include a specific font, font size, alignment, number format, border, fill, or frame. And although a style can include all of these, it doesn't have to. What it includes is up to you. You can save up to 16 styles per worksheet file. To create your own style:

1. Format a cell or group of cells in the normal manner.

2. Select the cells whose style you want to save.

3. Open the Style menu.

4. Select Named Style. The Named Style dialog box appears.

Type a name for your style.

Then click here.

5. Enter a style name using up to 32 characters, including spaces, in the Style name text box.

6. Click on the Define button.

7. Click on the Close button.

Once you have a named style, you can apply it to a cell by selecting that cell and then selecting the style from the Style selector on the status bar.

Just select a range and apply a style.

Style selector

Deleting a Named Style

If you want to delete a named style:

1. Open the Style menu.

2. Select Named Style. The Named Style dialog box appears.

3. Select the style you want to delete from the Existing Styles list.

4. Click on the Clear button.

5. Click on the Close button.

If the deleted style was used in the worksheet, that's okay. The cells with that style remain formatted in the deleted style.

Formulas and Functions

There's no point in throwing a lot of numbers onto a page without a formula that makes sense out of them. From simple formulas that add numbers to compute a total, to complex formulas that compute the future value of an investment based on a series of planned payments and a given interest rate, 1-2-3 has what you need. And in this section, you'll learn how to make the most of it with such topics as:

- Working with Formulas
- Copying Formulas
- Problems with Formulas
- Entering a Function
- Using Ranges in Functions and Formulas
- Problems with Functions

Cheat Sheet

Operators to Use Within Formulas

Operation	Operator	Example
Add	+	C1+4 (C1 plus 4)
Subtract	–	4–C1 (4 minus C1)
Divide	/	4/C1 (4 divided by C1)
Multiply	*	C1*4 (C1 times 4)
Exponentiation	^	C1^4 (same as $C1^4$)
Combine two text strings	&	B2&" Cost" (If B2 contains "Under," you get "Under Cost")
Equal to	=	B2=4
Less than	<	B2<4
Greater than	>	B2>4
Less than or equal to	<=	B2<=4
Greater than or equal to	>=	B2>=4
Not equal to	<>	B2<>4
If this is true, *and* that is true	#AND#	B2<4#AND#C3=9
If this is true, *or* that is true	#OR#	B2<4#OR#C3=9
If this is *not true*	#NOT#	#NOT#A1=0

Entering a Formula

1. Move to the cell in which you want to enter a formula.
2. Type a plus (+).
3. Type a cell address, a number, or a range name. You can click on a cell or select a range name from the Range Selector instead of typing it if you want.
4. Type an operator such as +, –, /, *, &, =, <, and so on.
5. Type the second cell address, a value, or a range name. Continue adding operators and operands until the formula is complete.
6. Press Enter or click on the Confirm button.

If you make a mistake, press Backspace to erase it, and then retype your formula. To cancel completely, click on the Cancel button or press Escape.

29

Working with Formulas

A *formula* is a calculation that computes a value. For example, you can create a formula that adds the values in a range. Formulas can be simple (such as adding two numbers) or complex (such as computing a loan payment based on a particular interest rate). 1-2-3 uses three types of formulas: numeric, text, and logical. In this chapter, you will learn how to enter all types of basic formulas.

Basic Survival

What Is a Formula?

As you learned in the opening paragraph, a *formula* is a calculation that computes some type of value. You can use formulas in your worksheets to do a variety of things, such as add expenses, compute your annual income, or add two labels together to create a text string. When you enter a formula into the worksheet, 1-2-3 displays the result in the cell and displays the formula itself in the contents box when that cell is selected.

The formula is displayed in the contents box.

The result is displayed in the cell.

The result of a formula is displayed with as many decimal places as the cell's format allows. Be careful; just because you set up a cell to display only two decimal places doesn't mean that there aren't more decimals there. Those invisible decimal places continue to be used in formulas involving that cell, which can throw off your totals if you aren't looking for it. There is a special *function* (utility) that you can use in a formula to round a number to a certain decimal place. If you use that function, you know that what is displayed is what is actually being used by the computer in your formulas, so your totals won't mysteriously be "off." See Chapter 34 for help.

1-2-3 automatically updates formulas.

Formulas are *dynamic*, which means that they are always active. When you put a formula in your worksheet to add two cells, and then you change the value in one of those cells, 1-2-3 automatically recalculates the formula to display the correct total. You can turn this automatic recalculation off and then recalculate manually whenever you want (see Chapter 31).

Of the three basic types of formulas (numeric, text, and logical), numeric formulas are probably the most common. With a numeric formula, you can add, subtract, divide, or multiply the *values* in any group of cells. Special characters (called *operators*) indicate what you want to do in the formula:

Operation	Operator	Examples
Add	+	C1+4 or C1+B5
Subtract	–	4–C1 or B5–C1
Divide	/	4/C1 or B5/C1
Multiply	*	C1*4 or C1*B5
Exponentiation	^	C1 ^ 4 (same as $C1^4$)

A text formula manipulates *text strings* or short pieces of text. With a text formula, you can add the contents of one cell to another and come up with a phrase, such as "Over Cost." You could also compare two cells to see if they contained the exact same text, such as "Jones, Pat." When used in formulas, text strings are placed within quotations. If you want to add a space between words, insert a space within the quotations, as in " Sales."

Operation	Operator	Example
Combine two text strings	&	B2& "Cost" (If B2 contains "Under," you get "Under Cost")

A logical formula compares two values and tells you whether that comparison is true or false. For example, you could ask whether the contents in cell C1 were less than B2, and you would get an answer: true if it was less than B2, or false if it wasn't. True is equal to 1 in the computer, and false is equal to 0. So if you had the logical formula +C1<B2 (Is C1 less than B2?) and the answer was true, you would see a 1 displayed in the cell. Otherwise, you'd see a 0.

Operation	Operator	Example
Equal to	=	B2=4
Less than	<	B2<4
Greater than	>	B2>4
Less than or equal to	<=	B2<=4
Greater than or equal to	>=	B2>=4
Not equal to	<>	B2<>4
If this is true, *and* that is true	#AND#	B2<4#AND#C3=9
If this is true, *or* that is true	#OR#	B2<4#OR#C3=9
If this is *not true*	#NOT#	#NOT#A1=0

Logical operators are usually combined with logical *functions*, special utilities that perform a comparison and then do something based on whether that comparison is true or false. For example, the @IF function can perform one action if the logical formula is true, and another if it is false. Very useful. See Chapter 32 for more help.

Entering a Formula

A formula consists of three things:

Operands Values (such as 12, 1.35, or 100.01) or cell addresses (such as B4, S98, or AA12) that contain values to act upon. You can also use range names (such as MAY_TOTALS).

Operators Mathematical, logical, or textual symbols that tell 1-2-3 what to do with the operands—for example, to add them together.

Separators Parentheses act as separators within a formula, controlling what part of the formula 1-2-3 calculates next.

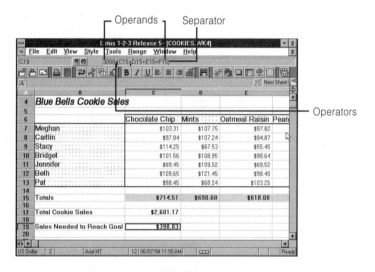

In this example formula, the operands include: 3000, C15, D15, E15, and F15. The operators include – and +.

Remember these rules when typing a formula:

- A formula always begins with a plus sign +. (Actually, you can use other things besides the plus, but why try to remember so many different things? Stay with the plus and you'll always be okay.)

- Don't use spaces in formulas, unless they are part of a text string, as in "The Big Sale."

- Don't use commas in formulas. For example, don't type +B2*1,345.

DON'T use spaces or commas in formulas

- Blank cells referred to in a formula are treated as if they contain 0 (zero).

- Formulas are recalculated automatically as values change unless recalculation is turned off.

Begin for-mulas with a plus (+)

So how do you enter a formula into a worksheet? Follow these steps:

1. Move to the cell in which you want to enter a formula.

2. Type a plus +.

3. Type a cell address, a number, or a range name. You can click on a cell or select a range name from the Range Selector instead of typing it in if you want. For example, type G4.

4. Type an operator, such as +, –, /, *, &, =, <, and so on. (See the previous section for a complete listing.) For example, type + to add two values.

5. Type the second cell address, a value, or a range name. For example, type 200. Your formula now looks like: +G4+200. Continue adding operators and operands until the formula is complete.

6. Press Enter or click on the Confirm button. Do *not* click on a cell to confirm the formula, because you'll just be adding that cell to the formula itself.

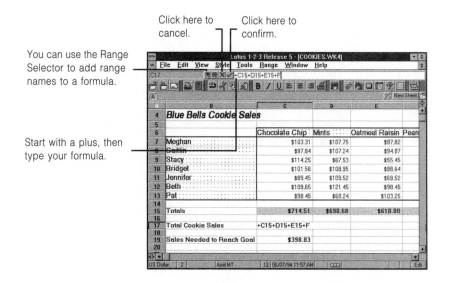

215

If you make a mistake, press Backspace to erase it, and then retype your formula. To cancel completely, click on the Cancel button or press Esc.

If the result of your formula is too big to be displayed in the cell, the cell is filled with asterisks. See Chapter 22 for instructions on making a column wider. If you get an error after entering a formula, see Chapter 31 for help.

You can copy similar formulas from one cell to another. For example, if you enter the formula to total the sales for June in one cell, you can copy that formula to the August and September columns. See Chapter 30 for more information on copying a formula.

Beyond Survival

When to Use Parentheses

When 1-2-3 calculates the result of a formula, it processes that formula in a particular order. First, 1-2-3 evaluates each operator according to its *precedence*. Operators with the same precedence are processed from left to right.

*precedence = * and / are calculated first, then + and −*

Operator	Operation	Order of Precedence
^	Exponentiation	1
* /	Multiplication and division	2
+ −	Addition and subtraction	3
= <> > >= < <=	Comparison tests	4
#NOT#	Logical NOT test	5
#AND# #OR#	Logical AND or OR tests	6
&	Text string concatenation	7

So what does all this mean to you? Bottom line: a formula might not produce the results that you expect. Consider this example:

$$+B2-A1*C3+B2/A1$$

If B2=6, A1=2, and C3=4, here's how 1-2-3 would evaluate the formula:

6–(2*4)+(6/2)

6–8+3

1

Use parentheses to override precedence

The multiplication and the division take precedence over the addition and subtraction, so they're done first. The formula is then evaluated from left to right, meaning that the subtraction is done next, and the addition is last. If you want to change the order of precedence (in this case, to have 1-2-3 perform the subtraction first), you must use parentheses.

For example, if you change the formula to this:

+(B2–A1)*(C3+B2/A1)

You get a different result:

(6–2)*(4+(6/2))

4*(4+3)

4*7

28

Because of the parentheses, A1 is subtracted from B2 first. Within the second set of parentheses, the order of precedence causes the division to be calculated first and then the addition. Lastly, the results of the two parenthetical operations are multiplied together. So you should put parentheses around the parts of a formula you want calculated first.

Nested parentheses (parentheses *within* parentheses) are evaluated from the inside out. For example, the formula

+(B2–(A1*C3))+B2/A1

results in:

(6–(2*4))+(6/2)

(6–8)+3

–2+3

1

By the way, a formula can begin with a parenthesis, so you could write our formula like this:

(B2–(A1*C3))+B2/A1

But again, it's much simpler to remember that formulas begin with a plus. The extra plus used in the earlier example:

+(B2–(A1*C3))+B2/A1

doesn't cause an error, so if you use pluses at the beginning of all your formulas, you'll have an easier time.

Displaying the Contents of One Cell in Another Cell

You can display the contents of one cell in another cell through a formula. This is a neat trick to use when you need to display the same data in more than one place within a worksheet (for example, if you needed to create a recap of important figures in another area of the worksheet—a long way away from the real data). Although this formula doesn't really calculate anything, it gets the job done:

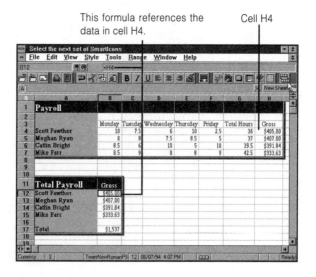

This formula references the data in cell H4.

Cell H4

1. Move to the cell in which you want to display the contents of another cell.

2. Type a + (plus sign).

3. Either click on the cell whose contents you want to display, or type that cell's address.

4. Press Enter or click on the Confirm button.

Controlling When Formulas Are Calculated

As you know, formulas are dynamic. That means that as you change data in a worksheet, 1-2-3 automatically adjusts formulas. Sometimes in a large worksheet, this automatic recalculation process can take a few minutes or even more. Although the recalculation process happens in the background (you don't have to wait for it to stop before you can continue), it does slow the computer down a bit. If you have a lot of changes to make, you may want to delay the recalculation process until you are through entering or editing your data.

To control when formulas are calculated:

1. Open the Tools menu.

2. Select User Setup. The User Setup dialog box appears.

3. Click on the Recalculation button. The Recalculation dialog box appears.

4. Click on Manual.

5. Click on OK. The User Setup dialog box reappears.

6. Click on OK again.

Press F9 to recalc

Now when you make changes to the worksheet, the formulas are not automatically recalculated. If recalculation is necessary because of the changes you made, the Calc indicator appears on the status bar. Simply press F9 at any time to recalculate the worksheet. You can also click on the Recalculation SmartIcon , located on the Audit SmartIcon set.

Cheat Sheet

What Happens When Formulas Are Copied

When a formula is copied, the cell references are automatically adjusted to fit the new column or row.

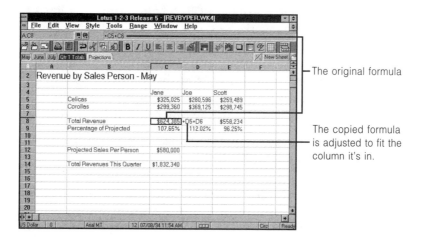

The original formula

The copied formula is adjusted to fit the column it's in.

Absolute vs. Relative Cell References

Sometimes when you copy a formula you don't want the cell references to be adjusted because you want the copied formulas to refer to a *specific* cell, column, or row. A cell reference that 1-2-3 does not adjust when copying formulas is called an *absolute cell reference* and one that is adjusted is called a *relative cell reference*.

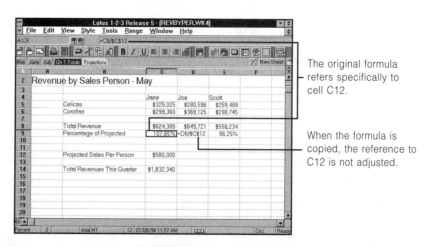

The original formula refers specifically to cell C12.

When the formula is copied, the reference to C12 is not adjusted.

Copying Formulas

30

You can copy formulas just like you can copy other types of data (see
Chapter 13 for help on copying). Copying formulas saves you the
trouble of entering similar formulas within a worksheet.

Basic Survival

**What Happens
When Formulas
Are Copied**

You can copy or move formulas to different areas of the worksheet or
even to a new worksheet. When you copy or move a formula, 1-2-3
automatically adjusts the cells it references to fit their new column,
row, or worksheet. A cell reference that 1-2-3 automatically adjusts is
called a *relative cell reference*.

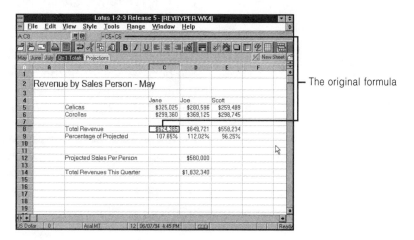

The original formula

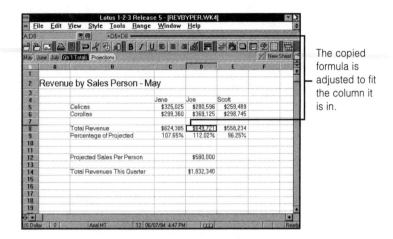

The copied formula is adjusted to fit the column it is in.

In this example, the formula entered in cell C8 is copied to cell D8. Because the formula is copied to a different column, the column letter in each cell reference is changed. So the original formula +C5+C6 becomes +D5+D6.

If you copied the formula to a different row, such as cell C9, the row number in each cell reference changes instead, giving us the formula +C6+C7. The row references are adjusted by one row, since the formula was copied one row down, from cell C8 to cell C9.

Absolute vs Relative Cell References

Sometimes when you copy a formula you don't want the cell references to be adjusted because you want the copied formulas to refer to a specific cell, column, or row. A cell reference that 1-2-3 does not adjust when copying formulas is called an *absolute cell reference*.

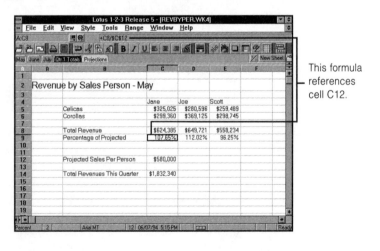

This formula references cell C12.

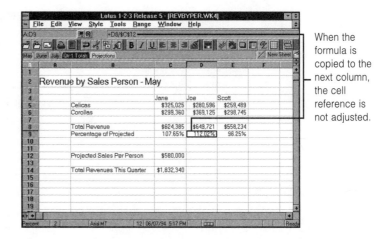

When the formula is copied to the next column, the cell reference is not adjusted.

Absolute cell reference = colrow

To prevent 1-2-3 from adjusting all or part of a cell reference when copying a formula, you enter a $ in the formula. You can place the $ anywhere: in front of a column letter, a row number, or a worksheet letter. Just be sure to place the $ *in front of all the parts* of a cell reference that you do not want 1-2-3 to adjust when that formula is copied.

In the example, the $ is placed in front of the column and the row, as in C12, because the formula refers to a specific cell; that reference should not be adjusted *at all*.

Sometimes you may want part of the cell reference to change. For example, you may want the row to change but not the column. This is called a *mixed cell reference*. To create a mixed cell reference, simply place the $ in front of only the part of the cell reference (the column or row) that you do not want adjusted.

223

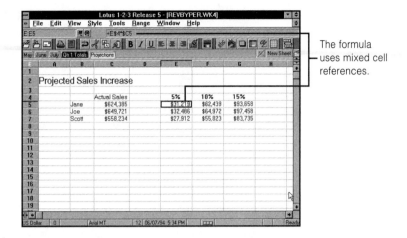

The formula uses mixed cell references.

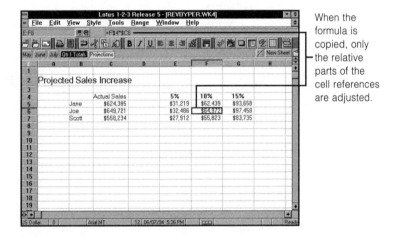

When the formula is copied, only the relative parts of the cell references are adjusted.

In this example, I used mixed references. In the part of the formula that refers to the percentages, the column reference was relative, while the row was not. That's so when the formula is copied down for each salesperson, the row is not adjusted. For example, when the formula is copied to cell F6, the formula does *not* become +F5*$C6.

In the part of the formula that refers to the actual sales for each salesperson, the row was relative, whereas the column was not. That's so that when the formula is copied across for each percentage, the column is not adjusted. For example, when the formula is copied to cell F6, the formula does *not* become +F$4*D6.

Beyond Survival

Copying Values and Not Formulas

Sometimes you may want to copy the result of a formula and not the formula itself. For example, maybe you're trying to build a recap area in a different part of the worksheet. If you copy the formula using normal methods, it will be adjusted (as normal), and it won't display the same value as before. So if you want the value to be the same in the new cell, copy the *value* and not the *formula*.

To copy the value (result) and not the formula:

1. Select the cells that contain the results (values) you want to copy.

2. Click on the Copy SmartIcon 🔲.

3. Move to the cell or range to which you want to copy.

4. Open the Edit menu.

5. Select Paste Special. The Paste Special dialog box appears.

Click here ——

6. Click on the Formulas as values option button.

7. Click OK. The value displayed in the first cell appears in the cell to which you copied it. The formula is not copied.

To copy values and not formulas, use Edit Paste Special.

225

Cheat Sheet

Circular References

- A *circular reference* is a formula that refers to the cell it's in. For example, if you typed the formula @SUM(B1..B4) in cell B2, you'd have a circular reference.
- To fix circular references, correct the formula so it does not refer to the same cell that the formula is in.
- To locate circular references, use the Audit feature.

Labels and Blank Cells in Formulas

- Normally, 1-2-3 assigns the value of 0 to blank cells or labeled cells referred to in a formula.
- Statistical functions (such as @AVG) ignore blank cells completely. However, they treat labeled cells as equal to 0, which can throw off your stats.
- Text functions, such as @LENGTH, display ERR if you refer to a blank cell.

Using Audit to Find Problems

1. If you are looking for formula or cell dependents, select a range to search. Otherwise, continue to step 2.
2. Open the Tools menu.
3. Select Audit.
4. Under Audit, select an option.
5. Under Produce a, select an option. You can have Audit create a report or highlight the appropriate cells for you to review. If you select Report at range, select an empty range in which Audit can produce the report.
6. Click OK.

31

Problems with Formulas

If you hear a beep after entering a formula, 1-2-3 is telling you that the formula does not make sense. You must correct the formula before it will be entered into the cell. Common problems to look for include typos, misspellings, spaces, and mismatched parentheses.

If you get an error message instead of a beep when entering a formula, the problem may be something more difficult to spot. In this chapter, you learn how to look for trouble spots in your worksheet and how to fix them.

Basic Survival

Oh, No, Not ERR!

1-2-3 displays ERR in a cell when you enter a formula that it cannot calculate for one reason or another. Here's a list of some of the most common types of problems and what you can do to eliminate them:

Problem	How to correct it
You divided by zero.	Sometimes you can't help this, like when the worksheet is empty of data. See the section in Chapter 34 for help.
Your formula looks like a date, for example, 12/31 or 15-Jan.	Use a plus sign or parentheses: +12/31 or (15–Jan).
You started your formula with a range name.	That's okay, but be sure to use a plus (as in +SALES) to indicate that this is a formula and not a label.

Important!

continues

227

Problem	How to correct it
You tried to add a label and a value.	If you use a formula such as C1&B3 to concatenate two text strings, be sure the two cells contain text and not values.
You referenced a range name that doesn't exist	Be sure the range name is spelled correctly. To create a range name, see Chapter 14.
You moved data into the first or last cell of a named range used in your formula.	When you use the drag and drop method to move data, you can sometimes mess up the ranges defined by a range name. If this has happened to you, simply redefine the range for that range name. See Chapter 14 for help.
You referenced a file that doesn't exist.	Check the spelling and the path (directory) to the file.
The formula refers to another cell that contains ERR.	Go fix the other cell. This one will be okay when the one with the problem is fixed
You used a range name when it wasn't appropriate.	Most formulas work with single cells, for example, +C1+E4. If you substitute a range name that stands for E4, it's okay. If you substitute a range name that stands for the range E4..E6, the formula

Problem	How to correct it
	+C1+TOTALS doesn't make any sense to 1-2-3. Instead, you could use some thing where a range is expected, as in +C1+@SUM(TOTALS).

Circular References

Circ ref is a formula that includes its own cell address

Probably the most common and frustrating error, a *circular reference* is a formula that refers to the cell it's in. For example, if you typed the formula +B2–E4*2 in cell E4, you'd have a circular reference because you are trying to reference the same cell (E4) into which you want 1-2-3 to place the results. In other words, you typed a formula into cell E4 that used cell E4 as part of the formula. When you have a circular reference, the word Circ appears on the status bar.

To correct a circular reference and remove the Circ indicator on the status bar, retype the formula in cell E4, using the correct cell reference: +B2–E3*2.

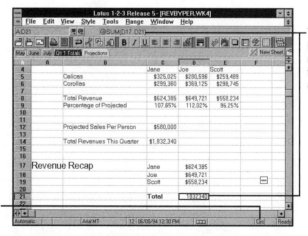

This formula includes a reference to the cell it's in, cell D21.

When you have a formula with a circular reference, this appears on the status bar.

If you spot the Circ indicator on the status bar and have trouble finding the formula which contains the circular reference, check out the Audit feature explained in the Beyond Survival section of this chapter.

Labels and Blank Cells in Formulas

Watch for Circ in status bar

What happens if you have a formula that includes a range of cells, some of which include labels or are blank? How does that affect the result of the formula?

Well, in arithmetic formulas, 1-2-3 simply assigns the value of 0 to any blank cell or cell that contains a label. It then calculates the result of the formula, using the value 0 for that cell. For example, in the following figure, the formula +C4+C5+C6+C7+C8 contains both a label cell (C4) and a blank cell (C7). They are both treated as 0, and the result is a total of 30.

Results ———— 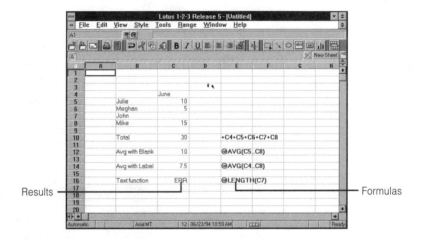 ———— Formulas

Statistical functions such as @AVG (a built-in formula that calculates the average of a range of cells) are a bit trickier. They ignore blank cells because they would throw off the result. For example, in the figure, the formula @AVG(C5..C8) includes cell C7 which is blank. The blank cell is ignored, and the average comes out to be 10 (30 divided by 3 cells). Label cells are *not* ignored, however, and are instead treated as 0. Of course, this could also throw off your statistics. For example, the formula @AVG(C4..C8) includes a cell with a label (C4) as well as a blank cell (C7). The blank cell is ignored, but the label cell is not, resulting in an average of 7.5 (30 divided by four cells). The thing to learn here is to be careful not to accidentally include blank or labeled cells in your formulas.

If you're using a text function (such as @LENGTH, which returns the length of a label as a number), you'll get an ERR if you include a blank cell. For example, the formula @LENGTH(C7) returns an error if cell C7 is blank. (By the way, you'll learn about @AVG, @LENGTH, and other functions in Chapter 32.)

Beyond Survival

Using Audit to Find Problems

Use Tools Audit to find circ. ref.

With the Audit feature, you can quickly discover errors and incongruities with formulas in your worksheet. It's especially useful in finding the source of that troublesome error, Circ (circular references).

Audit locates the following:

 All formulas   Locates every formula in a worksheet.

 Formula precedents   Locates the cells that are referenced in the range of selected formulas. For example, if you selected cell E3, which contained the formula +A2–(C3–C2), Audit would locate three cells: A2, C3, and C2.

 Cell dependents   Locates the cells whose formulas depend on the values in the range of selected cells. For example, if you selected cell C3, (using the previous example) Audit would locate cell E3, a cell that contains a formula using cell C3.

Circular references   Locates any cell in the worksheet that contains a formula which references the cell it is in.

 File links   Locates any cell in the worksheet that contains a link to another worksheet.

 DDE links   Locates any cell in the worksheet that contains a link to data created in another Windows application, such as Excel, Word for Windows, or Ami Pro.

To audit your worksheet:

1. If you are looking for formula or cell dependents, select a range to search. Otherwise, continue to step 2.

2. Open the Tools menu.

3. Select Audit. The Audit dialog box appears.

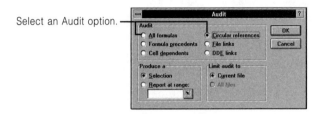

Select an Audit option.

4. Under Audit, select an option.

5. Under Produce a, select an option. You can have Audit create a report or highlight the appropriate cells for you to review. If you select Report at range, select an empty range in which Audit can produce the report.

6. Click OK.

You can quickly audit your worksheet by clicking on the appropriate SmartIcon located on the Sheet Auditing SmartIcon set. (See the previous listing for a picture of each icon.) However, 1-2-3 does not have a SmartIcon for auditing circular references. Instead, click on the Audit SmartIcon located on the Goodies SmartIcon set .

If you elected to produce a report displaying all formulas in the worksheet, you might see something like this, beginning at the range you selected.

Formulas
Current file
A:C15:@SUM(C7..C13)
A:C17:+C15+D15+E15+F15
A:C19:+C15/C17
A:D15:@SUM(D7..D13)

If you instructed Audit to highlight the cells for you instead, your screen might look something like this:

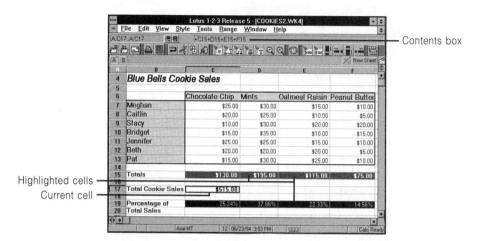

In our example, every cell that contains a formula is highlighted. You can review each of the highlighted cells by pressing Ctrl+Enter to move from cell to cell. The contents of the current cell appear in the contents box. When you're done reviewing the worksheet, press an arrow key or click anywhere in the worksheet.

Cheat Sheet

Entering an @Function Such as @Sum

1. Click on the cell in which you want to enter the @function formula.
2. Click on the @Function selector.
3. Select SUM from the menu.
4. Drag over the range of cells you want to add.
5. You can include more than one range by typing a comma and repeating step 4 as many times as you like.
6. Click on the Confirm button or press Enter.

Using the @Function List

1. Click on the cell in which you want to enter the @function formula.
2. Click on the @Function selector.
3. Select List All from the menu.
4. If you know the category of the @function you want, select it from the Category drop-down list box.
5. Select an @function from the @Functions list box.
6. Click OK.
7. Replace the placeholder arguments with actual data, such as a range address.
8. Click on the Confirm button or press Enter.

Customizing the @Function List

1. Click on the @Function selector.
2. Select List All.
3. Click on the Menu>> button.
4. To delete an @function from the menu, select it from the Current menu list and click Remove.
5. To add another @function to the menu, select it from the @Functions list and click on Add.
6. To add a separator line between groups of functions on the menu, select— from the Current menu list—the @function below which you want to add the separator line. Then click on Separator.
7. When you finish customizing the menu, click OK.

32

Entering an @Function

An *@function* is a type of built-in formula that you can use to create complex calculations. For example, instead of typing this long formula:

+A1+A2+A3+A4+A5+A6

With an @function, you could type this instead:

@SUM(A1..A6)

The @SUM function tells 1-2-3 to add the range you specify within the parentheses. There are many @functions you can use, including statistical @functions such as @AVG (which calculates the average of a range of cells), logical @functions such as @IF (which takes one action if something is true, and another if something is false), and mathematical @functions such as @COS (which calculates the cosine of an angle). For a listing of common functions and what they do, turn to Appendix B at the back of this book.

You enter @functions through the @Function selector. In this chapter, you learn about the most common @functions and how to enter them.

Basic Survival

Entering an @Function

The most common @function is @SUM. All @functions, by the way, begin with the @ sign and include a set of parentheses. Within the parentheses, you enter the *arguments* (parameters) for the @function. Some @functions have many arguments separated by commas. The @SUM @function only has one argument—the list of ranges you want the @function to add.

Functions look like: @name (argument1, argument2 etc.)

To add a range of numbers with the @SUM @function:

1. Click on the cell in which you want to enter the @function formula.

2. Click on the @Function selector.

235

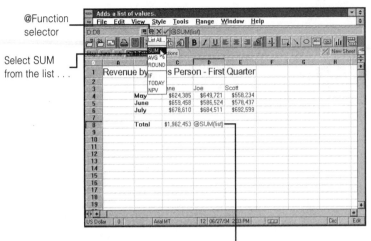

@Function
selector

Select SUM
from the list . . .

. . . and it appears in the cell, along with a placeholder for its argument.

3. Select SUM from the menu that appears. The @SUM function appears in the cell with its list argument highlighted.

4. Drag over the range of cells you want to add, or type the range address. The address of the cells you select replaces the list placeholder in the @SUM function.

5. Because @SUM accepts a list of ranges to add, you can include more than one range by typing a comma, and then repeating step 4 as many times as you like.

6. Click on the Confirm button or press Enter.

The @SUM function totals the amounts in the selected cells. The method used in selecting the range for the @SUM function is called *point and click*. You'll learn more about this method for entering formulas and @functions in Chapter 33.

Can enter @functions manually, instead of using @Function selector

If you want, you can type your functions by hand instead of using the @Function selector to enter them. For example, you can type @SUM(and either type in the actual range address or point and click to select a range. Finish with a right parenthesis,), and then press Enter or click on the Confirm button.

The @Function selector lists the most common @functions, such as @SUM, @AVG (which computes the average of a range of cells), @ROUND (which rounds a value to the specified decimal point), @IF (which performs one action if something is true, and another action if something is false), @TODAY (which calculates the current date), and @NPV (which calculates the net present value of a series of cash deposits). You can even customize this menu to include only the @functions you use the most—see the Beyond Survival section for more info.

You can use the @Function selector to input these other functions if you want. However, if you select one of these other @functions from the menu, you'll be presented with a different list of arguments. For example, the @IF @function includes these arguments:

@IF(*condition,x,y*)

The argument *condition* represents the thing you want to test for; for example, you could type B2<0 to test if B2 was less than zero. (For more help with logical formulas, see Chapter 29.) The argument *x* represents the action you want 1-2-3 to take if the condition is true; *y* represents the action to take if the condition is false. You enter the arguments by replacing the placeholders with actual data, such as a range, a value, a condition, or even a formula or another @function.

Some @functions don't have any arguments at all, which means there's nothing for you to enter. For example, the @function @TODAY() does not have any arguments. The parentheses, however, are still required.

Some @ functions, such as @TODAY(), have no arguments.

You can use one @function in another @function if you want, as long as the first @function produces the right kind of value for the required argument. For example, the formula

@ROUND(@SUM(C3..C6),2)

rounds the result of the @SUM function to two decimal places. Because the @ROUND function expects some kind of number as its argument, you can use the @SUM function since it produces a number result and not text.

Using the @Function List

If the @function you want to use is not listed on the menu that appears when you click on the @Function selector, you must use the @Function List dialog box. Again, you can customize the menu to include the functions you personally use the most. See the Beyond Survival section for details. To use the @Function List to select an @function which does not appear on the menu, follow these steps:

Reminder: customize @Function menu for @functions I use most

1. Click on the cell in which you want to enter the @function formula.

2. Click on the @Function selector. A menu of @functions appears.

3. Select List All from the menu. 1-2-3 displays the @Function List dialog box.

Select the category for the @function you want.

Select an @function from this list.

4. Initially, all @functions are displayed. If you know the category of the @function you want, select it from the Category drop-down list box. This narrows the listing for you, making it easier to locate the appropriate @function. For example, select Statistical from the list to display statistical functions, such as @AVG.

5. Select an @function from the @Functions list box. (You can get help on a particular @function by selecting it from the list and then clicking on the ? help button.)

6. Click OK. The @function appears in the contents box, complete with placeholders for the arguments.

Click ? for help.

7. Replace the arguments with actual data, such as a range address. Some arguments are not required, but are optional. For more information on which arguments are optional for the particular @function you've selected, consult 1-2-3 Help by clicking on the ? button at the top of the dialog box. In addition, common @functions are listed in Appendix B at the back of this book.

8. Click on the Confirm button or press Enter.

As with all formulas, the result of the @function, not the @function formula itself, is displayed in the cell. If you encounter an error, see Chapter 34 for help.

Beyond Survival

Customizing the @Function List

When you click on the @Function selector, 1-2-3 displays a list of the most common @functions. If the @function you want to use is not listed, you must select the List All option and proceed to the @Function List dialog box where you can select the @function you want.

Although they are the most common, the @functions listed on the menu may not be the ones you use the most. You can customize the @Function List so that it displays the @functions you find the most useful in your work. Here's what you do:

1. Click on the @Function selector. A menu of @functions appears.

2. Select List All. The @Function List dialog box appears.

3. Click on the Menu>> button. The @Function List dialog box expands.

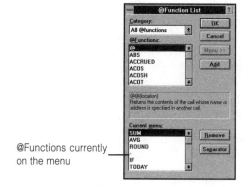

@Functions currently on the menu

4. The @functions currently included on the menu appear under Current menu. To delete an @function from the menu, select it from the Current menu list and click the Remove button.

5. To add another @function to the menu, select it from the @Functions list and click the Add button.

6. To add a separator line between groups of functions on the menu, from the Current menu list select the @function below which you want to add the separator line. Then click on Separator.

7. When you're finished customizing the menu, click OK.

The next time you click on the @Function selector, 1-2-3 will display the new menu selections. This is a permanent change which remains effective even after you exit 1-2-3. You can of course, change the @Function List again as often as you want.

Cheat Sheet

Selecting a Range While Entering a Formula or an @Function

1. Click on the cell in which you want to enter the formula or @function.
2. Begin typing the formula or, if you're entering an @function, select it with the @Function selector.
3. When you get to the point in the formula or @function where you need to type the range address, begin highlighting the range by clicking on the first cell of the range you want to select.
4. Press and hold the left mouse button.
5. Drag the mouse to the last cell in the range.
6. Continue entering the formula or @function.
7. When you're done, click on the Confirm button or press Enter.

Using a Named Range in a Formula or an @Function

1. Click on the cell in which you want to enter the formula or @function.
2. Begin typing the formula or, if you're entering an @function, select it with the @Function selector.
3. When you get to the point in the formula or @function where you need to type the range address, do one of the following:
   - Type the name of the range.
   - Click on the Navigator and select the named range from the list.

   or
   - Press F3 and select the named range from the list.
4. Continue entering the formula or @function.
5. When you're done, click on the Confirm button or press Enter.

33

Using Ranges in @Functions and Formulas

In Chapter 12, you learned that a *range* is a group of adjacent cells that you select to indicate that you want to perform some action on them. By selecting a range to use with a formula or @function, you can perform a calculation on that group of cells. In Lotus 1-2-3, there are several ways in which you can select a range while typing a formula. The most basic method is to simply type the address of the range to which you want to refer.

In this chapter, you learn two other methods for selecting ranges: the point and click method and the range name method. The point and click method requires the use of a mouse; the range name method requires you to name ranges within your worksheet and then refer to those names when typing a formula. If you forget how to name a range, refer to Chapter 14 for help.

Basic Survival

Selecting a Range While Entering a Formula or an @Function

Instead of typing in the address of a range when entering a formula or @function, use the point and click method of selection. This method requires a mouse, but it is simple to do.

1. First, click on the cell in which you want to enter the @function or formula.

2. Begin typing the formula or, if you're entering an @function, select it with the @Function selector.

Drag to select a range for a formula.

3. When you get to the point in the formula or @function where you need to type the range address, highlight the range with the mouse instead. Start by clicking on the first cell of the range you want to select.

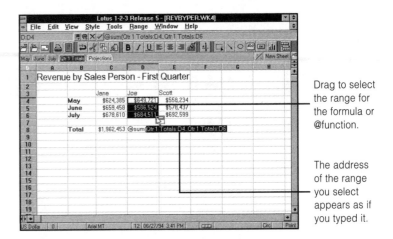

Drag to select the range for the formula or @function.

The address of the range you select appears as if you typed it.

4. Press and hold the left mouse button.

5. Drag the mouse to the last cell in the range and release the mouse button. The range is now selected. The address of the range you selected appears within the formula or @function you were entering.

6. Continue entering the @function or formula.

7. When you're done, click on the Confirm button or press Enter.

This is the easiest way!

Dragging to select a range of cells is much easier and more accurate than trying to type in the correct range address for a formula or @function. So remember to use the point and click method of selection whenever possible.

You can specify a *3-D range* in a formula or @function by following the instructions in Chapter 12 for selecting this type of range. A 3-D range includes the same cells in adjacent worksheets.

Beyond Survival

Using a Named Range in a Formula or an @Function

When working in a large worksheet, it's easier to name areas of the worksheet and use these names instead of actual cell addresses in your formulas or @functions. For example, you could name several subtotals in your worksheet, such as MAY_TOT, JUN_TOT, and JULY_TOT, and then use those range names in a formula that creates a grand total. Refer to Chapter 14 for help in naming ranges in your worksheet.

Using named ranges in formulas is especially convenient in large worksheets. You don't have to name every range in a worksheet, just the ones you think you might want to refer to later.

Name ranges first—then use them in formulas.

You should name your ranges first, before using them in a formula or @function. If you refer to a range name that does not exist in a formula or @function, you'll get an ERR. After you name the ranges, follow these steps to use the named ranges in a formula or @function:

1. Click on the cell in which you want to enter the @function or formula.

2. Begin typing the formula or, if you're entering an @function, select it with the @Function selector.

3. When you get to the point in the formula or @function where you need to type the range address, do **one** of the following:

- Type the name of the range.

- Click on the Navigator and select the named range from the list.

Press F3 or click on Navigator to see named ranges.

- Press F3 and select the named range from the Range Names dialog box.

Click on the Navigator and select   The named range is
a named range from the list.   added to your formula.

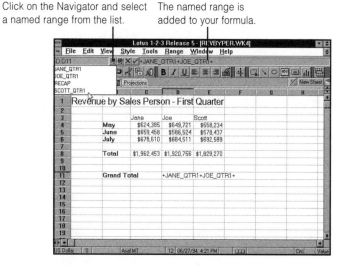

4. Continue entering the @function or formula.

5. When you're done, click on the Confirm button or press Enter.

Cheat Sheet

Problem	How to correct it
You divided by zero.	Sometimes you can't help this, like when the worksheet is empty of data. See the section later in this chapter for help.
You referenced a range name that doesn't exist.	Be sure the range name is spelled correctly. To create a range name, see Chapter 14.
You moved data into the first or last cell of a named range used in your @function.	When you use the drag and drop method to move data, it can sometimes mess up the ranges defined by a range name. If this has happened to you, simply redefine the range for that range name. See Chapter 14 for help.
You used an inappropriate argument.	If an @function calls for a label (text), don't refer to a cell that contains a value (or vice versa). A *label* is text typed in quotation marks, a cell that contains text, or some @function that produces a label. A value is a number, a cell that contains a number, or a formula or @function that produces a number. A *condition* is a logical formula such as B3<5 that evaluates to either true or false.
The @function refers to another cell which contains ERR.	Go fix the other cell. This one will be okay when the one with the problem is fixed.
You used a range name when it wasn't appropriate.	Most @functions work fine with ranges, but some expect to work with single cells. For example, @ROUND expects to work with a single cell, so the formula @ROUND(C3..C5,0) produces ERR.

34

Problems with @Functions

If you hear a beep after entering an @function, 1-2-3 is telling you that it can't evaluate the @function—in other words, it doesn't make any sense. Common problems to look for include typos, misspellings, spaces, and mismatched parentheses. For example, you should not put a space between arguments in an @function, as in @ROUND(C4, 0). Also, if you type text into an @function, as in @LENGTH("How long is this sentence?"), be sure to enclose the text in quotation marks. A cell that contains text is not enclosed in quotation marks, as in @LENGTH(C5).

If you get an error message instead of a beep when entering an @function, the problem may be something more difficult to spot. In this chapter, you learn how to find errors in your @functions and how to correct them. Some of the techniques used in correcting formulas apply here as well, so you may also want to review Chapter 31.

Basic Survival

Not ERR Again!

1-2-3 displays ERR in a cell when you've entered an @function that it cannot calculate for one reason or another. Here's a list of some of the most common types of problems, and what you can do to eliminate them:

Look for these problems!

Problem	How to correct it
You divided by zero.	Sometimes you can't help this, like when the worksheet is empty of data. See the section later in this chapter for help.

continues

Problem	How to correct it
You referenced a range name that doesn't exist.	Be sure the range name is spelled correctly. To create a range name, see Chapter 14.
You moved data into the first or last cell of a named range used in your @function.	When you use the drag and drop method to move data, it can sometimes mess up the ranges defined by a range name. If this has happened to you, simply redefine the range for that range name. See Chapter 14 for help.
You used an inappropriate argument.	If an @function calls for a label (text), don't refer to a cell that contains a value (or vice versa). A *label* is text typed in quotation marks, a cell that contains text, or some @function that produces a label. A value is a number, a cell that contains a number, or a formula or @function that produces a number. A *condition* is a logical formula such as B3<5 that evaluates to either true or false.
The @function refers to another cell which contains ERR.	Go fix the other cell. This one will be okay when the one with the problem is fixed.
You used a range name when it wasn't appropriate.	Most @functions work fine with ranges, but some expect to work with single cells. For example, @ROUND expects to work with a single cell, so the formula @ROUND(C3..C5,0) produces ERR.

Dividing by Zero

This section does not deal with a function problem, but rather with how you can cure a formula problem using a function. Clever, eh? Here's the problem: if you have a formula that divides some value by zero, you get an ERR. Obviously, if there's something wrong with the formula, you should fix it. But sometimes, there's not a problem with the formula, it's that the cell it refers to is blank. For example, if you enter the formula +C15/C17, and C17 does not contain any data, you get an ERR. Remember, blank cells are treated as if they equal zero in most formulas. So what do you do if you're creating a new worksheet and most of the cells are blank?

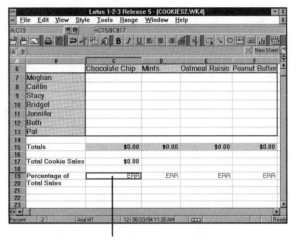

Cell C17=0, so this formula results in an ERR.

Well, you could just ignore the ERR, since you know the reason for it. But if you're giving this worksheet to your boss, you don't want it to look as if you don't know what you're doing, right? Or what if there's a chance that the cell might remain blank under certain circumstances? What you probably want is to display a zero instead of the ERR.

Mark this page. Cool trick!

To display a zero instead of the ERR message, you use a *logical* formula and the @IF function. A logical formula compares two values and tells you whether that comparison is true or false. For example, you could ask whether the contents in cell C1 were less than B2, and you would get the answer true if they were less than B2, or false if they weren't. True is equal to 1 in the computer, and false is equal to 0. To perform this bit of magic, you use the @IF function and a logical formula:

1. Double-click on the cell that contains the ERR caused by division by zero. In our example, double-click on cell C19.

2. Press Home to move to the beginning of the formula.

3. Press Delete to delete the plus sign.

4. Type @IF((that's @IF followed by the left parenthesis).

5. Click on the divisor cell. In this example, click on cell C17, which is being used as a divisor but is currently blank.

6. Type =0,0, (that's equals zero comma zero comma).

7. Now, press End to move to the end of the formula.

8. Type) (a right parenthesis).

9. Press Enter to accept the changes.

In our example, the resulting formula would now look like this:

@IF(C17=0,0,C15/C17)

What this formula means is "If cell C17 contains a zero, the result is zero; otherwise, the result is calculated by taking the contents of cell C15 and dividing by the contents of cell C17." So, if cell C17 is blank or zero, cell C19 displays a zero and not an ERR message. If cell C17 contains a value, the actual formula is carried out, and the result is displayed in cell C19.

Those Invisible Decimal Places

A common problem that you might run into is connected with the number of decimal points you choose to display in your worksheet formulas. For example, suppose you used a worksheet to calculate the gross pay for your small workforce, and that the gross pay is displayed with two decimal places. However, you choose to display the total with no decimal places. Regardless of what you choose, the value that 1-2-3 uses in its formulas is the entire number, not just what is displayed. That means that the total in your payroll worksheet would be correct.

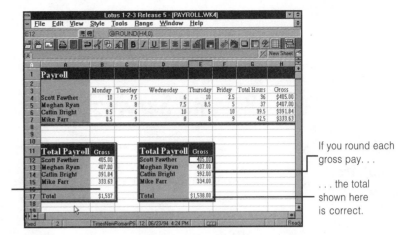

This total should
be $1,537.47.

If you round each
gross pay. . .

. . . the total
shown here
is correct.

To fix this problem, you should round off any numbers you don't want
to use fully. For example, let's assume that the reason you wanted to
display the total with no decimal places is that you wanted the result
rounded up to the next whole dollar. You could round just the total,
but the column would still not add up correctly. You should probably
round up each gross pay, and then add these rounded figures. That
way, your total would jive with the total of the gross pays shown on the
worksheet.

*Here's how
to round
totals!*

To round the result of a formula, you use the @ROUND function. A
function, which you learned about in Chapter 32, is a pre-programmed
formula built into 1-2-3. The function looks something like this:

@ROUND(x,n)

where x is the number or the formula you want to round, and n is the
number of decimal places to which you want to round. A formula that
calculates gross pay rounded to zero decimal places (up to the next
whole dollar) might look like this:

@ROUND(+G4*J4,0)

The +G4*J4 would calculate the gross pay by taking the total hours
times the hourly rate; the 0 would tell the @ROUND function to round
the result up to the next whole value (no decimal places). Since the
places after the decimal point are zero, you don't even have to display
them.

If you use a four digit hourly rate and you want the gross pay rounded up to the nearest penny, the formula would look like this:

@ROUND(+G4*J4,2)

Beyond Survival

Using @ERR to Keep From Entering Invalid Data

Good way to check for errors in data entry!

You can use a special function, @ERR, to prevent errors in data entry. This is especially useful when you're designing a worksheet for someone else to use. For example, suppose you're designing an expense worksheet, and your company doesn't issue checks for less than $20. If the total on the expense sheet is less than $20, you'd like to flag the error.

You use the @ERR function with another function, @IF. The @IF function has three arguments:

@IF(*condition, x,y*)

Condition represents some kind of logical formula. In this case, you can test to see if the cell that contains the total is less than 20 with the following formula:

@IF(@SUM(G10..G12)<20,*x,y*)

The formula @SUM(G10..G12) produces a total, which is then compared with the value 20.

The *x* argument represents the action you want 1-2-3 to take if the logical condition is *true*; the *y* argument represents the action you want 1-2-3 to take if it is *false*. To display an error if the total is less than 20, and to display the real total if it's not, use this formula:

@IF(@SUM(G10..G12)<20,@ERR,@SUM(G10..G12))

In English, this says to total the cells G10 to G12, and if they are less than 20 to display the ERR message in the cell. Otherwise, display the actual total.

Printing Your Worksheet

In most cases, printing your worksheet is as simple as clicking on a button. However, there are times when you might decide to print only part of your worksheet, or to print multiple copies of the entire thing. In this section, you'll learn all this and more:

- Printing Your Worksheet
- Previewing Before You Print
- Changing the Page Setup
- Adding Headers and Footers

Cheat Sheet

Printing the Entire Worksheet or File

1. If you want to print only one worksheet within a file, move to that worksheet.
2. Click on the File Print button 🖨.
3. Select Current worksheet to print the current worksheet only, or select All worksheets to print all the worksheets in the file.
4. Click on OK.

Printing a Selected Range

1. Select the range of cells or the collection of worksheets you want to print.
2. Click on the File Print button 🖨.
3. Choose Selected range.
4. Click on OK.

Stopping the Printer

Click on the Cancel button while it's visible.

or

Switch to Print Manager, select the worksheet, and then click on Delete. Click on Yes to cancel the printing of the worksheet.

35

Printing Your Worksheet

After all this hard work making your worksheet look perfect, you've reached the point of triumph: printing your result. Printing the entire worksheet is easy. And as an added bonus, when you print a worksheet, its charts and query tables print too. (A *chart* is a visual representation of your worksheet's data; see Chapter 39 for more information. A *query table* extracts and sorts specific information from your worksheet. See Chapter 45 for help in creating a query table.)

In addition, 1-2-3 offers several alternatives for printing your worksheet: for example, you can print a range instead of the entire worksheet. In this chapter, you learn how to print your worksheet or a range of cells. The Beyond Survival section teaches you how to print certain pages or multiple copies, among other things.

If you want to add special titles, print the worksheet sideways across the page. To preview your worksheet before you print, see the upcoming chapters for help before following the steps in this chapter.

Basic Survival

Printing the Entire Worksheet or File

Printing the entire worksheet is simple to do. Just follow these steps:

1. If you want to print only one worksheet within a file, move to that worksheet. Otherwise, these steps will print all the worksheets in the file. If you want to print a selection of worksheets (not just one worksheet, but not the entire file), see the next section.

2. Click on the File Print button ▣. Or you can open the File menu and select Print, or press Ctrl+P. The Print dialog box appears.

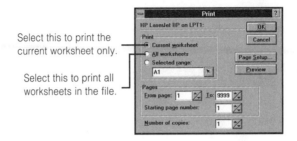

Select this to print the
current worksheet only.

Select this to print all
worksheets in the file.

3. Select Current worksheet to print the current worksheet only, or select All worksheets to print all the worksheets in the file.

4. Click on OK.

If you have a row or column within a worksheet that you don't want to print, see Chapter 21 for tips on hiding a column or a row.

Printing a Selected Range

If you want, you can print an area of the worksheet instead of the entire thing. For example, you could select the summary range in your worksheet and print only that. You can also print a selection of worksheets within a file, instead of printing only the current worksheet or all of them. Just make sure that whatever you want to print is completely selected (within the selected range).

If you have a row or column within a selection that you don't want to print, see Chapter 21 for tips on hiding a column or a row.

1. Select the range of cells or the collection of worksheets you want to print. If you're going to include print titles in your worksheet (see Chapter 38), do *not* include those row or column titles in your selected range. Doing so will make them print twice.

*Can also
select range
from dialog
box*

2. Click on the File Print button ![printer icon]. Or you can open the File menu and select Print, or press Ctrl+P. The Print dialog box appears.

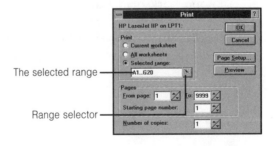

The selected range

Range selector

3. Choose Selected range.

4. Click on OK.

You can also select your range to print from the Print dialog box by clicking on the Range selector.

Stopping the Printer

Sometimes after you get started printing a worksheet, you notice something's wrong. Sometimes you just change your mind after deciding to print (especially after your boss walks in with updated figures). Whatever the reason, it's never too late to stop printing.

Stop printer with Cancel button

When 1-2-3 starts printing a worksheet, it displays a dialog box like the one here. Simply click on Cancel to cancel the printing process.

After this dialog box disappears, your worksheet may still be printing. That's because the printing process has been turned over to Print Manager, the Windows printing utility. To stop printing at this point, press Ctrl+Esc to access the Task Manager list. Select Print Manager. Select your worksheet from the print list, and click on the Delete button. You'll see a dialog box asking you if it's okay to cancel printing. Click on Yes. For good measure, let the last page print fully. Then turn your printer off and back on to reset it. (To print the last page, you may need to press the On-Line button to take your printer off line. Then press Form Feed.)

Beyond Survival

Printing Multiple Copies of Your Worksheet

Rather than spend a day waiting in line at the copier to make the copies of the budget worksheet you need for your next meeting, why not let 1-2-3 do the work for you? After all, stupid repetitive tasks like these are perfect for a PC—I mean, that's what they're for. To print multiple copies:

1. Click on the File Print button 🖨 . Alternatively, you can open the File menu and select Print, or press Ctrl+P. The Print dialog box appears.

257

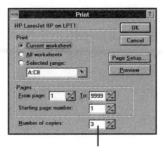

Select the number of copies to print.

2. Under Number of copies, select the number of copies you want 1-2-3 to print.

3. Make any additional selections as necessary.

4. Click on OK. 1-2-3 prints the selected number of copies, one after the other.

Printing Only Certain Pages

You don't have to print your entire worksheet if you don't want to; you can print only certain pages of it instead. You can even number those pages however you like!

1. Click on the File Print button [icon]. Or, open the File menu and select Print, or press Ctrl+P. The Print dialog box appears.

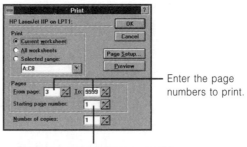

Enter the page numbers to print.

Enter the page number you want to appear on the first printed page.

2. Under From page, select the number of the first page you want to print.

3. Under To, select the number of the last page you want to print. If you leave this set to 9999, 1-2-3 prints from the first page you selected to the end of the worksheet.

4. If you want, under Starting page number, select the page number you want to appear on the first page printed.

5. Click on OK.

Inserting Manual Page Breaks

Put pg break in cell below or to right of actual break.

When you print your worksheet, 1-2-3 automatically prints as many columns and rows as it can on a page and continues printing additional columns and rows on additional pages until the worksheet is printed. When you use Print Preview (explained in the next chapter), you can see in advance exactly which columns or rows will print on each page. Sometimes you want to start a particular row or column on the next page, even though the current page is not yet full. By inserting manual page breaks, you control exactly what is printed on each page. A *manual page break* appears in the worksheet as a dashed line and tells 1-2-3 to start printing on a new page.

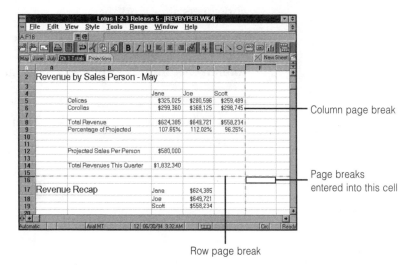

Column page break

Page breaks entered into this cell

Row page break

To insert a manual page break:

1. Move to the cell below the row or to the right of the column in which you want to place the page break.

259

2. Open the Style menu.

3. Select Page Break.

4. To add a page break above the current cell, select Row. To add a page break to the right of the current cell, select Column. To add both a row and a column page break, select Row and Column.

5. Click on OK.

Insert row break in cell A1 to start worksheet on new page.

1-2-3 normally prints one worksheet after another, without creating an automatic page break between them. To force each worksheet to print on a new page, insert a manual row page break in cell A1 of all worksheets after worksheet A.

To remove a page break, move to the cell containing the page break. Open the Style menu and select Page Breaks. Click on the Row or Column check boxes to deselect them, and then click on OK.

You can also create a page break by clicking on the Horizontal Page Break ▦ or Vertical Page Break ▥ buttons, located on the Printing SmartIcon set.

Cheat Sheet

Previewing Your Worksheet

1. Select the range or worksheets you want to print.
2. Click on the Print Preview button 🖽.
3. Make the appropriate selections in the dialog box.
4. Click OK.

Click this button in the Print Preview window	To
	Move to the next page
	Move to a previous page
	Zoom in
	Zoom out
	Access Page Setup
	Display the current page and the next page
	Display the current page and the next three pages
	Return to a single page display
	Print your worksheet
	Close the Print Preview window

36

Previewing Before You Print

Before you print your worksheet, it's a good idea to preview it first, to make sure that it will print exactly the way you want. Then if you need to add headers, footers, page breaks, or additional formatting, you can do so before you actually print. In this chapter, you learn how to preview your worksheet, and how to print from the preview window. You also find out how to access Page Setup to add headers, footers, and change the page orientation (Page Setup is explained in detail in the next chapter). The Beyond Survival section shows you how to zoom in on any section you want to examine your worksheet in detail.

Basic Survival

Previewing Your Worksheet

In the Print Preview window, you see your worksheet as it will appear when printed. From there, you can make changes prior to actually printing your worksheet. To preview a worksheet:

1. Select the range or worksheets you want to print.

2. Click on the Print Preview button 📊 or open the File menu and select Print Preview. The Print Preview dialog box appears.

Select what to preview.

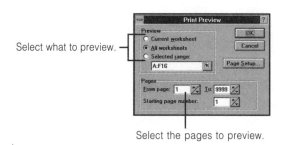

Select the pages to preview.

3. If you want to select a specific range, to preview only the current worksheet or all worksheets, or to preview only certain pages, make the appropriate selections in the dialog box.

Can also preview by clicking Preview from Print dialog box.

4. Click OK. The Print Preview window appears. You can also preview a worksheet by clicking on the Preview button within the Print dialog box.

Click here to close the Print Preview window.

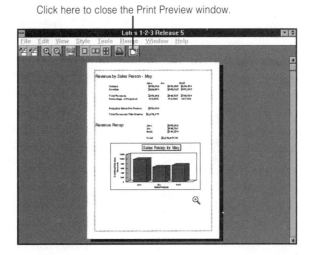

To . . .	Do this . . .
Move to the next page	Press Pg Dn or click ⌐.
Move to a previous page	Press Pg Up or click ⌐.
Zoom in	Click ⊕.
Zoom out	Click ⊖.
Access Page Setup	Click ▦. (Page Setup is discussed in detail in the next chapter.)
Display the current page and the next page	Click ▢▢.
Display the current page and the next three pages	Click ▦.

To . . .	Do this . . .
To display up to nine pages	Click ▦ again.
Return to a single page display	Click ▢.
Print your worksheet	Click 🖶.
Close the Print Preview window	Press Esc or click ▣.

Beyond Survival

Zooming In

To zoom, move mouse over page and click

The text displayed in the Print Preview window is tiny, so if you want to see a section of your worksheet close up, use the zoom feature.

To zoom in, click on the Zoom In button 🔍 press the plus key (+) on the numeric keypad or move the mouse pointer over the area you want to zoom in on the worksheet and click (the mouse pointer changes to a magnifying glass with a tiny plus sign in it). Once you've zoomed in, you can use the arrow keys or the scroll bars to view other areas of the page.

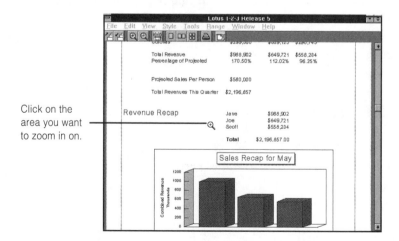

Click on the area you want to zoom in on.

To zoom back out again, click on the Zoom Out button 🔍 or press the minus key (–) on the numeric keypad.

265

Cheat Sheet

Changing the Page Margins

1. Click on the Page Setup button.
2. Under Margins, enter a measurement for Left, Right, Top, and/or Bottom.
3. Click OK.

Changing the Page Orientation

1. Click on the Page Setup button.
2. Under Orientation, select Landscape or Portrait.
3. Click OK.

Printing Data So It Fits on One Page

1. Click on the Page Setup button.
2. Under Size, select an option:

   Actual size: Prints data as it appears on-screen.

   Fit all to a page: Prints all data on one page.

   Fit columns to page: Prints all columns on one page; rows that do not fit on page one print on additional pages.

   Fit rows to page: Prints all rows on one page; columns that do not fit on page one print on additional pages.

   Manually scale: Shrinks or enlarges data by the percentage you specify. Valid percentages are 15%–1000%.
3. Click OK.

Centering Data on a Page

1. Click on the Page Setup button.
2. Under Center, select Horizontally, Vertically, or both.
3. Click OK.

37

Changing Page Setup

Simply printing your worksheet is easy; however, getting it to print exactly the way you want may require a few adjustments to the page setup. In the Page Setup dialog box, you can change the page margins, change the direction in which data prints across the page (orientation), and even shrink data to fit a single page. You can also add headers and footers, but they're discussed (along with print titles) in the next chapter.

In the Beyond Survival section, you even learn how to print the row and column markers with the worksheet data and how to print gridlines marking each cell. If you want to control which columns or rows appear on each printed page, you may need to insert *page breaks* as explained in Chapter 35.

Basic Survival

Changing the Page Margins

You can change the margins on the top, bottom, left and right sides of the page. You can even specify your measurements in millimeters or centimeters instead of inches if you want. Note that changing the margins affects the entire worksheet file. To change the margins:

1. Click on the Page Setup button ▦ located on the Printing SmartIcon set, or open the File menu and select Page Setup. The Page Setup dialog box appears.

Enter new margin settings as needed.

Don't set margins to less than 1/2".

2. Under Margins, enter a measurement for Left, Right, Top, and/or Bottom. Most printers require at least a .5" margin on all sides, so don't enter a setting less than that. To enter millimeters or centimeters, type mm or cm after the measurement.

3. Click OK.

You can also access the Page Setup dialog box by clicking on the Page Setup button from the Print or Preview dialog boxes or the Print Preview window.

Changing the Page Orientation

The orientation of a page describes the direction in which text prints. Normally, text prints across the width of the page (*portrait*), but you can make it print across the length of a page (*landscape*) instead. Landscape printing is especially useful for worksheets that contain a lot of columns, since you can fit more columns along the length (the 11" side) of a standard piece of paper than you can along its width (the 8 1/2" side). If just changing the orientation is not enough, try reducing the size of the data—see "Printing Data So It Fits on One Page" in the Beyond Survival section.

To change the orientation of the pages in a worksheet file:

1. Click on the Page Setup button [icon] located on the Printing SmartIcon set, or open the File menu and select Page Setup. The Page Setup dialog box appears.

2. Under Orientation, select Landscape or Portrait.

3. Click OK.

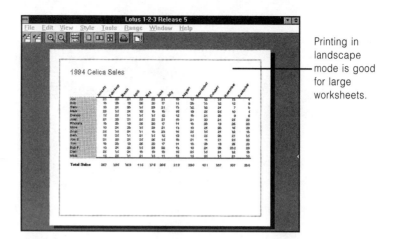

Printing in landscape mode is good for large worksheets.

You can also click on the Portrait 🔲 or Landscape 🔲 buttons located on the Printing SmartIcon set to change page orientation.

Beyond Survival

Printing Worksheet Elements

By default, the lines that surround each cell on-screen (gridlines) do not print. You can, however, print the cell gridlines when you print your worksheet. In addition, you can print the row and column markers (the worksheet frame), which is helpful if you're reviewing your formulas and you need to identify individual cells. You can also control whether drawn objects (such as arrows, text boxes, and charts) print with the worksheet data (normally, they do).

1. Click on the Page Setup button 🔲 located on the Printing SmartIcon set, or open the File menu and select Page Setup. The Page Setup dialog box appears.

2. Under Show, select the worksheet elements you want to print.

3. Click OK.

Cell gridlines

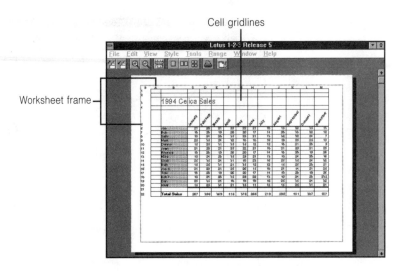

Worksheet frame

You can also access the Page Setup dialog box by clicking on the Page Setup button from the Print or Preview dialog boxes or the Print Preview window.

Printing Data So It Fits on One Page

You can reduce the size of data so that it all fits on one page. However, in the case of a large worksheet, reducing could make the data too tiny to read, so you can adjust the amount of the reduction to suit your taste and print the worksheet on two pages instead of one.

Remember this for large worksheets!

1. Click on the Page Setup button 🔲 located on the Printing SmartIcon set, or open the File menu and select Page Setup. The Page Setup dialog box appears.

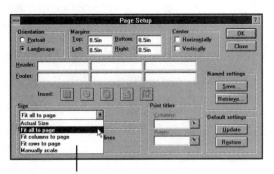

Select a suitable size.

2. Click on the Size drop-down list arrow and select an option.

> **Actual size:** Prints data as it appears on-screen.
>
> **Fit all to a page:** Prints all data on one page.
>
> **Fit columns to page:** Prints all columns on one page; rows that do not fit on page one print on additional pages.
>
> **Fit rows to page:** Prints all rows on one page; columns that do not fit on page one print on additional pages.
>
> **Manually scale:** Shrinks or enlarges data by the percentage you specify. Valid percentages are 15%–1000%.

3. Click OK.

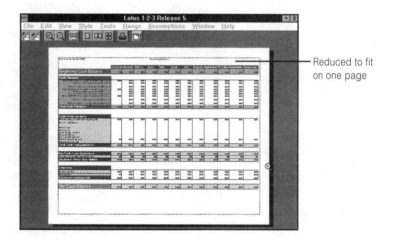

Reduced to fit on one page

If you're printing just a chart (as discussed in Chapter 40), you'll see different options under Size:

> **Actual size:** Data is printed as it appears on-screen.
>
> **Fill page:** The chart is reduced to fit on the page.
>
> **Fill page but keep proportions:** The chart is reduced to fit on a page, but its original proportions are maintained.

You can also use these SmartIcons, located on the Printing SmartIcon set, to reduce a worksheet: Fit columns to a page ▢, Fit rows to a page ▢, or Fit all to a page ▢.

Centering Data on a Page

Good trick for charts and presentations

You can center data on a page between the top and bottom margins, the left and right margins, or both. This is especially useful for presentations. To center data on a page:

1. Click on the Page Setup button ▦ located on the Printing SmartIcon set, or open the File menu and select Page Setup. The Page Setup dialog box appears.

2. Under Center, select Horizontally, Vertically, or both.

3. Click OK.

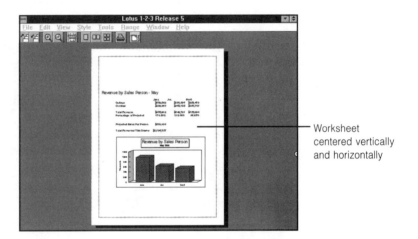

Worksheet centered vertically and horizontally

You can also center a page by clicking the Center Horizontally button ▦, the Center Vertically button ▦, or the Center Both button ▦, all located on the Printing SmartIcon set.

Cheat Sheet

Adding a Header or a Footer

1. Click on the Page Setup button ⊞ located on the Printing SmartIcon set, or open the File menu and select Page Setup.

2. In any of the three boxes under Header, type data or click on one of the buttons from the table below.

To enter this...	Click on this...	Or type this...
The print date	🗓	@
The time of printing	🕐	+
Page number	🖹	#
File name	🖺	^
Contents of a cell	🖽 and then type the cell address	\ followed by the cell address

3. Under Footer, repeat step 2 to add footer information.
4. Click OK.

Printing Column or Row Titles on Every Page

1. Click on the Page Setup button ⊞ located on the Printing SmartIcon set, or open the File menu and select Page Setup.

2. Under Print titles, click on the Range selector for Columns.

3. Select the column you want to use as titles.

4. Repeat steps 2 and 3 for row titles.

5. Click OK.

38

Adding Headers and Footers

A *header* prints at the top of all pages in a worksheet, while a *footer* prints at the bottom of all pages. Within a header or a footer, you can include such text as a title, your name, a page number, or the date the worksheet was printed.

Headers appear at the top of every page.

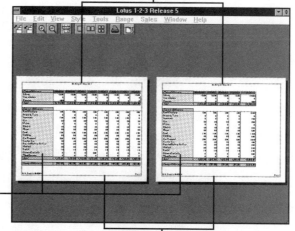

Titles can be used when data extends past one page.

Footers appear at the bottom of every page.

Use titles when worksheet extends to a second page

Titles are columns or row headings that you want repeated on each page of a worksheet. For example, in a big worksheet such as the one shown, it's nice to print the row headings on the second page, so you can understand what each row stands for. You can also repeat column headings, or both column and row headings if you like.

You can include a header, a footer, and titles in the same worksheet if you want.

Basic Survival

Adding a Header or a Footer

Within a header or a footer, you can type your own text or pull text from a cell in the worksheet. In addition, you can select from several buttons that add the page number, date printed, time printed, and other valuable data to your header or footer.

You enter header and footer information into any of three boxes in the Page Setup dialog box. If you enter data into the box on the left, it will print along the left margin of the header or footer. If you enter data into the center box, it is centered between the margins; while data you enter into the right box is aligned along the right margin. You can enter data for your header or footer in any or all of the three boxes, depending on the look you are trying to achieve.

To add a header or a footer to a worksheet file:

1. Click on the Page Setup button ⊞ located on the Printing SmartIcon set, or open the File menu and select Page Setup. The Page Setup dialog box appears.

This prints the contents of cell B103 in the center of the header.

This prints "Date Printed" followed by the actual date, left-aligned in the footer.

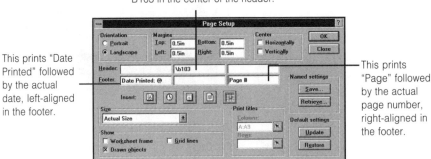

This prints "Page" followed by the actual page number, right-aligned in the footer.

2. In any of the three boxes under Header, type data or click on one of the buttons from the table below. You can even combine typed data with the data from a button. For example, you could type Page number – and then click on the Page Number button. The result would be this: Page number – #. The pound sign is replaced by an actual page number when the worksheet is printed.

To enter this...	Click on this...	Or type this...
The print date	🗓	@
The time of printing	🕐	+
Page number	▢	#
File name	▢	^
Contents of a cell	▦ and then type the cell address	\ followed by the cell address

3. Under Footer, repeat step 2 to add footer information.

4. Click OK.

You can also access the Page Setup dialog box by clicking on the Page Setup button from the Print or Preview dialog boxes or the Print Preview window.

Printing Column or Row Titles on Every Page

Adding column or row titles is equivalent to freezing titles on-screen, as explained in Chapter 9. Repeating column or row titles on a second page makes it easier for you to understand the worksheet by helping you keep track of the categories included in the columns or rows.

However, the trick to getting column or row titles right is to make sure you don't include them in your print range. For tips on selecting a print range, see Chapter 35.

Don't include titles in the print range!!!

To print column or row titles on every page of a worksheet:

1. Click on the Page Setup button 🗔 located on the Printing SmartIcon set, or open the File menu and select Page Setup. The Page Setup dialog box appears.

Select columns and or rows to repeat on every printed page.

2. Under Print titles, click on the Range selector for Columns.

3. Select the column you want to use as titles. For example, click in column A to use the titles in column A. You only need to select one cell in each column you want to use.

4. Repeat steps 2 and 3 for row titles. For example, in step 3, click in row 4 to use the labels along that row as titles.

5. Click OK.

You can also click on the Column Titles button 🗔 or Row Titles button 🗔 located on the Printing SmartIcon set to create print titles.

Beyond Survival

Saving Header and Footer Settings for Reuse

Save company header and footer to reuse!

If you often use the same kind of header or footer in your worksheets, save and reuse them. For example, if you prefer to place your company name centered in the header, with your name and the page number in the footer, enter these settings into a worksheet. Then save them and reuse them in other worksheets so you don't have to keep typing them. Saving your headers or footers saves all of the page setup settings, including page orientation, margins, and size, so you can reuse them too.

To save your page settings for reuse:

1. Click on the Page Setup button 🗔 located on the Printing SmartIcon set or open the File menu and select Page Setup. The Page Setup dialog box appears.

2. Enter your header, footer, and other page settings as normal.

3. Under Named settings, click on Save. The Save Named Settings dialog box appears.

Enter a file name

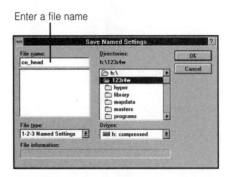

4. Under File name, enter a description for your settings using up to 8 characters. For example, you could enter CO_HEAD. (Use the underscore _ instead of spaces.) 1-2-3 automatically adds the .AL3 extension.

5. Click OK.

To reuse the saved settings at a later date, access the Page Setup dialog box and click on Retrieve under Named settings. Select a file name from the list and click OK. The saved settings replace those in the Page Setup dialog box. You can make changes to them, or simply use them as is by clicking OK.

You can save your settings as the default settings to be used with every worksheet if you want. Just create the settings you want. Then instead of saving them as a named setting, access the Page Setup dialog box and click on Update under Default settings.

Getting Graphical

One of the features that gave 1-2-3 its name is its ability to present your data in a visual form called a chart. Rows upon rows of numbers do not speak to your reader as well as a chart that presents trends and analyses. In this section, you'll learn about charts and more:

- Creating Your First Chart

- Changing Your Chart

- Formatting a Chart

- Adding Graphic Objects to a Worksheet

Cheat Sheet

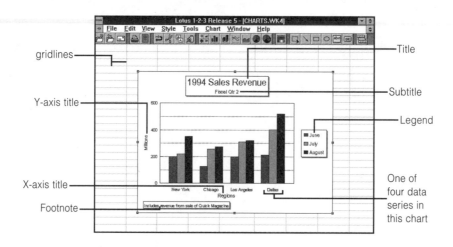

gridlines

Y-axis title

X-axis title

Footnote

Title

Subtitle

Legend

One of four data series in this chart

Creating a Chart

1. Select the data you want to chart.

2. Click on the Tools Chart button ▮▮▮.

3. Click in the worksheet to create a chart of the default size, or drag across the worksheet to drag the outline of the chart in the size you want.

Printing Just the Chart

1. Click on the chart to select it.

2. Click on the File Print SmartIcon 🖶.

3. Click OK.

Creating a Map

1. Select your map data.

2. Click on the Create Map SmartIcon located on the Goodies SmartIcon set 🌐.

3. Click in the worksheet.

39

Creating Your First Chart

A chart is a graphical representation of your worksheet data. The point of having a chart is to make the meaning behind a set of numbers more obvious. Charts help show relationships, changes, and trends within and between series of related values. There are many types of charts, which you'll learn about in this chapter. A chart also has many parts that you can customize, such as a title, subtitle, and legend.

Once you're familiar with the basic parts of a chart and the various chart types, you can advance to creating your first chart. If you work for a large corporation, you might find a map more effective than a chart. With a map, you can locate offices, regions, or divisions, and mark them with pertinent data, such as sales, growth percentages, client retention percentages, and so on.

Basic Survival

The Parts of a Chart

You already know how to create a worksheet, but how do you convert that data into a chart? Say, for instance, you're reading an expenditures worksheet, and you're looking up the supplies expenses for June. You'd most likely find the names of departments—such as "Supplies"— queued up along the leftmost column of the worksheet, while "June" and all the other months are in a row along the top. In your mind (or with your finger), you draw a line from "Supplies" to the right and from "June" down.

Let's say you want to chart the expenses for June for each department. The data in a chart is typically plotted against two axes. In our example, the departments (such as Supplies) would be placed along one axis, while the expense amounts for June would be plotted against the other axis. Categories of data, such as products, sales regions, months, years, or quarters, are usually plotted along the horizontal X-axis. Units of measure, such as dollars, percentages, sales units, and so on, define the scale for the vertical Y-axis. Here's a typical chart and its original data.

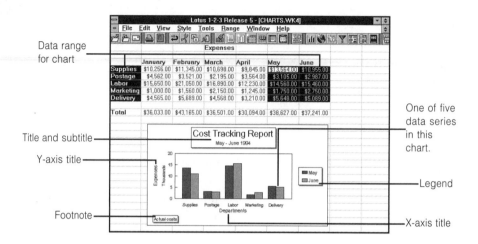

Data range for chart

Title and subtitle

Y-axis title

Footnote

One of five data series in this chart.

Legend

X-axis title

Title and subtitle The title can be taken from the worksheet or added manually. The second line of the title is called the subtitle.

X-axis and Y-axis titles These optional titles act as labels for the values plotted against each axis.

Data series A particular range of values within a chart (for example, the sales revenue for a single salesperson), a data series is a single row or column within the chart data.

Legend Typically found in a pie, clustered bar, or line chart (see next section), a legend provides a description for the separate data series in a chart.

Footnote An optional note that provides additional information about the chart.

Chart Types

There are several major chart types. Each is best suited for charting a particular type of data. In addition, most chart types come in a 3-D version (a chart with a third dimension—depth) for adding a bit of pizazz to your presentations.

Pie Good choice for illustrating the relationships between parts of a whole: for example, the percentages of revenue from each of five major products. The most popular product would have the largest slice of the "pie" in this type of chart.

Bar Good for comparing individual units: for example, the value of each stock in your portfolio. Each bar represents a different stock in this type of chart. Also good for illustrating changes over time, such as the change in home sales during the year. In this case, each bar might represent a month.

Line Good choice for illustrating trends and changes over time: for example, the rise in medical costs over the last ten years, or the rise and fall of stock prices over the last month.

Area Similar to a line chart. Good for emphasizing change in values,

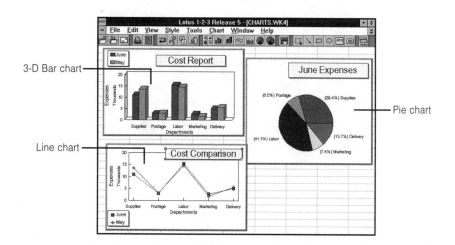

such as the rise in interest rates or the change in freshman enrollment.

XY Best choice for determining if a correlation between two data sets exists. The points in each data set are plotted, and if a solid line seems to emerge from the various points, you see the correlation.

HLCO Charts the high, low, closing, and opening values of the

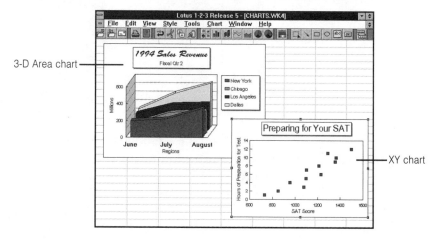

changing market value of stocks and other things that change in value over time (such as currency rates, temperature, artwork, gold prices, and so on). HLCO is a two-part chart that combines a highly function-alized line chart at the top, with a bar chart on the bottom. The line chart plots, along the horizontal X-axis, a series of *horizontal* lines. The length of each of these lines depicts the difference between the stock's highest and lowest prices for the day. Either a pair of so-called *whisker* ticks or a colored *candlestick* bar may be used to span the difference between the issue's opening and closing prices for the day. The lower portion of the HLCO chart is a simple bar chart, generally used to denote trading volume. Note here, though, that the Y-axis labels for this chart appear along the right side, as a way to stay separate from the Y-axis labels for the upper hi/lo chart.

Radar   Used in place of a bar or line chart, this type of chart is good at illustrating the similarity between data sets: for example, the SAT scores of a school compared against the national average. It's also good for plot-ting the changes in cyclic phenomena, such as the noise propagation in radio waves or the relative speed of a vehicle around a racetrack.

By default, 1-2-3 takes your chart data and creates a bar chart. In the

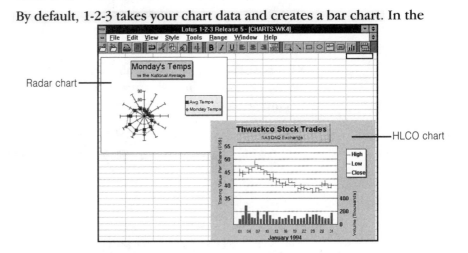

Radar chart

HLCO chart

Creating a Chart

next chapter, you'll learn how to change the chart type to best suit the type of data you're plotting. By the way, when you change the data used to create the chart, the chart itself is automatically updated.

To create a chart:

1. Select the data you want to chart. If possible, select the chart title, subtitle, and row and column titles along with the data cells. The row and column titles are the most important, since they contain the *axis references* for your chart.

2. Click on the Tools Chart button ▫▫▫ or open the Tools menu and select Chart.

3. Click in an empty area of the worksheet to create a chart of the default size, or drag across the worksheet to drag the outline of the chart in the size you want. Release the mouse button, and your chart is created.

Click in worksheet to create chart of default size

If a bar chart is just not your style, you can change the chart type. See

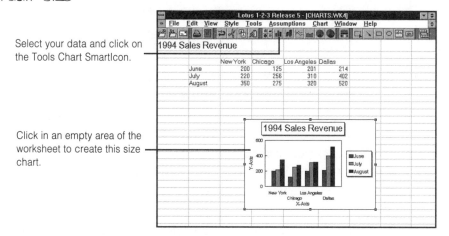

Select your data and click on the Tools Chart SmartIcon.

Click in an empty area of the worksheet to create this size chart.

Chapter 40 for help. Chapter 40 also contains information on adjusting the data ranges (and, therefore, the values the chart uses). If you want to move or resize the chart after creating it, you can (see Chapter 42 for information).

To delete a chart, click on the chart to select it, and then press Delete.

Beyond Survival

Printing Just the Chart

It's entirely possible, and in fact quite simple, to have 1-2-3 print out a copy of just the chart, aside from the worksheet. Here's how:

1. Click on the chart to select it.

2. Open the File menu and select Print or click on the File Print SmartIcon 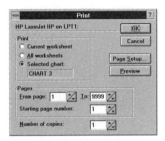. The Print dialog box appears.

3. Under Print, Selected chart should already be chosen for you. Click OK to begin the printing process.

Creating a Map

If you want to present your data by region or division, it might make more sense to use a map than a chart. 1-2-3 for Windows 5.0 comes with a set of standard maps, including those of the USA, Europe, Japan, Mexico, and Canada. Additional maps are also available at a nominal charge.

To create a map, you enter specific data into two or three columns. The first column contains map codes that indicate particular states or countries. You can find a complete listing of the map codes in the Help system. The second column contains whatever data you want to include on the map (for example, a region or division within your company). The third column (which is optional) contains some type of additional data, such as sales figures or growth percentages. The first column containing labels is represented on the map with various patterns such as stripes or crosshatching. The first column containing values is represented on the map with various colors. You can adjust the patterns and/or colors used on the map to suit your taste.

You can also add pin characters, placing them on the map at locations you specify. These characters can be anything—such as a flag or a star. Certain fonts contain a variety of characters from which you can choose. For example, the letter O in the Wingdings font is a flag. The star you see in the sample was made by pressing Alt+0171 using the Wingdings font. The Windows Character Map program, located in the Accessories group, can help you identify additional symbols that you can copy to 1-2-3.

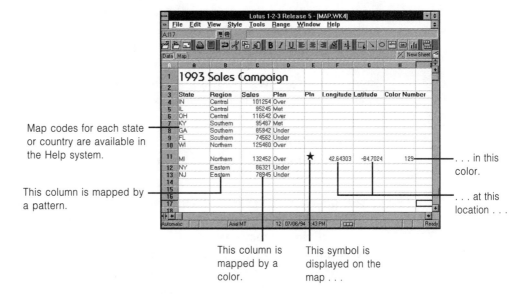

Map codes for each state or country are available in the Help system.

This column is mapped by a pattern.

This column is mapped by a color.

This symbol is displayed on the map . . .

. . . in this color.

. . . at this location . . .

Once you have your data organized correctly, you can create your map.

1. Select your map data. For the sample, I selected the range A3..H13.

2. Open the Tools menu, select Map, and select Insert Map Object. Or, click on the Create Map SmartIcon, located on the Goodies SmartIcon set . The mouse pointer changes to a globe.

3. Click in the worksheet at the point where you want to create the map. Do NOT drag the mouse pointer to create the map; just click. You can switch to another worksheet to create your map if you want.

Changing the Way Your Map Looks

Once you have your map, you can make adjustments to it with the Tools Map command or with the Map Viewer, a special program that allows you to manipulate elements of the map.

For hints on moving and resizing the map, see Chapter 42. Chapter 42 also covers ways in which you can also add text boxes, arrows, and other graphic objects to enhance your map.

To change the colors on the map, click on the map to select it, and then open the Tools menu and select Map. Select Color Settings. Use the Values column to adjust the cutoffs that determine which state/country/province gets what color. Use the Legend Labels column to change what appears in the Legend box, and use the Colors column to actually change the colors assigned to each level. You can change the pattern assignments in the same way with the Pattern Settings command.

Change the title by opening the Tools menu, selecting Map, and then selecting Ranges and Title. Under Title, type a new title for your map and press Enter.

Place pin characters on the map by adding some additional information to your map data. In the first column to the right of the regular map data, type the character you want to appear on the chart. You can use the Windows Character Map to create the character if you want. In the next two columns, type the exact location on the map in which you want to place the pin character. You can use the Map Viewer (coming up later in this section) to obtain this location. You can add one more column of data if you like; a number that represents the color you want the pin character to be. To get this color number, open the Lines and Color dialog box, move the cursor over a color, and look at the bottom of the dialog box where a number will appear. If you don't specify a color, 1-2-3 uses a color it thinks will look the best over that area of the map.

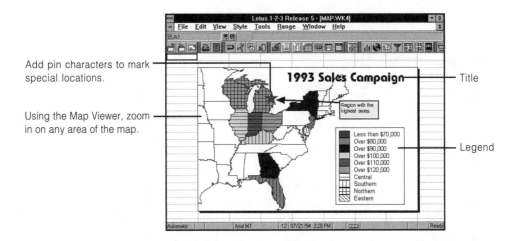

Add pin characters to mark special locations.

Using the Map Viewer, zoom in on any area of the map.

Title

Legend

By double-clicking on the map, you can access the Map Viewer. The Map Viewer is a special program that allows you to manipulate the separate parts of the map. With it, you can:

Zoom in on any area of the map. Just drag your mouse across the area to draw a rectangle. Release the mouse button, and 1-2-3 zooms in on the area you identified.

Move the title or the legend. Click on the title or legend, and then drag it wherever you want.

Center the map on a particular location. Just move the mouse pointer over the spot you want to be the center of your map. Then click the right mouse button and select Recenter from the quick menu.

Copy coordinates to create a pin location. To create a location for a pin character, you need the exact coordinates for that location on the map. Simply move the mouse pointer over the spot you want to place a pin character, and then click the right mouse button. Select Copy Coordinates. When you return to the worksheet, click on the Paste button to copy the coordinates to the correct location within your map data area.

Exit the Viewer and save your changes. Open the File menu and select Exit & Return to Worksheet.

Remember, to start the Map Viewer, double-click on the map. Before you start using the Map Viewer, you might want to maximize the window by clicking the Maximize button.

Cheat Sheet

Changing the Chart Type

1. Click on the chart to select it.
2. Open the Chart menu and select Type.
3. Under Types, click on a chart type.
4. Click on a chart style.
5. Under Orientation, choose Vertical or Horizontal. (Note that with some types of charts, the Orientation option is not available.)
6. Click on Include table of values if you want to include a copy of the spreadsheet data from which the chart was created.
7. Click OK.

Adjusting the Data Ranges

1. Click on the chart to select it.
2. Open the Chart menu and select Ranges.
3. Under Assign, select Individually.
4. Under Series, select the series you want to change. To add a new series to the chart, select one marked "Empty."
5. Under Range, click on the Range Selector button and select the range of cells for the series you chose in step 4.
6. Click on OK.

Changing Your Chart

Lotus 1-2-3 draws an entire bar chart automatically, based on the data you give it from your worksheet. Chances are, however, this isn't really the type of chart you're looking for, or it's too big, or in the wrong place for printing, or something. In this chapter, you learn how to correct your chart so it looks more like what you want. (To move, copy, or resize your chart, treat it like any other graphic object. See Chapter 42 for help.) The next chapter shows you how to add finishing touches such as titles, legends, and the like.

Basic Survival

Changing the Chart Type

Following the steps in Chapter 39, you created your basic bar chart. Problem is, a basic bar chart just won't do. Your job now is to uncover the type of chart that best represents the values, changes, and trends that were hidden within the worksheet numbers.

1. Click on the chart to select it. Selection handles (tiny black boxes) appear around the edges of the chart when it's selected.

2. Open the Chart menu and select Type. Or, click on the Chart Type SmartIcon, located on the Default Chart SmartIcon set, which appears whenever you select a chart ▥. 1-2-3 displays the Type dialog box.

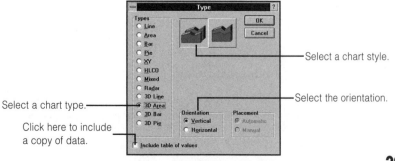

Select a chart type.

Click here to include a copy of data.

Select a chart style.

Select the orientation.

293

3. Under Types, click on a chart type. A set of example chart arrangements belonging to this type appears.

4. Click on a chart style.

5. Under Orientation, choose Vertical or Horizontal. This orientation only applies to rectangular charts; round charts such as Pie and Radar don't require orientation. For example, if you want your bars to be displayed from left to right across the chart, choose Horizontal.

Add a table of values to charts printed separately

6. Click on Include table of values if you want to include a copy of the spreadsheet data from which the chart was created. The spreadsheet data is added to the chart just below (or beside) the chart's plot area. This extra copy of the worksheet data might be helpful if the chart is designed to be printed separately from the rest of the worksheet.

7. Click OK. 1-2-3 automatically redraws your chart using the type and arrangement you requested.

Here's a shortcut for changing to the most often used chart types. Click once on the chart, and 1-2-3 automatically switches to the Default Chart SmartIcon set. Next, click on one of the chart styling tool buttons on the Default Chart SmartIcon set. The chart automatically changes to the style whose button you select. For example, click on the Pie chart button to change your chart to the pie chart style.

	Vertical bar chart
	Vertical 3-D bar chart
	Vertical line chart
	Vertical area chart
	Pie chart
	3-D pie chart

You can add other chart types to this set if you want; see Chapter 6 for more information.

Some types of charts are harder to change to because they require more information than regular bar charts. Specifically, to create an

HLCO chart, you need two sections in your worksheet: place the high, low, open, and close prices in one section or table within your worksheet, and the trading volume in another section. For clarity, your trading volume table should be directly beneath your high/low table so that each day's trading data appears on the same column of the worksheet. To create the HLCO chart, add data ranges to include the high, low, open, close, and trading volume ranges (ranges A to E; five ranges in all). See "Adjusting the Data Ranges" later in this chapter for help in adding the data ranges.

Create an HLCO or an XY chart using two tables

You use a similar process to create an XY chart; the XY chart compares the values in the two sections of your worksheet and graphs the similarities. To create an XY chart, you need at least two columns of data: a column that contains SAT scores, and another column that contains hours spent in preparation. The SAT column becomes the X-range, while the hours spent column becomes the A-range. Substitute other data to create your own XY chart.

Beyond Survival

Adjusting the Data Ranges

Here's how to change the data in the chart!

After you create a chart, you may decide that the chart is plotting the wrong sets of values. To correct this, you can change the ranges of cells to which the chart is referring, or you can bring in a series of values from a different table entirely. In any case, here's what you do:

1. Click on the chart to select it.

2. Open the Chart menu and select Ranges, or simply double-click on a bar, line, etc. in the chart. The Ranges dialog box appears.

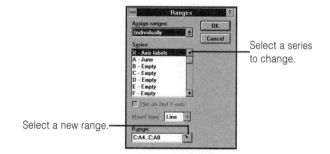

Select a series to change.

Select a new range.

3. Under Assign, select Individually. This enables you to correct individual data series or ranges as necessary.

4. Under Series, select the series you want to change. To add a new series to the chart, select one marked "Empty". If an "Empty" series is not available, you may have to replace an existing series with the data you need. Select that series instead.

5. Under Range, click on the Range Selector button. The Ranges dialog box momentarily disappears. Select the range of cells for the series you chose in step 4. Release the mouse button, and you return to the Ranges dialog box.

6. Click on OK. The changes you requested are immediately reflected in the chart.

Cheat Sheet

Adding a Chart Title or a Footnote

1. Click on the chart to select it.
2. Open the Chart menu and select Headings.
3. Type a title or subtitle on Line 1 or 2. Or use a title already in a cell by selecting the Cell check box and typing the cell address under Line 1 or 2.
4. Select a Placement.
5. Repeat steps 3 and 4 under Note to add a personal note to your chart.
6. Click OK.

Adding Axis Titles

1. Click on the chart to select it.
2. Open the Chart menu and select Axis. Then select either X-Axis, Y-Axis, or 2nd Y-Axis.
3. Under Axis title, type a title. You can use a title already in a cell by selecting the Cell check box and typing the cell address under Axis title.
4. Click OK.

Changing a Legend

1. Click on the chart to select it.
2. Open the Chart menu and select Legend.
3. Under Series, select a series whose legend label you want to change.
4. Under Legend entry, type the new entry for the data series you selected, or use a description already in a cell by selecting the Cell check box and typing the cell address under Legend entry.
5. Under Place legend select a location for the legend.
6. Click OK.

41

Formatting a Chart

After you create your chart, you'll probably want to dress it up a bit. After all, the chart was probably created to enhance your worksheet and add a touch of professionalism—so it makes sense to have it look as good as it can. This chapter teaches you how to add a title, subtitle, footnote, axis titles, or legend to your chart. If you hang around for the Beyond Survival section, you'll learn even more tricks for making your charts look their best, including adding color and a border.

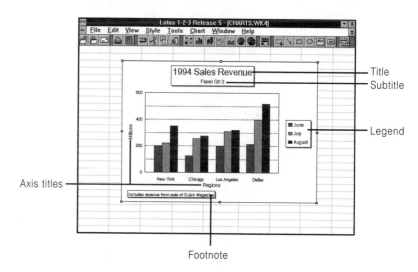

Basic Survival

Adding a Chart Title or a Footnote

If the range you selected when you created your chart included a title cell, then your chart already has a title. Even so, you can use the steps in this section to change your chart title. If your chart doesn't have a title, you can add a title without too much fuss. In addition, you can add a subtitle or footnote (a personal note explaining some detail) to your chart while you're at it.

1. Click on the chart to select it. Tiny handles (black boxes) appear along the edges of the chart.

2. Open the Chart menu and select Headings. The Headings dialog box appears. If your chart already has a title and you want to change it, you can also double-click on the title to open the Headings dialog box.

Type a title or select a cell.

Add a footnote.

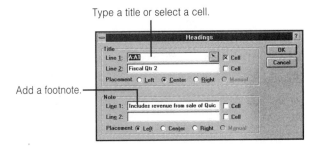

3. Under Title, type a title or subtitle on Line 1 or 2. You can use a title that's already in a cell by selecting the Cell check box and typing the cell address under Line 1 or 2.

4. Select where you want the title to appear in the chart by selecting a Placement option button: Left, Center, Right, or Manual.

5. Repeat steps 3 and 4 under Note to add a personal note (what Lotus also calls a footnote) to your chart.

6. Click OK.

Double-click on a title to change it

You can also double-click on the title to change it or to add a footnote. Just double-click on the title, and the Headings dialog box appears. Change your title or add a footnote as described above. Also, instead of selecting a placement for the title or footnote in the Headings dialog box, you can simply drag it to its desired location within the chart box. Just click on the footnote or the title, and drag them wherever you like within the chart.

Adding Axis Titles

Remember to do this!

When you create a chart, 1-2-3 uses the default axis titles, "X-axis" and "Y-axis." Since these are not terribly descriptive of the data plotted against each axis, you should probably change them. For example, if the amounts plotted against the Y-axis represent departmental expenses, change the Y-axis to "Expenses." To add axis titles:

1. Click on the chart to select it. Tiny handles (black boxes) appear along the edges of the chart.

2. Open the Chart menu and select Axis. Then select either X-Axis, Y-Axis, or 2nd Y-Axis. The appropriate dialog box appears.

Type a title.

3. Under Axis title, type a title. You can use a title already in a cell by selecting the Cell check box and typing the cell address under Axis title.

4. Click OK.

Double-click on an axis title to change it

You can also double-click on an axis title to change it. If you want to move or delete your axis titles, see the section, "Moving or Deleting Chart Elements."

Changing a Legend

A *legend* describes the various data series in a chart. 1-2-3 automatically adds a legend to any chart that requires it (such as a pie chart, or a bar or line chart with several data series). You can change the description for each legend entry by following these steps:

1. Click on the chart to select it.

2. Open the Chart menu and select Legend, or double-click on the legend to display the Legend dialog box.

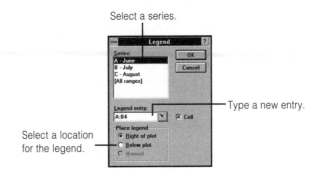

Select a series.

Type a new entry.

Select a location
for the legend.

3. Under Series, select a series whose legend label you want to change.

4. Under Legend entry, type the new entry for the data series you selected. If you want to use a description already in a cell, select the Cell check box and type the cell address under Legend entry.

5. Under Place legend, select a location for the legend.

6. Click OK.

If you have a pie chart, you can delete the legend and label each pie section directly on the chart. Simply select the chart, open the Chart menu, and select Data Labels. Under Show, select the Contents of X-data range option. Click OK. The legend is automatically removed and is replaced by appropriate labels next to each pie piece.

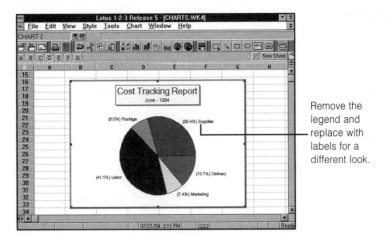

Remove the legend and replace with labels for a different look.

Beyond Survival

Moving or Deleting Chart Elements

You can reorganize your chart to suit your tastes by moving or deleting such chart elements as the title, legend, or footnote. For example, you can add interest to a pie chart by "exploding" (moving) a pie piece out of the pie to emphasize its importance.

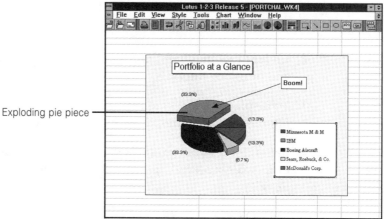

Exploding pie piece

To move a chart element, drag it.

To move a chart element, click on it and drag it to its new location. To delete a chart element, click on it and press Delete.

Changing the Scale

When you create a chart, 1-2-3 automatically sets the scale that runs along the Y-axis. For example, suppose you created a chart showing sales revenue for June, July, and August that was similar to the chart shown at the beginning of this chapter. If the revenue values ranged from 200 to 520 million, 1-2-3 might choose a scale that showed the values in 100 million increments. The upper limit of the scale might be set to 600 million, while the lower limit is usually set to 0. The tick marks running along the y-axis might be set at intervals of 200 million, resulting in two tick marks: one set at 200 million and the other at 400 million. Minor tick marks (those without labels) could be added at halfway points between these major tick marks, at 100, 300, and 500 million. You can change the scale's upper limit, lower limit, and major and minor intervals. To change the scale:

1. Double-click on the scale. The Y-axis dialog box appears.

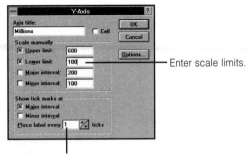

Enter scale limits.

Limit how often labels appear.

2. Under Scale manually, enter the upper limit, lower limit, major and/or minor intervals.

3. To display tick marks at minor intervals in addition to the major intervals, click on the Minor interval check box.

4. If you don't want the labels that identify the scale to appear at every major interval, increase the value under Place label every *x* ticks.

5. Click OK.

You can change the type of scale 1-2-3 uses by clicking on the Options button in the Y-axis dialog box. You can then select a *log scale* (a scale that increases logarithmically). You can select a 100% scale to display values as percentages of the upper limit.

You can also add gridlines to your chart to make the scale easier to follow. To add gridlines, click on the chart to select it. Open the Chart menu and select Grids. If the scale is located on the Y-axis, select an option from the drop-down list box under Y-axis. For example, select Both to display gridlines at both the major and minor intervals set by the scale. Click OK, and the gridlines appear.

Changing Fonts and Colors

To add real pizzazz to your chart, take the time to format it. This process is especially rewarding if you have a color printer. You can change the font style of any label on the chart. In addition, you can change the color of any element. You can also change the border of the plot area, legend, title, footnote, or the entire chart box if you like.

To change the font of a label, such as the X-axis labels:

1. Click on the label to select it.

2. Open the Style menu and select Fonts & Attributes. The Fonts & Attributes dialog box appears.

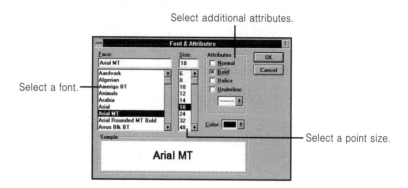

Select additional attributes.

Select a font.

Select a point size.

3. Select a font face and point size. Select additional attributes as necessary, such as bold, underline, or color.

4. Click OK.

To change the color or border of a chart element, such as the chart background or the plot area, follow these steps:

1. Click on the chart element to select it.

2. Open the Style menu and select Lines & Color. The Lines & Color dialog box appears.

Style/Lines
& Color to
change the
color or
border style
of any
element

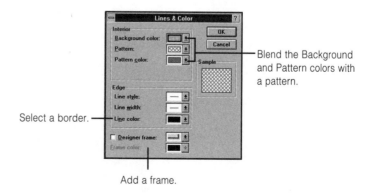

Blend the Background
and Pattern colors with
a pattern.

Select a border.

Add a frame.

3. Under Interior, select a Background color.

4. You can change the background color by blending it with a Pattern color and selecting a pattern.

5. Under Edge, select a style, width, and color. This changes the border of the selected chart element.

6. If you selected the chart itself, you can add a frame by selecting one under Designer frame. In addition, change the frame color if you want.

7. Click OK.

You can also change the color or border of a chart element by clicking on it, and then clicking on the Lines & Color SmartIcon .

Cheat Sheet

Drawing Lines, Arcs, and Arrows

1. Open the Tools menu and select Draw.
2. Select Line, Arc, or Arrow.
3. Click on the worksheet to establish the end point of the line, arc, or arrow. (Be sure to hold the mouse button down.)
4. Drag across the worksheet to the other end point. Release the mouse button, and the line, arc, or arrow appears.

Drawing Rectangles, Ellipses, and Polygons

1. Open the Tools menu and select Draw.
2. Select Rectangle, Rounded Rectangle, or Ellipse.
3. Click on the worksheet to establish the upper left-hand corner of your object. (Be sure to hold the mouse button down.)
4. Drag across the worksheet to the lower right-hand corner. Release the mouse button.

Adding a Text Block

1. Open the Tools menu and select Draw.
2. Select Text.
3. Click on the worksheet to create a text block of the default size. You can also click and drag the mouse pointer to create a text block of any size.
4. Type your text, or copy and paste the text from elsewhere in the worksheet.
5. Click in the worksheet when you're done.

42

Adding Graphic Objects to a Worksheet

A *graphic object* is something you draw on your worksheet, such as a line, arrow, rectangle, or text block. Want to point out your division's hot sales record? Draw an arrow to it. Want to explain the low revenue growth? Add a text block. To create this visual magic, you're going to need your mouse.

You can use graphic objects to enhance your worksheet, a chart, or a map. Once created, a graphic object can be moved, copied, deleted, or resized. The colors and borders of graphic objects can also be changed, as you learn in the Beyond Survival section.

Basic Survival

Drawing Lines, Arcs, and Arrows

Arrows are often used to point out important information within a worksheet. You can use lines and arcs and even freehand lines to create other effects. (To create a polyline, see the next section.)

1. Open the Tools menu and select Draw. A cascading menu appears.

2. Select Line, Arc, or Arrow from the cascading menu. The mouse pointer changes to a cross-hair.

3. Click on the worksheet to establish the end point of the line, arc, or arrow. (Be sure to hold the mouse button down.)

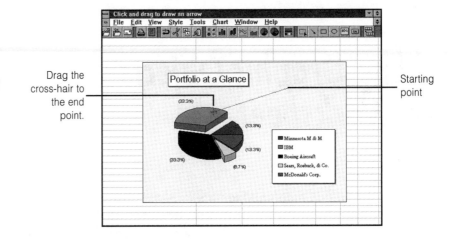

Click, then drag to create an object

Drag the cross-hair to the end point.

Starting point

4. Drag across the worksheet to the other end point. Release the mouse button and the line, arc, or arrow appears.

To create a freehand line:

1. Open the Tools menu and select Draw. A cascading menu appears.

2. Select Freehand from the cascading menu. The mouse pointer changes to a cross-hair.

3. Drag across the worksheet to create your freehand line. Release the mouse button to end the freehand line.

Use these SmartIcons to create your lines, arcs, or arrows:

SmartIcon	Name	Location
Arrow	Default Sheet	SmartIcon set
Line	Goodies	SmartIcon set

In addition, you can add these SmartIcons (which are not located on any particular set) to any existing set, or you can create a special set called Drawing (see Chapter 6 for help).

 Arc

 Double-Arrow

 Freehand Line

Drawing Rectangles, Ellipses, and Polygons

Use ellipses to surround an important figure with an oval ring. You can combine squares, rectangles, or polygons to add interest or to create a unique logo. To draw a rectangle or ellipse:

1. Open the Tools menu and select Draw. A cascading menu appears.

2. Select Rectangle, Rounded Rectangle, or Ellipse from the cascading menu. The mouse pointer changes to a cross-hair.

3. Click on the worksheet to establish the upper left-hand corner of your object. (Be sure to hold the mouse button down.)

4. Drag across the worksheet to the lower right-hand corner. To create a square or a circle, press and hold the Shift key as you drag. Release the mouse button and the rectangle or ellipse appears.

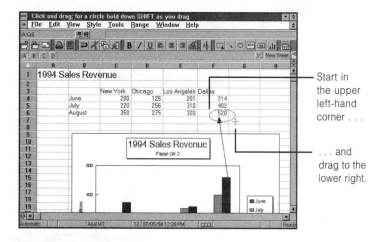

Start in the upper left-hand corner . . .

. . . and drag to the lower right.

To create a polygon or polyline (a line with several segments, each angled in a different direction):

1. Open the Tools menu and select Draw. A cascading menu appears.

2. Select either Polygon or Polyline from the cascading menu. The mouse pointer changes to a cross-hair.

3. Click on the worksheet to establish the first end point.

4. Drag across the worksheet to add a line. To add a line with a 45 or 90 degree angle, press and hold the Shift key while dragging.

Double-click to end polygon or polyline

5. Double-click to complete the polygon or polyline.

You can create an ellipse with the Ellipse SmartIcon 🔘, located on the Default Sheet SmartIcon set. In addition, you can add these SmartIcons to any set (see Chapter 6 for info).

▫ Rectangle

▫ Rounded Rectangle

◇ Polygon

╲ Polyline

Adding a Text Block

Think of text blocks as being similar to those yellow notes you can stick anyplace: use them to add comments and other information to your worksheet. You can position text blocks anywhere on your worksheet to draw attention to specific numbers, totals, or trends. To add a text block:

1. Open the Tools menu and select Draw. A cascading menu appears.

2. Select Text from the cascading menu. The mouse pointer changes to a cross-hair.

3. Click on the worksheet to create a text block of the default size. Or, click and drag the mouse pointer to create a text block of any size.

Type your text into the text block.

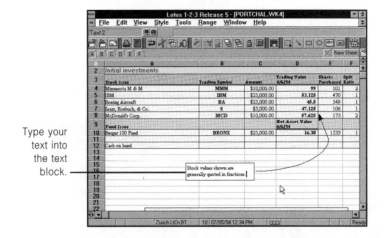

4. Type your text, or copy and paste the text from elsewhere in the worksheet. See Chapter 13 for help in copying text.

5. Click in the worksheet when you're done.

You can also click on the Text Block SmartIcon 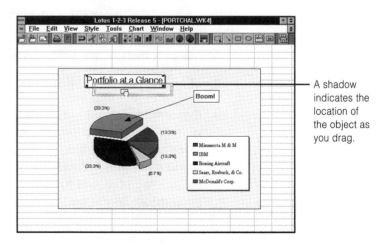 located on the Default SmartIcon set to create a text block.

To edit the text in a text block, double-click on it and edit as desired. You can style the text by selecting the text block and using the commands on the Style menu (such as Font & Attributes). However, all of the text within a text block retains the same font, color, or attributes, regardless of the amount of text you select to change.

Beyond Survival

Moving or Copying a Graphic Object

Your graphic object floats above the 1-2-3 worksheet. This means that your graphic object isn't really contained *within* your worksheet as much as it is *on top of* it. You can literally move any graphic object so that it obstructs your view of the cells in your table (why you'd want to, I don't know, but you can). Likewise, you can move a graphic object away from data cells so it doesn't obstruct your view of data. To move your graphic object by dragging:

1. Click on the graphic object to select it.

2. Hold your mouse pointer down and drag the pointer to the new location. A rectangular shadow, indicating the shape of the object, follows the mouse pointer.

A shadow indicates the location of the object as you drag.

Drag to move objects

3. Release the mouse button. The object is now moved to the new location.

To copy the object or to move the object to another worksheet or to another file, use the Clipboard:

1. Click on the object to select it.

2. Open the Edit menu and select Copy (to copy the object) or Cut (to move the object). You can also click on the Copy ⌧ or Cut ✂ SmartIcons.

3. Click in the worksheet at the place where you'd like to copy or move the object. You can switch to a different worksheet or open a new worksheet file if you want.

4. Open the Edit menu and select Paste or click on the Paste SmartIcon ⌧. The object appears.

By the way, if you copied your object, it is considered a separate copy from the original. This means that you can make changes to the copy without affecting the original.

Resizing or Deleting a Graphic Object

Drag a handle to resize object

You've probably already noticed that when you select a graphic object, tiny black boxes (called *handles*) surround the object on all sides. This happens anytime you click on a graphic object (such as a chart, or an arrow). The eight tiny boxes surround your graphic object when you click on it, as if to say, "You want *me*?"

These boxes are not just used as selection indicators; they also act as handles for resizing a graphic object (hence the name). To resize a graphic object:

1. Click on the graphic object to select it.

2. Move the pointer over one of the handles and click.

3. Continue to hold down the left mouse button, and then drag the pointer in the direction you want to move the handle (outward to make the graphic object grow, inward to make it shrink). A shadow line will follow your pointer, representing the new size of the graphic object. If you want to retain the graphic object's proportions, press and hold the Shift key as you drag a corner handle.

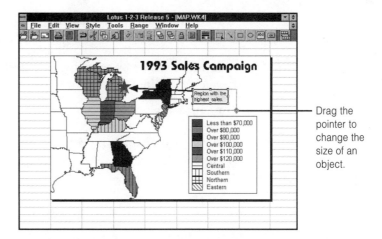

Drag the pointer to change the size of an object.

4. Release the mouse button. The graphic object is resized to fit the new border.

To delete a graphic object, click on it to select it and press Delete.

Changing the Color or Border Style of an Object

You can enhance the look of graphic objects by changing their color or border style. To change the color or border of a graphic object:

1. Click on the graphic object element to select it.

2. Open the Style menu and select Lines & Color. The Lines & Color dialog box appears.

Style/Lines & Color to change the color or border style of object

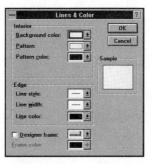

3. Under Interior, select a Background color.

4. You can change the background color by blending it with a Pattern color and selecting a pattern. To make the object transparent (so the cells that it covers show through), open the Pattern list and select T.

315

5. Under Edge, select a style, width, and color. This changes the border of the selected graphic object element.

6. Add a frame by selecting one under Designer frame. In addition, change the frame color if you want.

7. Click OK.

You can also change the color or border of a graphic object by clicking on it, and then clicking on the Lines & Color SmartIcon .

PART

8

Special Features

This final section explores the hidden power behind 1-2-3. With ease, you can manipulate your worksheet data to create complex analyses that can save you both time and money. If you deal with large amounts of data such as inventory or employee tracking, learn to utilize the database management features of 1-2-3. In this section, you'll learn about these topics:

- Checking Your Spelling

- Databasics

- Searching a Database

- Creating Macros

- Solving What-If Situations

- Creating Different Versions of the Same Worksheet

Cheat Sheet

Checking the Spelling of a Worksheet

1. Open the Tools menu and select Spell Check. The Spell Check dialog box appears.
2. Under Check, select Entire file.
3. Click OK.

What to Do When 1-2-3 Finds an Error

To replace the misspelled word with another word, select a spelling from the Alternatives list, or type a correction under Replace with and click on Replace. To replace all instances of this misspelling with the correction, click on Replace All.

To ignore the error, click on Skip. To skip all instances of this particular error, click on Skip All.

To add the word to the dictionary, click on Add to dictionary.

To cancel the spell check before it's through, click on Close.

When the spell check is complete, click OK.

43

Checking Your Spelling

Though your worksheet may contain mostly numbers, there is always some text in the labels, titles, footnotes, and so on. Don't spoil all of the hard work you've put into your worksheet with a misspelled word. Instead, check the spelling of your worksheet with Spell Check.

You can check the spelling of an entire worksheet file, a single worksheet, or a selected range. In this chapter, you learn how to perform all types of spell checks and what to do when Spell Check finds an error.

Basic Survival

Checking the Spelling of a Worksheet

While Spell Check checks the spelling of text, it also identifies duplicate words, such as "the the." When checking the spelling of an entire worksheet file, Spell Check not only checks the spelling of the text within cells, but also checks text in charts, text blocks, and query tables. (You'll find out what query tables are in Chapter 45; for now, just know that Spell Check checks *everything*.) To check the spelling of a worksheet file:

1. Open the Tools menu and select Spell Check or click on the Spell Check SmartIcon located on the Goodies SmartIcon set ![ABC] .

   1-2-3 displays the Spell Check dialog box.

   Click here to spell check entire worksheet file.

2. Under Check, click on the Entire file option button.

3. Click OK.

When Spell Check finds an error, this dialog box appears:

Misspelled word

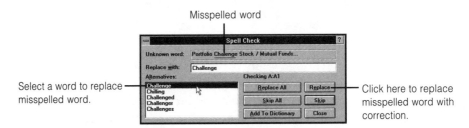

Select a word to replace misspelled word.

Click here to replace misspelled word with correction.

Select a correction, then click on Replace

To replace the misspelled word with another word, select a spelling from the Alternatives list, or type a correction in the Replace with text box and click on Replace. To replace all instances of this misspelling with the correction, click on Replace All.

To ignore the error, click on Skip. To skip all instances of the error, click on Skip All.

To add the word to the dictionary, click on Add to dictionary.

To cancel the spell check before it's through, click on Close.

When the spell check is complete, you see the message **Spell check complete!** Click on OK.

Beyond Survival

Checking the Spelling of a Range

Can spell check part of a file

You don't have to check the spelling of an entire worksheet. For example, if you're going to print just a chart, you may want to spell check only the chart. Or perhaps you might want to check the spelling of one worksheet, but not the entire worksheet file. To spell check part of a worksheet file:

1. Select the range, chart, text block, or query table whose spelling you want to check. To check the spelling of a single worksheet, simply move to that worksheet.

2. Open the Tools menu and select Spell Check or click on the Spell Check SmartIcon located on the Goodies SmartIcon set . The Spell Check dialog box appears.

Select a range to spell check.

3. Under Check, click on the Current Worksheet or Range option buttons.

4. Click OK.

When Spell Check finds an error, it displays a dialog box from which you can correct it. See the previous section for additional help.

Cheat Sheet

Creating a Database

1. Enter the field names for each column of the database.
2. Begin entering data on the row just under the field names. Do not skip a row.
3. Enter each record in the row just below the previous row.
4. You can add styles such as fonts, bold, or italics to the data in the database if you want.
5. Give your database a range name by selecting the database table, opening the Range menu, and selecting Name. Enter a name into the Name dialog box and click OK.

Adding Records to Your Database

1. Select a row within the range of the database. If you want to add lots of records, select several rows.
2. Open the Edit menu and select Insert.
3. Enter your new records in the blank rows.

Deleting Records in Your Database

1. Open the Tools menu and select Database. Select Delete Records.
2. Under Delete records from database table, click on the Range Selector. Select the entire table, including the field names row.
3. From the Fields drop-down list box, select a field to compare.
4. Select an operator from the Operator drop-down list box.
5. Enter a value to compare to in the Value box, or select it from the drop-down list box.
6. To enter additional criteria, click on the And or the Or button. Then repeat steps 5–7 to add the new criteria.
7. Click OK.

44

Databasics

A *database* is a collection of interrelated *records*. For example, a checkbook register is a collection of records (checks), each of which represents a single transaction. An address book is also a database. Each record in an address book records the name, address, and phone number of a single person or family.

Row = record, column = field in database

Each record is made up of *fields*. A field is a single piece of a record, such as a name, or a phone number. Records are placed in rows, with each field in a single column. *Field names* are column headings placed at the top of each column in the database. The entire area of the worksheet that contains the database is called a *database table*. You can include more than one database table in a worksheet if you want; however, the entire database table must fit on a single worksheet.

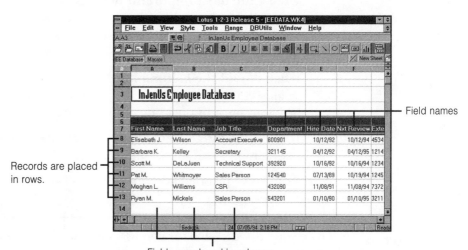

Field names

Records are placed in rows.

Fields are placed in columns.

Once you have a database, you can perform *queries* to locate specific records in the database, such as a listing of customers in Cincinnati. You can also sort your database (for example by last names in alphabetical order) and perform other functions. In this chapter, you learn how to create a database table and enter data. The Beyond Survival section teaches you how to sort your database.

Basic Survival

Creating a Database

Before you create your database, you should ask yourself a few questions:

What fields make up a single record? Examples of fields you might need for a customer database include: Company, Contact Name, Phone Number, Address, City, State, and ZIP. Each field belongs in a separate column, so enter the headings for each field at the top of each column.

How might you want the database organized? If you decide to sort an employee database by last name, last name should be treated as a separate field from first name. If you combine the two names into one field, such as "Jay Fairway," this record would appear with the J's—and not the F's—when you sorted the records.

What's the most important field, or the most often refer-enced field? If possible, place this field first in the database for convenience. Also, consider the forms from which the data might be taken. What order is used on the form?

What should the column headings be? Keep column headings small so they fit on a single row instead of two rows. (Column headings must fit on a single row at the top of the database table.)

What is the longest entry possible for each field? Use this information to set the widths for each column.

Now that you've planned how your database should look, you're ready to start entering data.

Entering Data

Once you have the plan for your database in mind, it's fairly easy to assemble it:

1. Enter the field names first. Begin by typing a label for each col-umn of the database. Don't use the same field name twice. Don't use names that can be mistaken as cell addresses, such as Q4. Although you can use spaces in field names, you might want to

avoid it. Also, avoid commas, semicolons, colons, hyphens, pound signs, exclamation points, and tildes (~) in field names.

. Once you have established the field names, begin entering each record in the database. Begin on the row just under the field names. Do *not* skip a row.

Enter each record in the row just below the previous row. Again, do not leave any blank rows within the database table. (Individual records can contain blank fields if necessary. For example, a record may not have an entry for a home phone number.)

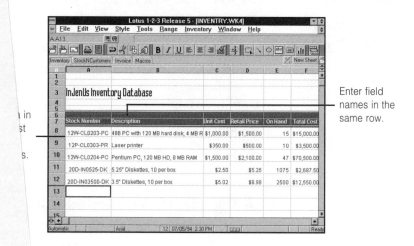

Enter field names in the same row.

 can add styles such as fonts, bold, or italics to the data in the base if you want.

greatest ease of use, give your database a range name. Select database table, open the Range menu, and select Name. Enter ne into the Name dialog box and click OK.

t to enter dates into your database, be sure to use one of the rmats:

onth-year   16-Oct-93

ay-month   16-Oct

Long international   10/16/93

Don't include field name row in sort selection!!!

When you have completed your database, you can sort the records in any order you want. First, select the data area of the data table. Do not include the row that contains the field names in the selection. Then open the Range menu and select Sort. Follow the directions later in this chapter under the section "Sorting Your Database" to select the fields to sort by and to complete the actual sort.

Beyond Survival

Adding or Deleting Records from the Database

After you create your database, you may find that from time to time you want to add new records or delete records you no longer need. The best way to add records is to insert new rows in the middle of the database. That way, the range you named for the original database is expanded to include the new rows. After you've added new records to your database, you can resort the database table using the instructions in the next chapter.

To add records:

1. Select a row within the range of the database. If you want to add lots of records, select several rows.

2. Open the Edit menu and select Insert, or click on the Insert Rows SmartIcon located on the Editing SmartIcon set ⊞ . The new rows are inserted in the middle of the database range.

3. Enter your new records in the blank rows.

To delete records, select the records you want to delete, and then open the Edit menu and select Delete. You can also click on the Delete Rows SmartIcon located on the Editing SmartIcon set ⊞ .

To delete a group of related records, you specify *criteria* that match the records you want to delete. Once the matching records are found, they are removed from the database table. (For more information on selecting criteria, see the next chapter.)

To delete records:

1. Open the Tools menu and select Database. Select Delete Records. The Delete Records dialog box appears.

Specify criteria for the records you want to delete.

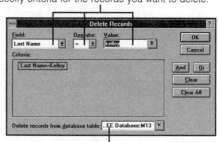

Enter database range or name.

2. Under Delete records from database table, click on the Range Selector. Select the entire table, including the field names row. If you named your table with the Range Name command, type the name of your database table instead of selecting it.

3. Select a field to compare to from the Fields drop-down list box. For example, select STATE to delete records from a particular state.

4. Select an operator from the Operator drop-down list box. For example, select = (equal to).

5. Enter a value to compare to in the Value box, or select it from the drop-down list box. For example, type **NY**.

6. To enter additional criteria, click on the And or the Or button. Then repeat steps 5–7 to add the new criteria. For example, click on Or and add the criteria STATE = IL. (In this example, records with an entry of NY or IL under the STATE field would be deleted.)

7. Click OK. The records you specified are deleted.

If the wrong records are deleted, click on the Undo button to undo the deletion ⟲. If you want to check your criteria before using the Delete Records command, see the section "Finding Records Without Creating a Query Table" in the next chapter. Once you're satisfied that your criteria identifies the correct records, repeat the steps here to actually delete the records.

Sorting Your Database

Once you have a database keyed in, you can sort the records any way you want. For example, you might want to sort an address database by ZIP code, or a check register database by check number. You can sort a database using more than one field, or *sort key*. For example, you could sort a client database by both city and state.

A sort can be performed in ascending order (from A to Z) or descending order (from Z to A). To sort your database:

1. Select the rows in your database. Don't select the row that contains the field name labels. To sort a query table (discussed in detail in the next chapter), click on it to select it.

2. Open the Range menu and select Sort. The Sort dialog box appears. To sort a query table, open the Query menu and select Sort.

When sorting a database, don't select the row of field names.

Select a sort key. —

Select a sort order. —

Click here to add a sort key.

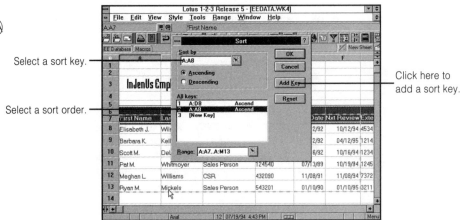

3. Under Sort by, type the address of any cell located within the column you want to use as the primary sort key. For example, select a cell in the Last_Name column to sort by last name. You can also click on the Range Selector and then click on a cell in the column you want to use as a sort key. If you're sorting a query table, simply click on the Sort by down arrow and select a field from the list.

4. Select a sort order: Ascending (A to Z) or Descending (Z to A).

5. Click on Add Key.

6. Repeat steps 3, 4, and 5 for additional sort keys. For example, add a secondary sort key for First_Name.

7. Click on OK to begin the sort. The records are rearranged within in the order you specified.

You can remove sort keys from the Sort dialog box by clicking Reset. If the sort does not work as you expected, immediately click on the Undo button ⏎.

If you add or delete records from your database, you'll need to resort the database. Just open the Range menu and select Sort. Verify that the selected range is correct (which it should be, if you followed the earlier directions for adding and deleting records) and click OK. The database is resorted for you. To resort a query table, simply select it, open the Query menu, and select Refresh Now.

Cheat Sheet

Performing a Query

1. Open the Tools menu and select Database. Select New Query.
2. Under Select database table in query, click on the Range Selector. Select the entire table, including the field names row.
3. Click on Set criteria button.
4. Click on Clear to remove old criteria.
5. Select a field to compare to from the Fields drop-down list box.
6. Select an operator from the Operator drop-down list box.
7. Enter a value to compare to in the Value box, or select it from the drop-down list box.
8. To enter additional criteria, click on the And or the Or button. Then repeat steps 5–7 to add the new criteria.
9. Click on OK.
10. To display selected fields in the query table (instead of all the fields in the database table), click on Choose Fields.
11. Select the fields you want to delete from the query table, and then click on Clear. To add a field, click on Add, and then select the field from the list and click OK to return to the Choose Fields dialog box. When you're through, click OK.
12. Under Select location for new query table, enter the range in which you want 1-2-3 to place the result of your query.
13. Click on OK.

Finding Records Without Creating a Query Table

1. Open the Tools menu and select Database. Select Find Records.
2. Under Find records in database table, click on the Range Selector. Select the entire table, including the field names row.
3. Specify your criteria as described in the previous section.
4. Click OK.

45

Searching a Database

Using 1-2-3 to store your database information is only half the fun. You can also use it to *query* your database—in other words, to locate specific records for you. For instance, you can query your database to locate:

All invoices over $100

All customers located in either New York or Illinois

All PC sales to new clients who bought more than one PC

The specifics about the records you want 1-2-3 to locate are called *criteria*. Once you have established your criteria, 1-2-3 locates the records you requested and places them in a *query table*, a separate area of the database. You can sort, print, and perform other functions on the query table without affecting the original database table. If you don't want to create a query table but you still want to locate specific records, see the section, "Finding Records Without Creating a Query Table."

Basic Survival

Determining Your Criteria

To query your database, you must be specific. In other words, you have to tell 1-2-3 exactly what to look for:

Match all records where the TOTAL field is greater than 100.

Match all records where the STATE field is equal to NY or IL.

Match all records where the UNITS field is greater than 1, and the STATUS field is equal to New.

Important!

These specifics are called *criteria*. When setting up criteria, you use specific operators to tell 1-2-3 how to compare data to your criteria:

Operator	Description
=	Equal to
< >	Not equal to
>	Greater than
<	Less than
< =	Less than or equal to
> =	Greater than or equal to

For example, the first criteria would look like this:

TOTAL > 100

If you have more than one criteria, you have to tell 1-2-3 whether a record needs to match all criteria, or if it needs to match only one of the criteria. To combine criteria, you use either the AND or the OR criteria. For example, the second criteria would look like this:

STATE = NY **OR** STATE = IL

This criteria tells 1-2-3 to find records where the STATE field contains either NY or IL. The third criteria would look like this:

UNITS > 1 **AND** STATUS = New

This criteria tells 1-2-3 to find any record where the UNITS field is greater than 1, and the STATUS field contains "New." *Both* criteria must be met for that record to be considered a match.

Performing a Query

Once you've determined the criteria you want to use, it's simple to perform a query on your database. Remember that once 1-2-3 locates the records you want to find, it copies them to another area of the worksheet, called a *query table*. You can resort the records in the query table, print the query table, and perform other functions on it. To create your query:

1. Open the Tools menu, select Database, and select New Query. Or, click on the New Query SmartIcon located on the Goodies SmartIcon set . The New Query dialog box appears.

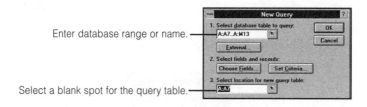

Enter database range or name. ——

Select a blank spot for the query table. ——

2. Under Select database table in query, click on the Range Selector. Select the entire table, including the field names row. If you named your table with the Range Name command, type the name of your database table instead of selecting it.

3. Click on the Set criteria button. The Set Criteria dialog box appears.

Select your criteria. ——

AND means records must meet all criteria. OR means records must meet any one criteria.

4. Click on Clear to remove old criteria.

5. Select a field to compare to from the Fields drop-down list box. For example, select STATE.

6. Select an operator from the Operator drop-down list box. For example, select = (equal to).

7. Enter a value to compare to in the Value box, or select it from the drop-down list box. For example, type **NY**.

8. To enter additional criteria, click on the And or the Or button. Then repeat steps 5–7 to add the new criteria. For example, click on Or and add the criteria STATE = IL.

9. When you're done adding criteria, click on OK. You're returned to the New Query dialog box.

10. To display selected fields in the query table (instead of all the fields in the database table), click on Choose Fields. The Choose Fields dialog box appears.

Select a field to remove. ——

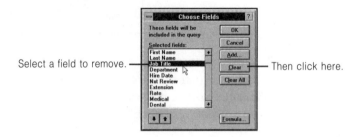

—— Then click here.

11. Select the fields you want to delete from the query table, and then click on Clear. To add a field, click on Add. Then select the field from the list, and click OK to return to the Choose Fields dialog box. When you're through, click OK. You're returned to the New Query dialog box.

12. Under Select location for new query table, enter the range in which you want 1-2-3 to place the result of your query. You can enter the cell address of the upper left-hand cell if you want. You can also select a range by clicking on the Range Selector.

13. Click on OK. 1-2-3 locates any matching records and copies them to the range you selected for the query table.

You can format your query table. ——

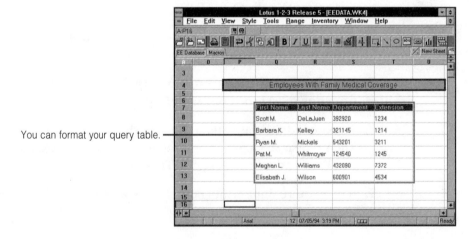

If the range you selected is not large enough to contain all of the records, you may need to expand the query table to see them. Simply click on the query table to select it, and then drag its border outward to expand the edges of the query table and reveal the hidden data.

You can format the query table by clicking on it to select it and then performing any of the formatting commands discussed in Part IV. You can also change the query table in other ways:

- To change the criteria for the table, click on the query table to select it. Then open the Query menu and select Set Criteria. Modify the criteria as necessary and click OK.

- To change the fields included in the query table, click on the table to select it. Then open the Query menu and select Choose Fields. To delete a field from the query table, select it then click on Clear. To add a new field to the query table, click on the Add button. Select a field, then click OK. To rearrange the order of a field within the table, click on it, then click on the arrow buttons at the bottom of the dialog box to move the field up or down within the list. Click OK when you're done.

- To delete the query table, click on it to select it, and then press Delete.

- To sort the records in the query table, follow the directions under "Sorting Your Database" in Chapter 44.

Anytime you make changes to your database (for instance, adding or deleting new records), update your query table by clicking on it to select it. Then open the Query menu and select Refresh Now.

Remember to update query table when you change database

Beyond Survival

Finding Records Without Creating a Query Table

If you don't want to create a separate query table in your worksheet, you can still locate the records you want. Basically, you follow almost the same steps that you do to create a query table. 1-2-3 locates the records you want and simply highlights them in the database table.

1. Open the Tools menu and select Database. Select Find Records. The Find Records dialog box appears.

Select your criteria.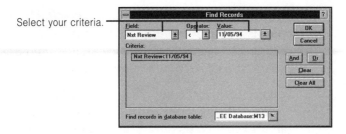

2. Under Find records in database table, click on the Range Selector. Select the entire table, including the field names row. If you named your table with the Range Name command, type the name of your database table instead of selecting it.

3. Specify your criteria as described in the previous section.

4. Click OK. 1-2-3 finds matching records and highlights them in the database.

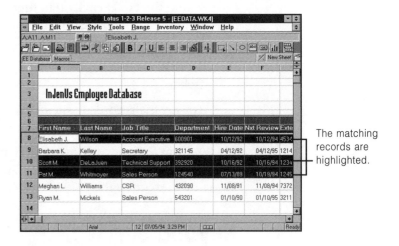

The matching records are highlighted.

To review the matching records use the following keys:

Key combination	What it does
Ctrl+Enter	Moves you to the next matching record.
Ctrl+Shift+Enter	Moves you to the previous matching record.

336

Key combination	What it does
Enter	Moves you to the next field in the current record.
Shift+Enter	Moves you to the previous field in the current record.
F2	Enables you to edit the contents of the current cell.

Press **Esc** or click within the worksheet to deselect the highlighted records and return to normal.

Cheat Sheet

Recording a Macro

1. Click on the Show/Hide Transcript SmartIcon {::} located on the Macro Building SmartIcon set.
2. Click on the Transcript Window, open the Edit menu, and select Clear All.
3. Click on the Record Macro SmartIcon {▶}.
4. Perform the actions you want to record.
5. Click on the Record Macro SmartIcon again {▶}.
6. Select the commands in the Transcript Window. Click on the Copy SmartIcon [A].
7. Click in the worksheet where you want to copy the macro commands.
8. Click on the Paste SmartIcon [].

Naming Macros

1. Move to the first cell in the macro.
2. Open the Range menu and select Name.
3. Under Name, type the macro name.
4. Click on Add.
5. Click OK.

Running Your Macro

To run a backslash macro, press Ctrl plus the letter assigned to the macro.

To run a range name macro, click on the Run Macro SmartIcon [] or press Alt+F3. Select your macro from the list and click OK.

46

Creating Macros

Macros are small programs that let you automate a series of commands. For example, you could create a macro that opens a specific file, or that formats selected text to be a certain size and font. Then, by pressing a series of keys or clicking on a button, you could run the macro. The steps you would ordinarily have to perform manually would be carried out by the macro automatically.

You create macros to save you time in repetitive tasks, such as typing in your company name and address, or entering a complex formula that you use all the time. Macros are flexible fellows that you can use for all sorts of things. For example, you could create a macro that selects a range and then prints it, or that prompts a user for data and then enters that data in the worksheet. A macro is a set of specific instructions. When you run a macro, 1-2-3 carries out these instructions as if you were entering each command individually.

Store macros in a separate worksheet.

Macro commands are placed into consecutive cells.

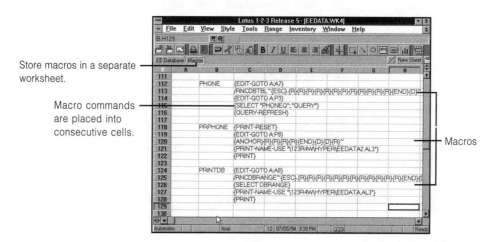

Macros

To record a macro, you simply turn on the recorder and enact the steps needed to perform the task you want to record. These macro functions (steps) are then copied to the worksheet as a series of commands, one per cell. Each macro command is surrounded by braces {}, so it is easy to identify. For convenience, you usually store your macros in a separate worksheet, away from your data.

Basic Survival

Recording a Macro

Before you record your macro, you'll probably want to set up a separate worksheet for storing your macros. This makes it easier to correct problems and to keep your macros organized.

Plan out the macros!

It's also best to plan out what you want to record, so you don't make any mistakes while recording the steps you want to save in your macro.

When you record a macro, the macro commands appear in a special window called the Transcript Window. Once the macro is complete, you copy the recorded commands from this window into the worksheet. (You can write a macro by typing commands manually, but it is more difficult. For help, see the 1-2-3 Help system.)

To record a macro:

1. Open the Tools menu, select Macro, and select Show Transcript. Or, click on the Show/Hide Transcript SmartIcon located on the Macro Building SmartIcon set ⌨. The Transcript Window appears.

2. Clear the contents of the window by clicking on the Transcript Window, opening the Edit menu, and selecting Clear All. If the Transcript Window is already cleared, skip this step.

3. Open the Tools menu, select Macro, and select Record, or click on the Record Macro SmartIcon ⏺. The word Rec appears in the status bar.

4. Perform the actions you want to record. For example, select commands or move around the worksheet. You can even enter, copy, or move data.

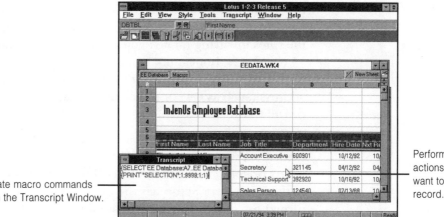

Appropriate macro commands appear in the Transcript Window.

Perform the actions you want to record.

5. Open the Tools menu, select Macro, and select Stop Recording. Or, click on the Record Macro SmartIcon again.

6. Select the commands in the Transcript Window, and click on the Copy SmartIcon.

7. Click in the worksheet where you want to copy the macro commands. If you want to add a new worksheet for storing macros, do so now.

8. Click on the Paste SmartIcon.

Once the macro commands are copied to the worksheet, you can edit them or add additional macro commands manually if you want. Just be sure that commands are stored in consecutive cells and that you don't skip a row. Once the macro is complete, assign it a name as explained in the next section.

Naming Macros

After creating a macro, you need to give it a name so you can run it. There are some rules to follow when naming a macro:

Backslash names   If you name your macro with a backslash and a single letter, as in \P, you can run the macro by pressing only two keys: Ctrl+P, for example. This is convenient for macros you use often, like a macro that prints a selected range within the worksheet.

Name common macros \letter

Range names   Name macros you use less frequently with ordinary range names. If you read Chapter 14, you might remember the rules involving range names: range names can contain up to 15 characters, but cannot contain spaces or the characters ! , ; . + – * / & > < @ # {. Also, don't use anything that looks like a cell address (such as Q4) or the name of a key (such as HOME, END, or DELETE).

Name autoexecute macro \0

Autoexecute macro   You can select one macro in your worksheet file to automatically execute (run) when the worksheet is first opened. Name that macro \0 (backslash zero), and as long as the Tools User Setup has the option Run autoexecute macro turned on, that macro will run automatically when the worksheet is opened.

To name your macro:

1. Move to the first cell in the macro.

2. Open the Range menu and select Name. The Name dialog box appears.

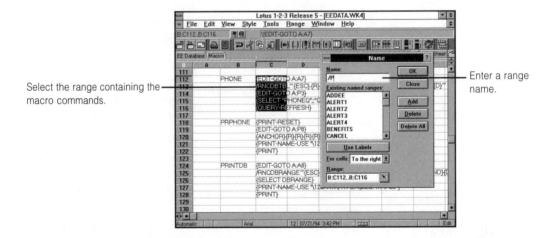

Select the range containing the macro commands.

Enter a range name.

3. Under Name, type the macro name. For example, type **\P**.

4. Click on Add.

5. Click OK.

See the next section for instructions on running your macro.

Running Your Macro

Run backslash macro by pressing Ctrl+letter

Once you've named your macro, you can run it. When you run it, 1-2-3 executes the commands it contains one by one, row after row. 1-2-3 stops executing commands when it encounters the first blank row in the macro range.

To run a backslash macro, press Ctrl plus the letter assigned to the macro. For example, to run a macro named \N, press Ctrl+N.

To run a range name macro, click on the Run Macro SmartIcon located on the Macro Building SmartIcon set [🔲]. Alternatively, you can press Alt+F3, or you can open the Tools menu, select the Macro, and select Run. The Macro Run dialog box appears. Select your macro from the list and click OK.

Select a macro to run.

You can halt a macro while it's running by pressing Ctrl+Break.

Beyond Survival

Fixing Problems with Macros

Use trace and step modes to find problems

If your macro does not perform as expected, you can review each command one at a time until you find the problem. This is called *step mode*. You can also use *trace mode* to find errors in macros. With trace mode, the command being executed is displayed in a special window. By combining step and trace modes, you can control the execution of the macro and view each command as it is executed. Follow these steps to combine step and trace modes:

1. Open the Tools menu and select Macro. Select Single Step. The word Step appears in the status bar. Alternatively, you can click on the Step Mode SmartIcon [🔲].

2. Open the Tools menu, select Macro, and select Trace, or click on the Trace Mode SmartIcon 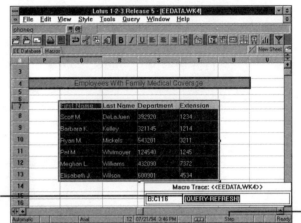. The Macro Trace window appears.

3. Run the macro. Press Enter to execute each command in turn. As a command is executed, it appears in the Trace Window.

The command being executed appears in the Trace Window.

Step mode is on.

4. When you find an error, stop the macro by pressing Ctrl+Break, and then Esc. Edit the macro and correct the error.

5. Run the macro again to retest it. Once it's running okay, turn step and trace modes off by repeating steps 2 and 3.

Cheat Sheet

Using Backsolver

1. Open the Range menu and select Analyze. Then select Backsolver.
2. Under Make cell, type the address of the cell that contains the formula you want to backsolve.
3. Under Equal to value, enter the value you want the formula to equal after Backsolver adjusts the variables.
4. Under By changing cell(s), type the range whose values you want Backsolver to change to make the formula equal the value you specified.
5. Click OK.

Using What-If Tables

1. Open the Range menu and select Analyze. Then select What-if Table.
2. Select the number of variables from the Number of variables drop-down list box.
3. Under Table range, click on the Range Selector. Select the table, including the formula you want to solve, the input values, and the blank cells in which you want to place the results.
4. Under Input cell 1, click on the Range Selector. Select the first input cell.
5. Repeat for additional input cells.
6. If you're creating a 3 variable what-if table, enter the address of the cell that contains the formula.
7. Click OK.

47

Solving What-if Situations

If you're using a worksheet to analyze data, you're bound sooner or later to run into what-if situations. For example, what if I reduce expenses by 10%? What if we sell over 10,000 units? What if I can afford a monthly payment of $800? You can use 1-2-3 to solve these problems for you, and much more.

In this chapter, you'll learn how to solve simple what-if situations using Backsolver, What-if tables, and the Solver. In the next chapter, you'll learn how to analyze complex situations using the Version Manager.

Basic Survival

Using Backsolver

Backsolver is good for solving what-if situations that involve one variable. Backsolver works backwards from a result to find the correct variable that creates the situation you desire. For example, suppose you were trying to buy a house. After analyzing your expenses, you decide that you can afford an $800 monthly payment. If you can obtain a loan at a 9.5% interest rate, what price house can you afford?

Backsolver can change more than one variable to solve the problem, provided it changes them all by the same percentage. For example, you could have Backsolver adjust all of last year's sales figures to equal this year's goal of $3,500,000.

Use Backsolver for what-if situations with one variable

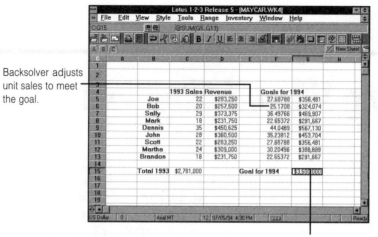

Backsolver adjusts unit sales to meet the goal.

Goal for 1994

To use Backsolver:

1. Open the Range menu and select Analyze. Then select Backsolver. The Backsolver dialog box appears.

2. Under Make cell, type the address of the cell that contains the formula you want to backsolve. You can also click on the Range Selector and select the cell.

3. Under Equal to value, enter the value you want the formula to equal after Backsolver adjusts the variables.

4. Under By changing cell(s), type the range whose values you want Backsolver to change to make the formula equal the value you specified. You can also click on the Range Selector and select the cell or cells.

5. Click OK. Backsolver solves your problem and changes the value in the indicated cell(s).

Using What-If Tables

If you have a formula you want to solve that involves changing several variables by different amounts, you should use what-if tables. What-if tables adjust up to three variables to arrive at the result you want. For example, you could use a what-if table to calculate the pay amounts for loans of varying percentages and loan lengths, such as 20 or 30 years. The results are placed in a table.

Can solve problems with up to three variables with what-if tables

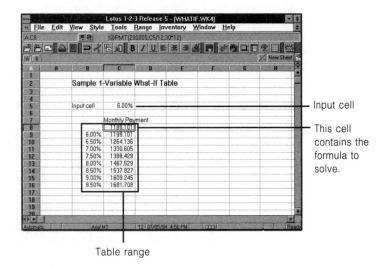

Input cell

This cell contains the formula to solve.

Table range

You must set up your what-if table in a specific way, depending on the number of variables you plan to use. All what-if tables include a formula cell, input cells (where 1-2-3 places the values as it generates the table), and input values (cells containing the variables you want to test in the formula). A three variable what-if table requires a 3-D range. Follow the examples closely to set up your what-if table.

This cell contains the formula to solve.

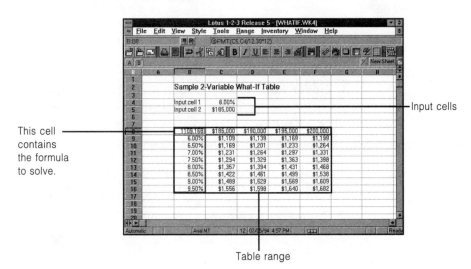

Input cells

Table range

349

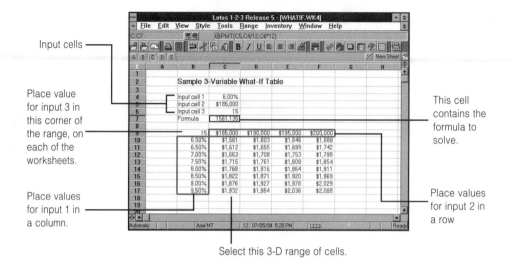

Input cells

Place value for input 3 in this corner of the range, on each of the worksheets.

Place values for input 1 in a column.

This cell contains the formula to solve.

Place values for input 2 in a row

Select this 3-D range of cells.

To create a what-if table:

1. Open the Range menu and select Analyze. Then select What-if Table. The What-if Table dialog box appears.

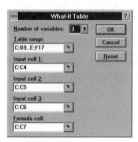

2. Select the number of variables (1, 2, or 3) from the Number of variables drop-down list box.

3. Under Table range, click on the Range Selector. Select the table, including the formula you want to solve, the input values, and the blank cells in which you want to place the results. Do not select the input cells. You can also type in the range address if you like.

4. Under Input cell 1, click on the Range Selector. Select the first input cell. You can also type in the cell address if you like.

5. Repeat for additional input cells.

6. If you're creating a 3 variable what-if table, enter the address of the cell that contains the formula.

7. Click OK. 1-2-3 substitutes the input variables into the formula and calculates the table.

You might want to chart the results of your what-if table to make your analysis of the results easier to understand. If so, see Chapter 40 for instructions on how to create a chart.

Beyond Survival

Using Solver

You can use Solver to find solutions to complex problems. For example, if you had a worksheet that contained your school's festival sales, you could have Solver determine the maximum profits by varying the number and mix of the foods sold at the festival. The formulas you use to express your problem can be algebraic, such as total sales or cost of food sold. They can also be logical, expressing relationships such as "Profit at least $10,000" or "Average attendance between 3,000 and 5,000."

For complex problems, use Solver

With Solver, you define *adjustable cells,* cells that contain values Solver can adjust to solve the problem. You set up *constraints*, logical formulas that specify the conditions you need Solver to satisfy with whatever answers it finds. In addition, you can identify an *optimal cell*, a cell whose value you want Solver to maximize as it solves the problem.

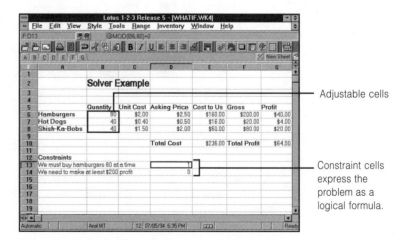

Adjustable cells

Constraint cells express the problem as a logical formula.

In the sample, the two contraints are expressed like this:

Constraint	Entered in cell	As this formula
Must purchase hamburgers in boxes of 80 each	D13	@MOD(B6,80)=0
Need to make a minimum of $200 profit	D14	+G10>=200

When Solver finishes, it presents an answer like the one shown here.

Solver's solution ⎯⎯⎯⎯⎯

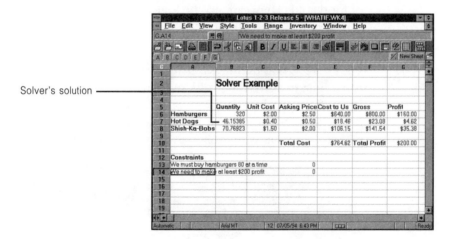

To use Solver:

1. Set up the problem in the worksheet. Identify the adjustable and constraint cells, and an optimal cell if there is one.

2. Open the Range menu and select Analyze. Select Solver. The Solver Definition dialog box appears.

3. Specify the address of the adjustable cell(s) under Adjustable cells, or click on the Range Selector and select the range.

4. Specify the address of the constraint cell(s) under Constraint cells, or click on the Range Selector and select the range.

5. Specify the address of the optimal cell (if there is one), or click on the Range Selector and select the cell.

6. Under No. of answers, select the number of answers (guesses) you want Solver to find.

7. Click on Solve. 1-2-3 works on your problem and then displays the Solver Answer dialog box

Click here to change the definition of the problem.

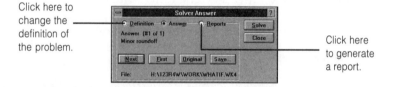

Click here to generate a report.

First, drag the dialog box out of your way by clicking on the title bar and holding down the mouse button as you drag. The initial "answer" to your problem appears in the adjustable cells. Click on Next to see the next possible solution. Continue to click on Next to view additional solutions one at a time. To return to the first solution, click on First. To view your original values, click on Original.

To see a report of the possible solutions, click on the Reports option button at the top of the dialog box. Select a report from the list, and then click on Table.

If you want to change your definition of the problem and try again, click on the Definition option button and change the definition as described earlier. Then click on Solve.

To exit Solver, click on the Close button.

Cheat Sheet

Creating a Version

1. Enter data for the first version into the range.
2. Move the cursor into the range.
3. Click on the Version Manager SmartIcon, located on the Goodies SmartIcon set ⊞.
4. Click on Create.
5. Change the version name and/or add a comment if you want.
6. Change the sharing level if you want.
7. Click OK.

Flipping Between Versions

1. Click on the Version Manager SmartIcon, located on the Goodies SmartIcon set ⊞.
2. Under Named range, select a range whose version you want to change.
3. Under With version(s), select a version for the range.

Creating a Scenario

1. Click on the Version Manager SmartIcon, located on the Goodies SmartIcon set ⊞.
2. Click on To Index.
3. Press and hold the Ctrl key as you click on versions.
4. Click on Scenario.
5. Enter a name under Scenario name.
6. Add a comment if you want. Change the sharing option if necessary.
7. Click OK.

48

Creating Different Versions of the Same Worksheet

You can perform more complex analyses with Version Manager than you can with Solver, Backsolver, or What-if Tables. With Version Manager, you create a named range such as INCOME, and then create different versions of the range with different values. For example, you could create High, Low, and Expected versions of a range called IN-COME and then display whatever version of the INCOME range you want to work with within your worksheet. How is this beneficial? It gives you the freedom to play with the numbers in a worksheet without damaging it. For example, you could create a worksheet listing the expected income for quarter two. Then you could name the range and create additional *versions*, maybe with high income figures or really low income figures. Then you could display one of these versions (such as Low income) and analyze how those figures affect the worksheet as a whole.

By changing the values in the INCOME range, you are in effect creating several versions of the worksheet itself, although 1-2-3 doesn't actually create separate worksheets. What it does is store the changing values for each version and then displays those values in the original worksheet when you select them. For example, when you select High income, the values for that version of the worksheet are plopped into the INCOME range. Formulas that depend on those values are recalculated. Select another version of the INCOME range, such as Low income, and the worksheet is magically transformed with new values.

In addition, you can create versions of additional ranges in the same worksheet. For example, you could create similar versions (High, Low, and Expected) of a range called EXPENSES, and then combine versions of the different INCOME and EXPENSES ranges to create Best Case, Worst Case, and Most Likely scenarios.

Basic Survival

Creating a Version

You can only create different versions of a named range, so be sure to name the range you want to play with first (see Chapter 14 for help). Then use Version Manager to create the different versions of the range, complete with unique values. Once you create the different versions of your range, you can flip between the "worksheets" that are created as a result of the changing values.

To create a version of a named range:

1. Enter data for the first version into the range.

2. Move the cursor into the range.

3. Click on the Version Manager SmartIcon, located on the Goodies SmartIcon set ⊞. You can also open the Range menu and select Version. The Version Manager dialog box appears.

Click on Create. ——

4. Click on the Create button. The Create Version dialog box appears.

Change the version name if you want.

Add a comment. ——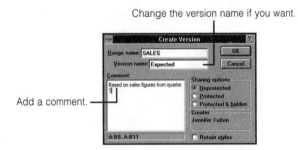

5. The range name should already appear under Range name. You can change the version name and/or add a comment if you like. For example, instead of "Version1" change the version name to "10% Increase."

6. Change the sharing options if you want. For example, if you select Protected, no one can change the values in the version. If you select Protected and hidden, the version is not displayed in the version list (but it is accessible through the Index).

7. Click OK. The version is saved.

Add additional versions with Version Manager

The Version Manager dialog box remains on-screen so you can create additional versions of the range. For example, to create a second version with different values, click in the worksheet and change the values in the range. Click on the Create button again and follow the steps above.

You can create different versions of more than one range in the worksheet. Just repeat the steps here with a different named range.

Flipping Between Versions

When you flip between versions, the values in the worksheet change to match those of the version you select. You choose the version you'd like to review from the Version Manager dialog box.

Select a range to view.

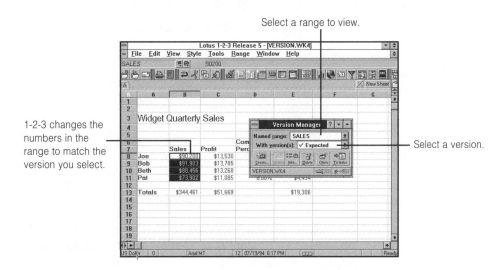

1-2-3 changes the numbers in the range to match the version you select.

Select a version.

If you don't like one version, try another.

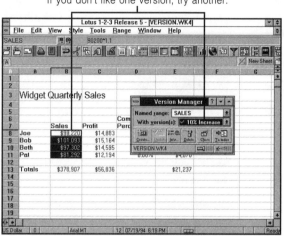

To change to a different version of a named range:

1. Click on the Version Manager SmartIcon, located on the Goodies SmartIcon set ⊞. You can also open the Range menu and select Version. 1-2-3 displays the Version Manager dialog box.

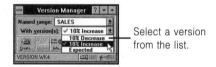

Select a version from the list.

2. Under Named range, select a range whose version you want to change.

3. Under With version(s), select a version for the range. The worksheet changes to reflect the new values.

You can also use the To Index to switch between versions. From the Version Manager dialog box, click on the To Index button. Select the version you want to review and click on Show.

Beyond Survival

Creating a Scenario

You can combine different versions of several ranges to create a scenario. For example, you could combine a version of high sales figures with low returns to create a best case scenario.

Scenario combines selected versions of different ranges into one worksheet

To create a scenario:

1. Click on the Version Manager SmartIcon, located on the Goodies SmartIcon set 🖾. You can also open the Range menu and select Version. The Version Manager dialog box appears.

2. Click on To Index. The Index dialog box appears.

Select the versions you want to combine from this list.

Then click on Scenario.

3. Press and hold the Ctrl key as you click on versions to select them.

4. Click on Scenario. The Create Scenario dialog box appears.

Change the scenario name if you want.

Add a comment.

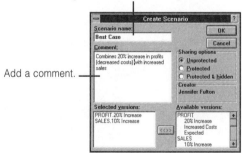

5. Enter a name under Scenario name.

6. Add a comment or change the sharing option if you want.

7. Click OK.

To switch to a scenario:

1. Click on the Version Manager SmartIcon, located on the Goodies SmartIcon set ⊞. You can also open the Range menu and select Version. 1-2-3 displays the Version Manager dialog box.

2. Click on To Index. The Index dialog box appears.

3. Click on the sort button at the top of the dialog box. Select Scenario sort.

4. Double-click on the scenario you want to display.

A

Installing Lotus 1-2-3 for Windows

If you haven't yet installed Lotus 1-2-3 for Windows, follow these steps to install the program with ease. Before you install, you should make copies of the installation diskettes. That way, if something happens to them, you'll have an extra copy you can use.

To copy a diskette, write-protect it first. To write-protect a 5.25-inch diskette, stick a write-protect tab over the side notch. To write-protect a 3.5-inch diskette, slide the write-protect tab up so that the hole is exposed. Then in Windows, double-click on the File Manager icon from the Main group. Open the Disk menu, and select Copy Disk. Select the appropriate diskette drive and click OK. Place the original program diskette in the drive and press Enter. Replace the original diskette with a blank diskette when prompted. Repeat for the remaining program diskettes.

When you have copied the program diskettes, install the program using these steps:

1. Start Windows if it isn't started already.

2. Open the Program Manager's File menu and select Run. The Run dialog box appears.

3. Under Command line, type **A:INSTALL** or **B:INSTALL** depending on your disk drive.

4. Click OK.

5. The Installation program displays its opening screen. Type your name and company name (if applicable), and then press Enter.

6. You're asked to confirm your name and company name. Click on Yes or press Enter.

7. Next, you'll see the Installation Options screen. Select the Default features option (this is the easiest option to use). If you're worried about space, use the Minimum features option, which installs only the minimum features needed to run 1-2-3. Use the Customize features option only if you feel comfortable enough with 1-2-3 to select just the features you'll need to use. Click on Next to continue.

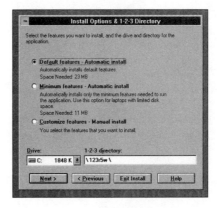

8. You're asked which program group you want to add the 1-2-3 program to. Press Enter to accept the default of Lotus Applications.

9. Now you're ready to install. Press Enter.

10. You'll be prompted when to remove the first disk and to insert the next one. Just follow the on-screen instructions.

11. Towards the end of the installation, you'll be asked whether you want 1-2-3 to modify the AUTOEXEC.BAT file on your PC. It's best to just click Yes or press Enter. If you want to try to modify the file yourself, click Make Copy instead.

12. If you've asked 1-2-3 to make changes to the 1-2-3 file, you'll need to restart your PC for the changes to take effect. Click on Restart. If you currently have other programs running, click on Done. Then when you've safely exited those programs and Windows, you can restart your computer and run 1-2-3.

B

Table of 1-2-3 Worksheet Functions

Below is a list of the most common Lotus 1-2-3 built-in functions. The type of data and the order in which it should be typed is included inside the parentheses next to each function. (Optional parameters are in *italics*.) The function syntax (the sequence of parameters) is followed by a brief description.

Mathematical Functions

@ABS(value)	Calculates the absolute value of a number.
@INT(value)	Rounds a number down to the nearest integer.
@MOD(dividend, divisor)	Calculates the remainder or *modulus* of a divisor and a dividend.
@PI	Used in the place of the value pi.
@ROUND(value, *places*)	Rounds a value to a specified number of places.

Statistical Functions

@AVG(range)   Calculates the
                                     mean average of a
                                     group of numbers.

@COUNT(range)   Counts the number
                                     of cells in a range
                                     that contain entries.

@MAX(range)   Returns the maxi-
                                     mum value in a
                                     range of cells.

@MIN(range)   Returns the mini-
                                     mum value in a
                                     range of cells.

@SUM(range)   Calculates the sum of
                                     a group of cells.

Financial Functions

@DDB(cost, salvage, life,   Calculates deprecia-
period)   tion using the
                                     double declining
                                     balance method.

@FV(payment, interest   Calculates the future
rate, term)   value of an investment

@IPAYMT(principal,   Calculates the
interest rate, term,   interest paid for a
start_period, *end_period*,   particular payment.
type, future value)

@IRATE(term, payment,   Calculates the
present value, *type, future*   interest rate required
value, guess)   for a present value to
                                     become a greater value.

@NPER(payment, interest rate, future value, *type*, *present value*)	Calculates the number of payments required to pay off a loan at a given interest rate.
@PPAYMT(principal, interest rate, term, start_period, *end_period*, *type, present value*)	Calculates the amount of principal being paid during any payment period.
@PMT(principal, interest rate, term)	Calculates the payment amount required for an investment to be paid off given a specific term and interest rate.
@PV(payments, interest term)	Calculates the present value of a rate, series of cash flow transactions.
@SLN(cost, salvage, life)	Calculates depreciation using the straight line method.
@SYD(cost, salvage, life, period)	Calculates depreciation using the sum of the years' digits method.

Logical Functions

@IF(condition, value if true, value if false)	Tests whether a condition is true or false, and then carries out some action depending on the result of the test.
@ISERR(address)	Tests whether a cell contains an error.
@ISSTRING(address)	Tests whether a cell contains a string.

Calendar Functions

@DATEVALUE(text)	Converts a text string into a valid date.
@DAY(date)	Returns the day within the date specified.

@MONTH(date)	Returns the month within the date specified.
@NOW( )	Returns the current date and time.
@TIMEVALUE(text)	Converts a text string into a valid time.
@TODAY( )	Returns today's date.
@WEEKDAY(date)	Returns the day of the week based on the date specified.
@YEAR(date)	Returns the year within the date specified.

Index

E

Edit menu commands
  Clear, 206
  Clear All, 340
  Copy Back, 97
  Delete, 144, 155
  Insert, 128, 154, 326
  Paste Special, 225
  Undo, 32
editing cells, 73
Ellipse SmartIcon, 312
ellipses, 28, 311
End key, 61, 73
enlarging
  query tables, 335
  SmartIcons, 40
entering
  @functions, 235-240
  data, 59, 65-70
  data in a series, 69-70
  dates, 68
  document information, 116
  formulas, 210, 215
  labels, 67
  times, 68
  values, 65-66
@ERR@function, 252
ERR messages
  displaying zero instead of, 249-250
  in formulas, 227
Evenly spaced SmartIcon, 184
Exit command (File menu), 52-53
Exit Windows command (File menu), 52, 55
exiting
  1-2-3 for Windows, 52-54
  Help, 46
  Windows, 52
extensions, 103

F

F1 (help) key, 44-45
F4 key (range selection), 84
F5 (Go To) dialog box, 61
Fast Format command (Style menu), 205
Fast Format SmartIcon, 206
fast formatting, 205
field names, 323
fields, 323
  changing in query tables, 335
  prioritizing, 324
file links (Audit), 231
File Manager, 8
File menu commands
  Close, 52, 54, 76
  Doc Info, 116
  Exit, 52-53
  Exit Windows, 52, 55
  Open, 119
  Page Setup, 267-272, 276
  Print, 255, 257, 288
  Print Preview, 263
  Properties, 8
  Protect, 189, 192
  Run, 362
  Save, 104
File New SmartIcon, 114
File Print SmartIcon, 288
files
  contiguous files, selecting, 122
  extensions, 103
  nonexistent referencing, 228
  opening worksheets, 119-124
  password protection, 107-108
  sealing, 189-190
  Spell Check, 319

Spell Check for parts of, 320-321
  unsealing, 191
  worksheets
    moving between, 136
    names, 103-104
    viewing, 137
fills, 197-198
financial functions, 367-368
Find Records dialog box, 335
Floating SmartIcons, 34
Font & Attributes command (Style menu), 172
Font & Attributes dialog box, 172
Font & Attributes SmartIcon, 174
font selector (status bar), 13
fonts, 169-175
  changing, 170
  changing in labels, 305
  default (Arial MT), 170
Fonts & Attributes command (Style menu), 305
Fonts & Attributes dialog box, 305
footers, 275-279
  inserting, 276-277
  saving, 278-279
footnotes (charts), 284, 299-300
For Upgraders command (Help menu), 45
format selector (status bar), 13
formats, default, 179
formatting, 203-208
  cells, 173-174
  charts, 299-306

G

O

P

X

Y

Z

What Are You Looking At?

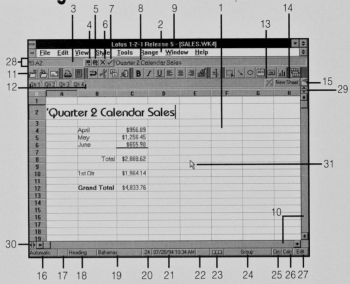

The Parts of a 1-2-3 for Windows Screen

1. Worksheet area
2. Menu bar
3. Selection indicator
4. Navigator
5. @Function selector
6. Cancel button
7. Confirm button
8. Contents box

9. Title bar
10. Scroll bars
11. SmartIcons
12. Worksheet tabs
13. Tab-sheet arrows
14. New Sheet button
15. Hide/Show Tabs
16. Format selector

17. Decimal selector
18. Style selector
19. Font selector
20. Font-Size selector
21. Date-time/Height-
     width indicator
22. Mail button
23. SmartIcons selector

24. Status indicator
25. Circ indicator
26. Calc indicator
27. Mode indicator
28. Edit Line
29. Horizontal Splitter
30. Vertical Splitter
31. Mouse pointer

The Parts of a Chart

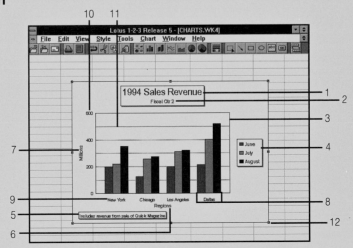

1. Title
2. Subtitle
3. Plot area
4. Legend

5. Note or footnote
6. X-axis label
7. Y-axis label
8. Data series

9. Data labels
10. Scale
11. Gridlines
12. Selection handles

Common Functions

Below is a list of the most common Lotus 1-2-3 built-in functions. There is also room below to add your own favorites:

@INT(value)	Rounds a number down to the nearest integer.
@ROUND(value, *places*)	Rounds a value to a specified number of places.
@AVG(range)	Calculates the mean average of a group of numbers.
@SUM(range)	Calculates the sum of a group of cells.
@DDB(cost, salvage, life, period)	Calculates depreciation using the double declining balance method.
@PMT(principal, interest rate, term)	Calculates the payment amount required for an investment to be paid off given a specific term and interest rate.
@IF(condition, value if true, value if false)	Tests whether a condition is true or false, then carries out some action depending on the result of the test.
@NOW()	Returns the current date and time.
@TODAY()	Returns today's date.

_____

_____

_____

_____

_____

_____

_____

_____

Quick Steps for Common Tasks

Opening an Existing Worksheet

1. Click on the Open File button .
2. Click on the file you want to open in the file list.
3. Click OK.

Closing a Worksheet

1. Open the File menu and select Close, or press Ctrl+F4.
2. If you have forgotten to save your work, you'll see a dialog box. Just click on Yes, and then type a file name if prompted.
3. Begin work on a new worksheet or open an existing worksheet.

Starting a New Worksheet

1. Open the File menu and select New.
2. Select a SmartMaster from the list, or select the Create a plain worksheet option.
3. Click OK.

Adding a New Worksheet

1. Move to the worksheet after which you want to add a new worksheet.

2. Click on the New Sheet button New Sheet.

Moving Around the Worksheet with the Mouse

- Click on a cell to move the cell pointer there.
- Click on the scroll arrows to move left or right one column, or up or down one row.
- Click between the scroll arrows to move a whole screen.
- Drag the scroll box to move a variable amount.

Moving Around the Worksheet with the Keyboard

To move here:	Press this:
One cell in any direction	Arrow key
One whole screen up or down	PgUp or PgDn keys
One whole screen left or right	Ctrl+arrow key
To cell A1 of the current worksheet	Home
To cell A1 of the first worksheet	Ctrl+Home
To the last cell with data	End, then Home
To the last cell with data in the indicated direction	End, then arrow key
To a specific cell	F5 (Go To)

More Quick Steps for Common Tasks

Undoing a Command

1. Don't make any more changes or issue any commands.
2. Click on the Undo button .

Selecting a Range

1. Click on the upper left-hand cell in the range.
2. Press and hold the left mouse button.
3. Drag down and/or to the right to select additional cells.

Selecting a Non-Contiguous Range (Collection)

1. Select the first range in the collection.
2. Press and hold down the Ctrl key.
3. Select additional ranges.

Selecting a 3-D Range

1. Select the range within the first worksheet.
2. Press and hold the Shift key.
3. Click on the tab of the last worksheet in the range.

Preview a Worksheet Before Printing

1. Select the range or worksheets you want to print.
2. Click on the Print Preview button .
3. Click OK.

To move to the next or a previous page, click or .

To zoom in or out, click or .

To access Page Setup, click on .

To display the current page and the next page, click .

To display the current page and the next three pages, click .

To return to a single page display, click .

To print your worksheet, click .

To close the Print Preview window, click .

Printing a Worksheet

1. If you want to print only one worksheet within a file, move to that worksheet.
2. Click on the File Print button .
3. Select Current worksheet or All worksheets.
4. Click OK.